MW00463503

THE PARISH MANAGEMENT HANDBOOK

A Practical Guide

for Pastors,

Administrators,

and Other

Parish Leaders

The Parish Management Handbook

EDITED BY CHARLES E. ZECH

TWENTY-THIRD PUBLICATIONS
185 WILLOW STREET • PO BOX 180 • MYSTIC, CT 06355
TEL: 1-800-321-0411 • FAX: 1-800-572-0788
E-MAIL: ttpubs@aol.com • www.twentythirdpublications.com
Bayard

Twenty-Third Publications
A Division of Bayard
185 Willow Street
P.O. Box 180
Mystic, CT 06355
(860) 536-2611
(800) 321-0411
www.twentythirdpublications.com

Copyright ©2003 Charles Zech. All rights reserved. No part of this publication may be reproduced in any manner without prior written permission of the publisher. Write to the Permissions Editor.

ISBN:1-58595-270-2
Library of Congress Catalog Card Number: 00-2003104395
Printed in the U.S.A.

CONTENTS

2/17   chapt 2 & 4
3/3   chapt 6
3/17   chapt 8
3/31   chapt 7

INTRODUCTION

Until the late 1960s administration in most Catholic parishes was straightforward. The parish was led by a pastor, who was assisted by one or more priests serving as assistant pastors. The parish school featured a large number of religious sisters, one of whom served as the school principal. Parish tasks were divided up among the priests, with the sisters lending their assistance with some extra-school activities, such as religious education. Laypersons typically volunteered their time to provide specific skills, such as bookkeeping or playing the organ for liturgies. The only paid laity on the parish staff were the maintenance people and, perhaps, the rectory housekeeper, although they too were frequently volunteers. Laity serving in parish leadership positions were almost non-existent.

This strongly mechanistic structure was characterized by the pastor making all of the major and many minor decisions and passing them downward. The pastor's authoritarian and directive leadership style was consistent with compliance-induction theory of leadership defined as " the process by which an agent induces a subordinate to behave in a desired manner" (Bennis 1959). Communication channels were almost exclusively vertical.

By the end of the 1960s the Catholic Church began to experience three trends that have dramatically changed the face of parish staffing (Schoenherr and Young 1992; Davidson et al. 1997; Starke and Finke 2000; D'Antonio et al. 2001). One was the resignation of priests and sisters in the ten years following Vatican II, which deprived the U.S. Church of some potentially creative leadership. A second has been the decline in new religious vocations, both to the priesthood and to vowed religious orders of sisters and brothers. This has meant that, not only do relatively few parishes have the luxury of being staffed by more than one priest, but some parishes don't even have one resident priest. Their pastor has other responsibilities, and a vowed religious, layperson, or deacon administers the day-to-day activities of the parish. Fewer religious sisters means that many parish schools function with entirely lay staffs, including the principal. Lay staff, both volunteer and paid, many of them in leadership positions, require the pastor to assume an expanding and more complex leadership role in the temporal as well as spiritual life of the parish.

The third trend has been the realization by the laity through the teachings of the Second Vatican Council that they are the people of God, that through their baptism they share in the Church's priesthood, and that they have both a right and a responsibility to be involved in church and parish administration. The Church's teaching in *Lumen Gentium*, the Dogmatic Constitution on the Church, is that the relationship between the laity and the clergy is one of communion, of support, and of interdependence.

Some laity have chosen to carry out their responsibility as volunteers, some as part-time paid staff, while others have chosen to become full-time professional lay ministers. Currently it is estimated that nearly 30,000 persons serve in lay ministry positions (Murnion and DeLambo 2000), with another 35,000 in training (Bendyna and Gautier 2001).

The last two decades have seen the publication of a number of studies describing who our lay ministers are (Walters 1983; Murnion 1992; Walters, Smith, and Macotta 1993; Fox 1997, 1999; and Murnion and DeLambo 2000). We've learned that, compared to the overall Catholic population, lay ministers are more likely to be female, to have a college education, and to be white. More recently, attention has turned to the education and formation of lay ministers (Elsesser 1986; Fahey and Lewis 1992; O'Meara 1999; and Schuth 1999). The U.S. bishops have been especially active in teaching about both the theology supporting the concept of lay ministers and their education and formation (NCCB 1980, 1995, 1998, 1999).

Lay ministers fill a diverse assortment of roles in today's Catholic parishes, ranging from pastoral associate to religious education director to liturgical minister. They are an essential component in the day-to-day functioning of most parishes. Pope John Paul II has stated, "We see a true source of hope in the willingness of a considerable number of lay people to play a more active and diversified role in ecclesial life…" (NCCB 1999).

With this "true source of hope" comes the responsibility to ensure that our lay ministers receive adequate training. One weakness in the education/formation of most lay ministers is the need for practical information on the nuts and bolts of parish leadership (Scheets 1995). It should be noted that this is a frequent complaint about the preparation that our priests receive, as well (Conway 2002).

With the priest shortage, many priests are becoming pastors within 2-4 years of ordination and have not had the time to acquire "on-the-job" training for the administrative responsibilities that are expected of them. Others are being asked to pastor more than one parish, and thus must rely heavily on the lay staff in each parish to keep the parish functioning smoothly.

In still other cases, non-priests (sisters, brothers, deacons, or laypersons) are receiving appointments as pastors. The education offered those studying for both the priesthood and lay ministry tends to be heavy on the areas of theology, Scripture, Church history, and spirituality, but light on practical parish topics such as managing volunteers and staff, legal issues, raising money, management systems, etc. Observers have been decrying for years the absence of a course on practical, parish management in seminaries. Others have argued that four years to form our priests spiritually and even less time to form our lay ministers leaves little time for practical parish administration courses. They argue that the appropriate time for priests to be educated in administrative and management skills is after ordination, shortly before they're assigned their first pastorate, and lay ministers could be asked to undertake continuing education in pastoral management.

Clearly, the current situation, where pastors and lay church workers frequently must learn about these topics while holding the responsibility of the position—typically through experience rather than education—needs to be addressed. This is an especially critical issue to those pastors and lay ecclesial ministers assigned to large, complex parishes with many organizations, programs, volunteers, and staff.

The Parish Management Handbook

With this in mind, a team of Catholic scholars, including diocesan personnel, seminary and university professors, and parish consultants, has written a book on practical issues that arise in parish leadership. This is no academic tome, but rather a hands-on, easy-to-understand guide to the most vexing issues faced by those holding parish leadership positions, whether they are ordained or lay, and for which they are likely to have had minimal training.

The *Handbook* contains nine chapters, each focusing on a specific practical parish issue. Chapter One, written by Mark Fischer of St. John's Seminary in Camarillo, CA, introduces the notion of a local theology of church management by reflecting on the Donatist controversy of the fourth century. Fischer is able to show the connection between that controversy (along with the theology of local church management) and topics covered in this book.

Chapter Two, also written by Mark Fischer, discusses parish pastoral councils. Fischer traces the history of parish pastoral councils and the development of their primary purpose, which, he argues, is to engage in pastoral planning. Fischer also tackles some practical matters related to parish pastoral councils, including the selection of councillors, their relationship with the pastor and parish staff, and their spiritual formation.

Sister Janet Baker wrote Chapter Three, which addresses parish decision-making processes. In the chapter she addresses the power that decision-making processes have in shaping the life of the parish. Sister Janet discusses practical issues, including a comparison of various decision-making methods and the importance of dialogue and discernment. She concludes by taking up some frequently asked questions about decision-making processes, including keeping the group on time and on task, making meetings more productive, and reaching a decision when a large number of people are involved in the process.

Parish human resource issues are the topic of Chapter Four, written by Robert Miller. Miller offers insights on important personnel issues, such as recruiting and interviewing staff (and volunteers), establishing appropriate compensation systems, developing and training parish personnel, composing job descriptions, and performance appraisal and discipline.

Related to parish personnel issues are parish legal issues. In Chapter Five, Sister Mary Angela Shaughnessy takes up the task of alerting us to pitfalls that parishes face in civil law. Along with personnel issues, Sister Mary Angela speaks to contracts, negligence and safety, sexual harassment, and dealing with volunteers.

Michael Cieslak ponders parish leadership in Chapter Six. Among the issues that he considers are the effect of a change in pastoral leadership on parish finances, the impact of pastoral leadership on parish vitality, and the importance of matching a pastor's leadership style with the needs of the parish.

Chapter Seven is devoted to the implementation of a parish stewardship program. Charles Zech describes the specifics of stewardship. First, a brief overview of the concept is presented, followed by a consideration of its theological underpinnings. Then Zech presents practical issues involved with introducing and promoting a parish-wide stewardship effort, including a discussion of the roles played by the key players (pastor, staff, pastoral council, finance committee, and stewardship committee) and an analysis of the typical tools used to educate parishioners on stewardship (time and talent fairs, lay ministry booklets, lay witness talks, etc.). The chapter ends with "Ten Ways To Increase Parish Giving."

Ed Gaffney and Terri Sorter put a unique spin on parish conflict management in Chapter Eight. They present a scripturally based, four-step process for Christian conciliation: glorify God, take responsibility for your own actions, consider the other person's perspective, and seek forgiveness while being willing to extend it.

They apply this technique to a typical parish setting.

Finally, in Chapter Nine, Father Francis Kelly Scheets recognizes parishes as social systems that can be grouped into four categories. The pastor's primary role is different in each type of parish. Moreover, each category of parish has different information needs and communication and accountability issues. This chapter discusses the data needs of each type of parish. What kinds of data need to be collected? How can this data be turned into information (the two are not synonymous)? How can this information be used to improve parish effectiveness by identifying those current tasks that could be done differently or abandoned altogether, as well as new tasks that should be undertaken? How do we know if our parish programs and staff are effective? And finally, what is the appropriate amount and mechanism for communicating that information to parishioners to ensure accountability?

Audience

The Parish Management Handbook is written for both clergy and lay leaders. It can be very helpful in seminaries, and we hope it will be a useful asset for current pastors and those priests anticipating a pastorate in the near future. Likewise, it should be a vital resource for those already in lay ministry positions and those currently pursuing a degree or certificate. It will make an excellent auxiliary textbook/assigned readings book for the many lay ministry programs already in place. Members of professional organizations such as NCCL and NALM will also find the book to be very useful. It is written at the non-specialist's level, yet doesn't insult the readers' intelligence. It strives to impart practical knowledge on complex topics in an understandable and useful manner.

References

Bendyna, Mary E. and Mary L. Gautier. 2001. "Spiritual Formation of Lay Ecclesial Ministers: A CARA Report for the Secretariat for Family, Laity, Women, and Youth." Washington D. C.: Center for Applied Research in the Apostolate.

Bennis, W.G. 1959. "Leadership Theory and Administrative Behavior: The Problems of Authority," *Administrative Science Quarterly* 4, pp. 259-301.

Conway, Daniel. 2002. *The Reluctant Steward Revisited.* St. Meinrad, IN: St. Meinrad Seminary.

D'Antonio, William V., James D. Davidson, Dean R. Hoge, and Katherine Meyer. 2001. *American Catholics: Gender, Generation, and Commitment.* Walnut Creek, CA: AltaMira.

Davidson, James D., Andrea S. Williams, Richard A. Lamanna, Jan Stenftenagel, Kathleen Maas Weigert, William J. Whalen, and Patricia Wittberg. 1997. *The Search for the Common Ground.* Huntington, IN: Our Sunday Visitor.

Elsesser, Suzanne, ed. 1986. *Preparing Laity for Ministry.* Washington D.C.: United States Catholic Conference.

Fahey, Charles J. and Mary Ann Lewis. 1992. *The Future of Catholic Institutional Ministries.* New York: Third Age Center, Fordham University.

Fox, Zeni. 1997. *New Ecclesial Ministry: Lay Professionals Serving the Church.* Kansas City: Sheed & Ward.

_____. 1999. *Forging a Ministerial Identity.* Chicago: National Association for Lay Ministry.

Murnion, Philip J. 1992. *New Parish Ministers: Laity and Religious on Parish Staffs.* New York: National Pastoral Life Center.

_____ and David DeLambo. 1999. *Parishes and Parish Ministers: A Study of Parish Lay Ministry.* New York: National Pastoral Life Center.

National Conference of Catholic Bishops. 1980. *Called and Gifted: The American Catholic Laity.* Washington D.C.: United States Catholic Conference.

_____, Committee on the Laity. 1995. *Called and Gifted for the Third Millennium.* Washington D.C.: United States Catholic Conference.

_____, Subcommittee on Lay Ministry. 1998. *Together in God's Service: Toward a Theology of Ecclesial Lay Ministry.* Washington D.C.: United States Catholic Conference.

_____. 1999. *Lay Ecclesial Ministry: The State of the Questions.* Washington D.C.: United States Catholic Conference.

O'Meara, Thomas Franklin. 1999. *Theology of Ministry.* New York: Paulist Press.

Scheets, Francis Kelly. 1995. "Improving Data-Literacy Among Diocesan Administrators," *The Jurist* 55 (1), pp. 369-80.

Schoenherr, Richard and Lawrence Young. 1992. *Full Pews and Empty Altars: The Demographics of the Priest Shortage.* Madison: University of Wisconsin Press.

Schuth, Katarina. 1999. *Seminaries, Theologates and the Future of Church Ministry: An Analysis of Trends and Transitions.* Collegeville, MN: The Liturgical Press.

Stark, Rodney and Roger Finke. 2000. "Catholic Religious Vocations: Decline and Revival," *Review of Religious Research* (December), pp. 125-45.

Walters, Thomas. 1983. *National Profile of Professional Religious Education Coordinators/Directors.* Washington D.C.: National Conference of Diocesan Directors.

_____, Wayne Smith, and Sylvia Macotta. 1993. *A Hopeful Horizon.* Washington, DC: National Catholic Education Association.

1

THE DONATIST CONTROVERSY AND A LOCAL THEOLOGY OF CHURCH MANAGEMENT

Mark F. Fischer

Some people might deny that parish management is theological. To them, management belongs to the realm of law and practical administration. Theology, by contrast, is a kind of knowledge that is always and everywhere true. From this viewpoint theology has nothing to do with the contingent affairs of parish administration, where judgments are made according to a congregation's changing situation. Theology, they would add, is also more important than administration. Where theological principles and administrative issues collide, theology trumps administration. The good parish manager, they would say, should merely observe the law and obey the pastor.

This chapter disputes that view. It argues that a wise parish manager should be a local theologian. Such a manager understands the faith of parishioners. Managers who appeal to universal theological truths, without regard for their applicability to the local situation, may betray those truths and destroy communion in the parish. Good principles of parish management, as we shall see, are rooted in local theology. When wise administrators apply theological principles with careful regard for the local situation, they manifest the Christian character of a parish.

To make this point, we will examine the events in fourth-century Carthage that led to the Donatist schism. In North Africa, an inability to resolve local differences provoked an appeal to Rome. This appeal, valid but premature, weakened the integrity of African church officials. Donatism is a case study of poor administration that had dire consequences.

We shall see the relevance of the Donatist crisis by comparing it to a contemporary parish, St. Brigid's. Part I will show the parallels between the two crises. Part II will examine the administrative issues and explain why an appropriate local solution is always preferable to an appeal to higher authorities. Part III will show how canon law supports the rights of the parish church and the concept of local theology. Let us begin with St. Brigid Church—a real example in which names have been changed—to understand the crisis that the Donatists faced.

Part I: St. Brigid's and the Donatist Controversy

At St. Brigid Church, Bill Bonaducci is the business manager. Retired from General Tire as a division vice president, Bonaducci has been a eucharistic minister for twenty years. After his retirement he has had more time to give to his parish. The former pastor at St. Brigid, Monsignor Clark, needed someone with Bonaducci's expertise to help with the budget and parish accounts. Bonaducci was happy for the chance to serve. He is not a trained theologian, but is an avid reader of church history. He wants to know how God is present in the concrete reality of St. Brigid's. He tries to ground his administrative decisions in what can be called a local theology of St. Brigid Church.[1] Bonaducci's local theology was tested in a crisis that occurred two years ago.

1. The Frustrated School Board

St. Brigid has a thriving parochial school. Strong parental support and a supplement from the parish bingo keep it on a firm financial footing. Two years ago, the school principal announced her retirement. Monsignor Clark asked the school board to plan a retirement party. In addition, he asked the board to help prepare a job description for a new principal, to interview applicants, and to recommend those who were suitable. The very capable school board immediately got to work. Several people applied for the job of principal, and Monsignor Clark and the board began to interview them. Bill Bonaducci occasionally sat in on the interviews.

Then, in the middle of the outgoing principal's last year, Monsignor Clark became ill with cancer. The school board continued to interview applicants without him and submitted its recommendations. But before Monsignor Clark could act on them, he resigned his pastorate for medical reasons. The bishop appointed a new pastor, Father Jack Manly. He presided at the outgoing principal's retirement party. Bill Bonaducci assisted the board with an Italian buffet at the parish hall, where Monsignor Clark presented the outgoing principal with a gift of appreciation.

Then the crisis began. The new pastor, Father Manly, did not accept the school board's recommendations for the new principal. He hired Marie Courtois (whom he had known when she was principal at another parochial school) as the new principal of St. Brigid. This angered the school board. Its members had worked hard to attract applicants, interview them, and recommend qualified people. They had no confidence in Marie Courtois, who had not been an applicant.

As the fall term began, relations between the new principal and the school board—never warm to begin with—cooled steadily. The board members resented the pastor's appointment of Marie Courtois and did not hide their dissatisfaction from the other school parents. Although Father Manly clearly stated that he had confidence in Courtois, the school board members scrutinized her every decision and were quick to criticize. The new principal felt that the board was undermining her.

Marie Courtois turned to Bill Bonaducci for help. She described the chilly relations she had with the school board. She explained that, although she enjoyed Father Manly's support, it was not enough. The board members viewed him as a partisan who had ignored their recommendations. The board, however, trusted the business manager. Marie Courtois thought that the members might accept Bill Bonaducci as a facilitator of school board meetings.

Bonaducci appreciated the importance of the new principal's request. Although the appointment of Marie Courtois was perfectly legal, he knew that the board felt slighted by Father Manly. Bonaducci saw the potential for division in the parish, where the opposition of a resentful board might damage confidence in the parochial school. St. Brigid faced, not a legal issue, but an administrative crisis. It was a crisis with theological implications, reminiscent of the Donatist controversy of the fourth century. With his love of Church history, the school board's refusal to accept Marie Courtois reminded Bonaducci of the refusal by Carthaginian Christians to accept their new bishop in the year 311.

The Donatist controversy is a complicated story. Readers impatient with historical examples might want to skip ahead. But Donatism offers a salutary example. Whoever wants to see how a failure to grapple with local management can lead to theological disaster, read on.

2. The Donatist Controversy

The Donatist controversy shows what can happen when church leaders disengage instead of resolving their differences. The Donatists wrongly taught that sanctity, the personal holiness of the believer, is necessary for the administration of sacraments and church membership. The Church condemned Donatism, saying that the sinful minister is less important than the ministry, which belongs primarily to

Christ. This argument clarified an important issue. But its focus on the universal tended to obscure the local. The Donatists were more than just heretics. They also criticized (with some justification) the corruption of church leaders. Today, some scholars believe that the Roman response to Donatism harmed the churches of North Africa.[2] Rome, they say, acted less like a sister church and more like the appellate court for North Africa. This weakened the collegial structure of African Christianity. It may even have paved the way for the inroads of Islam in the seventh century. Let us turn to the facts of the Donatist controversy.

The Facts of the Case
The authority of the Catholic hierarchy in North Africa reached a low point in the year 311, when a council of seventy local bishops declared invalid the ordination of a certain Caecilian as Bishop of Carthage. The African bishops had no confidence in Caecilian because of his moral cowardice in the face of imperial persecution. He had been the deacon of the previous bishop of Carthage, Mensurius, who was himself suspected of collaboration with the empire. In 304, during the persecution under Diocletian, Bishop Mensurius had fecklessly surrendered Church property to imperial authorities. For that betrayal many of the faithful despised him as a *traditor*, a coward who gave up sacred books and vessels to save his skin.[3]

Things had been different a hundred years earlier. In 213, the African theologian Tertullian had extolled the glory of martyrdom. He taught that flight from persecution was not permissible.[4] In many ecclesiastical circles of Bishop Mensurius' time, however, that heroism had cooled. Indeed, Mensurius looked with suspicion on the enthusiasts who were willing to die for the faith. He forbade his flock to do anything that would deliberately court martyrdom. Indeed, he cynically suspected that some members were less interested in dying for the faith than in the luxuries and wealth an accused martyr might gain from sympathetic Christians during a long legal process. His deacon, Caecilian, himself carried out Bishop Mensurius' wishes. Caecilian cooperated with imperial forces by discouraging Christian resistance and the cult of the martyrs. His rebuke to a wealthy Spaniard named Lucilla, for kissing the bones of a martyr who had not been officially recognized, earned him her lasting enmity. Moreover, Caecilian interfered with the Christian sympathizers of the imprisoned. He prevented them from bringing food to their comrades in jail. All this was not long before 312, the year of Emperor Constantine's conversion. The imperium did not seem as hostile to Mensurius and Caecilian as it had to Tertullian in the previous century.

Those who refused to collaborate with the emperor during the persecution of 304 despised Bishop Mensurius. After Mensurius died, Deacon Caecilian was duly chosen by the Carthaginian citizenry (but not by the ordinary people). Three neighboring bishops (one of whom was an accused *traditor*) ordained Caecilian as the new Bishop of Carthage. Many Christians bitterly recalled his efforts and those of his predecessor to cooperate with imperial authorities. Some presbyters who were custodians of Church property refused to reveal its whereabouts to the newly consecrated Caecilian. Secundus of Tigisis, the Primate of Numidia, summoned a council of seventy bishops. Its members, calling themselves the Church of the Martyrs, declared that a *traditor* such as Caecilian could not act as a bishop. They consecrated a second bishop, Majorinus. Eventually they excommunicated those who were loyal to the public sinner, Caecilian. They taught that any person initiated into the faith by such *traditores* needed to be rebaptized.

Attempts at a Solution

The facts of the Donatist controversy enable us to see a parallel between it and the situation at St. Brigid. Just as the Carthaginians refused to accept Caecilian as their bishop, so the members of the St. Brigid School Board refused to accept Marie Courtois as their new principal. The board members had good reason to be angry. They had, under the direction of the former pastor, interviewed applicants for the position of principal and had submitted their recommendations. But the new pastor, Father Manly, not only rejected the recommendations, but appointed a principal who had never even applied for the post. Marie Courtois was tainted by her association with Father Manly, just as Deacon Caecilian was tainted by his association with Bishop Mensurius.

Bill Bonaducci accepted Courtois's invitation to serve as mediator and to facilitate meetings of the school board. He had two aims. The first was to help the school board maintain its effective role. In the past, the board members had capably reviewed the school budget and contributed to institutional planning. Bonaducci knew that the school needed their help. His second aim was to overcome the alienation of the school board members. They were angry at what they perceived as an insult to their integrity. There were rumors that the board might protest the appointment of Courtois, damage her reputation and that of Father Manly, or even lead a boycott of the school. Bonaducci did not want the board members to walk out. He wanted them to keep talking with the pastor and the principal. That was the first remedy he sought.

In ancient North Africa, disputants also sought remedies as the controversy heated up. The Church of the Martyrs eventually took the name of Donatus, the eloquent and forceful bishop who succeeded Majorinus. He insisted on rebaptizing Christians whose faith had weakened under persecution and who subsequently repented. But Donatus was never recognized in Rome as Bishop of Carthage. In 312, after Constantine's conversion, the emperor showed himself to be a Christian by (among other things) granting economic assistance to the Catholic clergy of North Africa. He chose Bishop Caecilian as the legitimate distributor of these economic benefits, giving him powers of discretion and allowing him to exclude rival claimants. The party of Majorinus and, later, Donatus wanted its share, but had no process of appeal in Carthage.

So they appealed to the emperor. Constantine first deferred to Pope Miltiades (or Melchiades), who heard the case in Rome with fifteen Italian bishops. They declared Caecilian, not Donatus, to be Bishop of Carthage. This infuriated the Donatist bishops in Africa, whose congregations would not accept "Catholics." In Donatist eyes, the word "Catholic" had come to mean the "Church of the Traditors," the unholy communion of pusillanimous traitor-bishops with the Roman Empire. So the Donatists, after Pope Miltiades' death, appealed to the newly elected Pope Silvester, who ordered a new ecclesiastical trial. But this second trial, held at Arles in 314 and attended by bishops and representatives of 40-50 dioceses (but not by the pope himself), also found in favor of Caecilian. Finally the Donatists appealed for a decision from the emperor himself. At Milan in 315 Constantine heard arguments by the opposing sides, and he found Caecilian innocent. But Constantine's efforts to unite the African church by ecclesiastical pronouncement were a failure.

St. Augustine was Donatism's best-known opponent. Writing around 412, a century after the Donatists' rejection of Bishop Caecilian, Augustine had abandoned hope for a local solution. Rome had to refute Donatism by teaching that it is not the human minister but Christ who administers the sacraments. "Whether a man receive the sacrament of baptism from a faithful or faithless minister," wrote Augustine, "his whole hope is in Christ."[5] This was among the earliest expressions of the doctrine that the grace of baptism stems from the *opus operatum*, from the effectiveness of the work of Christ himself, independent of the worthiness of the minister. This is the standard treatment of Donatism in theological textbooks. But the arguments of Augustine did not win over the Donatists. Eventually the imperial military had to quell the Donatist revolt, and its bishops and clergy were exiled from Africa. Peter Brown called Donatism "a great church driven underground"[6] by the alliance of the Catholic Church and the empire.

Legitimacy of the Dispute

At St. Brigid Church, Bill Bonaducci might well have taken the same stand that Augustine took against the Donatists. He might have dismissed the claims of the St. Brigid School Board. The board members felt that Father Manly had wronged them by not consulting before the appointment of Marie Courtois. But the pastor believed that the board had no reason to be upset. Bonaducci might have simply agreed that Father Manly had every right to hire a principal without consulting the board. Even if the school board members felt that Father Manly had shown bad faith by not consulting them, canon law and diocesan regulations did not oblige him to consult. And even though the school board had no confidence in the new principal, the appointment of Marie Courtois was undoubtedly valid. About the board's anger, Bonaducci might have brusquely replied, "Get over it."

It is a credit to his administrative acumen that he did not. When he learned that the board members were going to make a formal protest to the diocesan department of education, he telephoned each member. The members argued that department guidelines clearly recommended consultation with the school board before the appointment of a principal. Bonaducci knew, however, that the guidelines were advisory, not obligatory. A formal protest by the board would have hardened its position, he suspected, to no avail. The diocese would have supported Father Manly, humiliating the board further.

At the same time, however, Bonaducci felt compassion toward the board members. Privately, he felt that Father Manly should have consulted them. He believed that Father Manly, by appointing Marie Courtois without consulting the board, put her into an impossibly awkward position. Although he did not express this feeling to the board, he was able to dissuade the members from making a formal protest. He promised to arrange a meeting to work out the grievances.

Seventeen centuries earlier, at the time of the Donatist controversy, there was little evidence of conciliation. The Donatists took a hard stance, and their opposition to Bishop Caecilian must have seemed honorable and even courageous. Caecilian's moral authority was weak from the start. Although he was duly elected and validly appointed, his link to his predecessor, Bishop Mensurius, had tarnished him. Caecilian's early collaboration with imperial authority, and his refusal to support its victims, deprived him of credibility. His consecration by an accused *traditor* diminished the little moral authority that he had. His attempts to distribute imperial funds may even have struck his enemies as influence peddling. His administration of the Church in Carthage led to scandal and division. The opponents of Caecilian undoubtedly saw themselves as supporters of a faith untainted by imperial influence. Their faith, sincere and upright, resolutely insisted on public credibility.

The Donatist Church of the Martyrs reverberated with other North African movements, such as Montanism and Novatianism. They emphasized adherence to the Holy Spirit and resisted accommodation with the world. Bishop Caecilian represented neither of these. His moral authority was almost nonexistent. Instead of being rebuked for cooperating in the imperial persecution of 304 and for his association with an accused *traditor*, Bishop Mensurius, Caecilian was rewarded and became bishop-elect after Mensurius' death. He did not seek the approval of African bishops who had remained faithful during the persecution, but arranged his consecration by another accused *traditor*, Felix of Aptonga (or Autumna). Shortly thereafter, Constantine freed the clergy (newly regarded as public servants) from the obligation of shouldering municipal expenses and granted them monetary benefits. The Catholic Church's support for Caecilian, the distributor of imperial funds, may have looked like a cynical effort to protect its assets.

The Donatist Church, by contrast, may have regarded Constantine's gift as a payoff to Caecilian for services to the imperium during the period of persecution. Undoubtedly the Donatists saw him as a merely valid representative of a corrupted church catholic that now sought to buy the allegiance of whatever clergy would vow obedience. Donatism was Spirit-led and counter-cultural; Catholicism was compromised by its links to the State. Donatism stood in the tradition of martyrdom and of faithful witness; Catholicism represented accommodation with the world and a preoccupation with material gain. Donatism maintained what today we would call a zero-tolerance policy toward immoral compromises with an oppressive regime; Catholicism stood for tolerance toward the lapsed. When we ask which party held more firmly to the dangerous memory of Jesus' passion and death, Donatism seems to have had an edge.

If today we regard the Donatist controversy as merely a textbook illustration of heresy, we fail to understand it. Donatism was more than a North African threat to orthodoxy and to the universal Church. Indeed, the Donatists had legitimate grievances. We make a mistake if we examine the controversy solely at the universal level, neglecting the local. The local dimension reveals the theological importance of church management. If the grievances of the Donatists could have been resolved at the local level, we might today speak of Donatism as a local protest movement, not a heresy.

Part II: Church Management and Local Theology

How might a good pastor-administrator have allayed the grievances of the Donatist party? The answer to this question is speculative. No one can return to ancient Carthage and repair the schism of the fourth century. But it is possible to imagine what might have happened. In Part II we will compare the facts of the Donatist crisis to the recent situation at St. Brigid Church, where wise parish administration prevented division. Let us begin there before we turn to North Africa. Then, after speculating about what good administration might have accomplished with the Donatists, we can turn to the underlying question. It is the question of application. Why is the application to a local situation of universal principles essential to a theology of parish administration?

1. Applications of Administrative Science

Bill Bonaducci calmed a tempestuous situation at St. Brigid by kindness and astute management. He began by acknowledging the complaints of the school board. Members were aggrieved because Father Manly had not consulted before appointing the new principal. And they were aggrieved with Marie Courtois because she was not the board's choice. They had had no say in her appointment. She was to them an unknown.

After acknowledging the board's complaints, Bonaducci began to search for ways to employ the talents of the board. He sought opportunities for the board to make a contribution to St. Brigid School. He wanted to restore the relationship of trust that had once existed between the board and the principal.

No one can say how Bonaducci's approach, the approach of a pastoral administrator, might have worked in another situation. As I said, we do not know if it might have made a difference with the Donatist controversy. However, we can outline Bonaducci's approach and imaginatively apply it to fourth-century Carthage.

Restoring Equanimity at St. Brigid

Bill Bonaducci recognized that the crisis at St. Brigid was, first of all, a crisis of leadership. Father Manly and his appointee, Marie Courtois, were new to the parish. Although they had the legal right—the bishop having entrusted Father Manly with the parish, and the new pastor having appointed the principal—nevertheless their moral credibility was low. By contrast, the school board comprised established parishioners. They had been in the parish a long time. Their children were enrolled in the school. The members were angry because they believed that the new pastor had violated their trust.

Bonaducci appreciated the importance of law. So he persuaded Father Manly (who dislikes confrontation) to attend the first school board meeting and present Marie Courtois to the members. Manly emphasized her competence. Where she had been principal, he said, the parish did not even need bingo to balance the school's books. Manly apologized for not consulting the board before appointing Courtois. "I heard that you had interviewed applicants and made recommendations to Monsignor Clarke," he said, "but from the moment that the bishop appointed me pastor, I wanted Marie on my parish team." By getting Father Manly to introduce Marie Courtois and to apologize, Bonaducci was hoping to disarm the board and underline the new principal's right to be there.

Courtois then led the rest of the meeting. Her businesslike manner, courtesy, and attention to detail revealed the qualities for which Father Manly had chosen her. Before the meeting, Bonaducci and Courtois had brainstormed about the agenda. They agreed that the principal needed to share responsibility with the board for school decision making. So Courtois requested the board's help in assessing the school's needs and establishing a new tuition schedule. She laid out a plan for evaluating various aspects of the school—maintenance, personnel policies, and facilities development—over the next nine months. Each of the board members had at least one child in the school and knew that this request had financial consequences. The members were impressed with the principal's vision and her willingness to involve the board in school decisions.

After the first board meeting, several members continued to resist Marie Courtois. In their eyes, she could never measure up to the applicants for the position of principal whom they had interviewed. She would always remain the pastor's appointee, the one who had circumvented their search process. But Courtois, with Bonaducci's help, had gotten off on the right foot. The board members knew that she was giving them serious attention. Although significant differences with the board lay ahead (as we shall see), Courtois' efforts at the first meeting blunted the force of the board's resentment. Bonaducci's knowledge of leadership, personnel supervision, and conflict management had helped Courtois defuse a potentially explosive situation.

Managerial Solutions in Carthage

These skills were noticeably lacking in the way that the church of North Africa handled the Donatist crisis. Poor management led to heresy and schism. For the purposes of developing a theology of church management, however, we need not reject the Catholic interpretation of Donatism. We need not reject the doctrine of the permanent character of baptism, the priority of Christ over the human minister of the sacraments, or the doctrine of *ex opere operato*. It is enough to respect the apparent good intentions of the Donatist party. We will begin with some speculations about how a local theology might have led to better managerial decisions regarding Donatism. Would greater attention to the needs of North African Christians, and to the selection of their bishops, have resolved the crisis?

Textbooks usually treat the Donatist controversy as a case that enabled the Church to articulate a universal principle: even a minister in mortal sin can validly administer the sacraments.[7] But the Donatist controversy, examined at the local level, illustrates more than the principle of sacramental efficacy. It raises questions about church management. Once we examine the Donatist controversy in light of the managerial disciplines, the Catholic response seems less than exemplary.

Human resource management. Bishop Mensurius appointed Deacon Caecilian to suppress Christian opposition to imperial forces in Carthage. Caecilian was reportedly worse than the imperial persecutors. How well was he supervised? Could Mensurius have dampened Caecilian's ardor?

Information gathering. Caecilian apparently believed that North African Christians would accept him after his consecration as bishop. The records show that he was chosen by "the whole citizenry"—but not by the ordinary people, who had Donatist sympathies. Did he know nothing about the Donatists' mounting disapproval of him?

Consultation. One of Caecilian's three consecrators was Felix of Aptonga, himself an accused *traditor*. The normal number of consecrators was twelve. Wouldn't it have been more prudent to consult with some of the seventy Donatist bishops before going ahead with the episcopal ordination?

Conflict management. Caecilian publicly humiliated Lucilla, the wealthy Spaniard, for kissing the bones of an unofficial martyr. Granting the need for uniform liturgical practices, could Catholic officials have curbed with greater sensitivity the enthusiasm of those who revered the martyrs?

Stewardship. Part of Caecilian's clash with the Donatists was the disposition of funds provided by Constantine. Would Caecilian have been less repugnant to the Donatists if he had articulated a clear policy of budgeting and income distribution?

Leadership. The charismatic leader, whose gifts are recognized by followers, is stronger than the delegated leader, whose position has been given by superiors. How effective was the delegated leadership of Caecilian, who tried to motivate his followers by distributing imperial largesse?

Decision making. After the consecration of Caecilian, the Donatists summoned the Council of Seventy, elected Majorinus, and appealed to Constantine and Pope Miltiades. Wouldn't the principle of subsidiarity have dictated a local solution?

Liability. One of the ways to diminish legal liability is to create policies in the event of conflict. There should be clear avenues of appeal. The fact that the Donatist controversy generated multiple appeals—to the Lateran, Arles, and Milan—suggests that the church lacked clear appeal policies.

In short, these questions about church management suggest that Donatism was not just a heresy that the Catholic Church needed to eradicate on the universal level. It was also a local problem with political and economic dimensions. The principle of subsidiarity suggests that problems should be solved at the lowest appropriate level. In the case of Donatism, Caecilian's opponents too quickly appealed to Rome. Could the Carthaginians have solved the dispute in Africa? Would it not have been preferable to seek a local solution among the college of North African bishops?

That the Donatists themselves appealed to Rome suggests that Carthage already viewed itself in 312 as a minor daughter of the Roman church rather than as a peer. Rome was the center of the world, religiously and politically. After the conversion of Constantine it became the distribution point for economic benefits. So it was natural for the Donatists to appeal to Rome. But had they solved the Donatist controversy in a local way, it might have strengthened African Christianity. An application of a contemporary understanding of the local church and of wise managerial principles may even have forestalled the schism.

2. The Local Dimension of a Theology of Church Management
Bill Bonaducci persuaded the St. Brigid School Board not to do what the Donatists did. He talked them out of protesting to the diocese Father Manly's appointment of Marie Courtois. The diocese would almost certainly have rejected the board's protest. Bonaducci also worked with the new principal in developing a work plan for the board. According to this plan, the board would share responsibility for preparing the budget and establishing a tuition schedule. This avoided another

problem that dogged the Donatists. They had no say in the distribution of imperial funds to church officials. Their opposition to Bishop Caecilian meant that they would probably receive nothing. By contrast, Bonaducci and Courtois planned to share responsibility with the board about finances. They included the board members in decision making.

Bonaducci was wise to seek conciliation at the parish level. By doing so, he affirmed the principle of local theology. Every locale has its own way of understanding how God leads a congregation. Problems that can be solved at St. Brigid's should not be solved by diocesan officials. In the Donatist controversy, however, local theology was overshadowed. The Donatists appealed to Rome, and Rome took the side of Bishop Caecilian. The Donatists were rejected, and the schism widened. It is not always necessary to solve disputes by appealing to higher authorities. What is the proper relation between the local church and Rome, between the parish church and the diocese?

It is appropriate for managers like Bonaducci to defer to their superiors. Managers ought to accept the proper decisions of ecclesial authorities as binding upon parishes. Bonaducci rightly has to answer to Father Manly. The pastor in turn is assigned by the bishop, and the bishop is appointed by the pope. Our aim is not to define exceptions or identify areas where Bonaducci need not obey. Rather, our concern is to show the importance, managerial and theological, of Bonaducci's local decisions. The term "local church" usually refers to the diocese, not the parish, but for our purposes we are considering the parish as the local church. There managers like Bonaducci deserve a broad scope for exercising judgment in their daily work.

Our example has been the Donatist heresy. Rome, as the universal Church's authoritative voice, rightly condemned Donatism. But Rome is not identical to the universal Church. Although the Bishop of Rome has primacy within the college of bishops, the universal Church is truly present in the other dioceses as well. Other churches—local churches—enjoy a rightful autonomy in the areas where they can and should govern. Prior to the Donatists' appeal to Pope Miltiades, their controversy was a matter for the local church. Before Donatism became a heresy, it was a movement of legitimate protest that cried out for adroit management by the bishops of North Africa. There, in the region surrounding the provincial capital of Carthage, the universal Church was truly present, just as it was present at Rome. There the Christian principles of forgiveness, justice, and charity could have been exercised. The North African Church could have managed the Donatist controversy better.

We will return to this point in Part III. For now, let us explore the meaning of the local theology in which managers such as Bill play an important role. Let us first examine the inner foundation of a local theology of church management. What is the basis for understanding St. Brigid Church as a locus of theology?

Rahner's Parochial Principle

Some might object that it is pretentious to speak of a local theology of parish management. Bill Bonaducci is a manager, they will say, not a theologian. He is not equipped to understand what he does from a properly theological viewpoint. Only an academic theologian or church official can be said to do real theology.

This objection, I would argue, discourages Catholics from reflecting on their local situation. It prevents them from participating fully in the effort to make the parish what it is meant to be, namely, a sacrament of communion. It wrongly suggests that theology is exclusively a professional enterprise, limited to those with specific credentials. Theology is more than that. It is the effort of faithful people to understand what they already believe. To be sure, Bill Bonaducci is not a writer of theological books and articles. But he is an official in the parish, committed to its mission and engaged in trying to make it accord with the gospel.

One of the obstacles to a theology of the local church, and especially of church management, is the neglect of the "parochial principle." The parochial principle is Karl Rahner's way of expressing the theological structure of the parish. There, he said, a pastor is competent to exercise the care of souls who gather in a given locale. Rahner summed it up this way: "One man is in charge of the whole pastoral work done among a group of people who are collected together under him because they have their home on the same soil."[8] Today we might balk at the phrase, "in charge of the whole pastoral work," because it seems to contradict the idea of collaborative ministry. But Rahner did not mean that the priest alone does pastoral work. Pastors undoubtedly rely on their staffs. Rahner's point was rather that the parish, and the pastor to whom it is entrusted, cannot be characterized as mere stand-ins for the diocese and the bishop. Parishes are more than franchises, we can say, and pastors are more than branch managers. Indeed, the parish is "the diocese in miniature," said Rahner. It is the place where Christians find a home and become a people.

Rahner radicalized the parochial principle in his 1956 contribution to a collection of essays on the parish. There he argued that the parish is more than a transitory representation of the universal Church, defined as the perfect society founded by Christ with a permanent existence. The parish, said Rahner, is rather "the highest degree of actuality of the total Church."[9] Undoubtedly the total or universal Church has a unique dignity. It endures by divine right, sacred tradition, apostolic succession, and ecclesiastical law. At the same time, however, this church is unfinished. It must become what it is meant to be. "It must translate itself from a certain potentiality into a definite, determined actuality," claimed Rahner, "and the whole enduring essence of the Church is directed to this event."[10] It takes place in the parish.

For that reason, we can say that the parochial principle is the inner foundation of a local theology of church management. Local decisions help to make the parish a sacrament of Christ. According to the parochial principle, the parish priest is more than a legitimate proxy for the bishop as the real pastor of the entire diocesan flock. The parish business manager does more than carry out the directives of others, functioning without theological consequence. The pastor and other managers help to make the parish a sign and instrument of communion. The parish does more than "represent" the universal Church. In a radical sense, the parochial principle means that the parish is the "event" of the universal Church.

Applying Rahner's Insight

Bill Bonaducci knows that St. Brigid Church is where his parishioners encounter Jesus Christ. So he tries to make the parish's decisions their decisions. When they feel excluded, as the school board did, he tries to make amends. He consults them, replies promptly to their inquiries, and shares their concerns with the pastor. Although Bonaducci loves the universal Church, he appreciates that an appeal to church authority does not always resolve disputes. He knows that a theology that remains at a universal level is incomplete. The parochial principle teaches that the parish is where people encounter God. Parish managers must connect their decisions to the faith of parishioners.

If they fail to do so, then others may make the connection for them. These others may view the parish as merely a proxy for the diocese or wherever they imagine the real church to be. This undermines the parish and damages its ability to be a sign and instrument of communion. Good managers appreciate that the parish is more than a mere exemplar, representative, or illustration of a reality that exists elsewhere. People encounter Christ in the concrete locale of the parish, and especially in the communion of parishioners for which the Eucharist is the greatest sacrament. That encounter, we can say in Rahner's word, "actualizes" the universal Church. There it becomes a concrete event. This insight found expression in *Lumen Gentium* 26, which stated that "The Church of Christ is truly present in all legitimate congregations of the faithful."

The key word is "legitimate." It means "valid" or "established by law," that is, by canon law. Such law gives the diocese and the parish their legal existence. To be sure, canon law is a human construct. It does not express the entirety of the mystery of the Church, for the Church is more than a juridically founded society. But canon law does give the parochial principle its validity. It establishes parishes. It entrusts them to pastors. It entitles each member of the faithful to call upon a priest. If we want to know how the parochial principle (as the inner foundation of a local theology of church management) really exists, then we must see how canon law supports it.

Part III: The Relevance of the Law

When a new conflict arose at St Brigid (this time, as we shall see, about bingo), Bonaducci knew that a curt defense of parish decisions in the name of canon law would not suffice. No school board member who complained about Father Manly's unwillingness to consult was ever satisfied to hear, "The pastor has a legal right to do it his way." The law exists to serve justice. When Bonaducci heard the school board's complaint, his first goal was to understand it. He wanted to weigh it and take appropriate action. To be sure, a legal defense of parish practice is appropriate, but never as an end in itself. The basic end of all parish activity is to maintain the parish's communion in Christ. All managerial decisions, including legal ones, should serve that end.

At the same time, however, Bonaducci recognized the importance of canon law. In it the Church has enshrined rules to govern and maintain the Christian community. The 1983 revision of canon law supports a theology of church management, we can say, because it codifies the Second Vatican Council's emphasis on the local church. This is rather surprising, for one would suspect the opposite. One would suspect that canon law, the law of the universal Church, exclusively would emphasize conformity, especially conformity with Roman expectations. But that is not the case. The law introduces social principles, rights and obligations, as well as ways of claiming those rights, all of which strengthen a local theology of church management. The law suggests how the parish, by exercising its rights, can be a more effective sacrament of communion.

This chapter does not intend to demonstrate the relevance of canon law to every field of church management (e.g., budgeting, supervising personnel, and consultative decision making). It is enough to show how the law clarifies the concept of local theology. To do that, we will first describe the principles and rights that are relevant to local theology, and the means provided by the law for vindicating those rights. Then we will show the law's relevance to the example of the Donatist controversy and apply it to church management today, in situations like that of St. Brigid.

Social Principles

How do the social principles enshrined in canon law support a local theology of management? James Coriden has enumerated four such principles: the right of association, the common good, the principle of solidarity, and that of subsidiarity.[11] To be sure, these principles apply universally. Catholics everywhere have the right to join or create societies, to participate in a search for the common good, to build up groups in solidarity with one another, and to enjoy respect and self-determination. The application of these principles is universal. At the same time, however, each of them strengthens the idea of the local church. The principles support the idea that parishes and dioceses are not poor reflections of the universal Church, but that the Church of Christ is truly present in them.

Consider the example of the Donatist Church. If North African Christians in the fourth century had had an understanding of the principles of solidarity and subsidiarity, the Donatist controversy might have resolved itself in a far different manner. The Donatists themselves might have delayed their appeal to the emperor. A delay would have given them time to work out their grievances with Caecilian in Carthage. The Catholics, for their part, might have applied the techniques of conciliation and decision making, techniques founded upon the principle of solidarity. Such techniques would have recognized the Donatists' legitimate complaints. The Catholics then might have generously conceded the scandal of Caecilian's collaboration with the enemy, the shortcomings of his leadership style, and his selective distribution of imperial funds. The fourth-century application of principles embodied today in canon law might have delayed or even avoided the schism.

Why are the social principles of canon law relevant to parish managers? They indicate general commitments—theological commitments—that the Bill Bonaduccis of today ought to make their own. Parish managers should not fear parishioners who meet to discuss the future of the parochial school or the religious education program. They should not worry when parishioners feel different than the pastor about the rectory renovation. Parish groups that express support for one another should not be cause for alarm. Parishioners who want diocesan policies applied in a way suitable to the parish recognize the value of local decision making. Good managers rejoice when their people show initiative and take responsibility. In Bill Bonaducci's eyes, the parishioners of St. Brigid are not adversaries but partners in a communion.

Rights and Obligations

St. Brigid Church, we can say, has its own personality. Canon law grants it rights that distinguish it from the universal Church. These rights reinforce a local theology of the parish. They suggest that St. Brigid's has its own standing and is distinct from the diocesan or universal Church. To be sure, the law does not regard the parish as an independent entity. St. Brigid's stands in communion with the wider Church. But the very fact that canon law grants it distinct rights indicates that St. Brigid's has a dignity that should not be infringed. It is a dignity that the universal Church pledges to support.

The 1983 code states that parishes are "juridic persons." They are entities with a legal personality, writes Coriden, and they enjoy many of the rights and obligations afforded by the code to individuals.[12] For example, the parish has a right to exist and cannot be suppressed without due process. Every parish is obliged to maintain communion with the diocesan church, contributing to and receiving assistance from it. At the same time, it enjoys a fundamental equality with every other parish. Its members have a right to hear the Word of God, to celebrate the sacraments, and to receive the care of a pastor and his associates, who are themselves bound by canonical standards. Parishes are entitled to devote themselves to apostolic activities, to be consulted, to be educated in faith, to exercise their own mission, to grow spiritually, and to acquire what they need to achieve their mission. These rights and obligations of individuals suggest the dignity of the parish. It is not merely an object of the church's law, but an active subject or juridic person as well.

If the rights and obligations of the local church had been clear in fourth-century North Africa, the Donatist controversy may have turned out differently. Consider, for a moment, the Donatists' fundamental objection to the appointment of Bishop Caecilian. They believed that he was unworthy to lead. His valid consecration did not make up for his lack of moral authority as a collaborator with the church's persecutors. But the Donatists were unable to make this point in a convincing way. Indeed, by consecrating Majorinus as their own bishop, they violated the obligation to maintain communion. Their premature appeal to Rome showed a lack of patience. Writing a century later, Augustine could dismiss the Donatist Council of Seventy as "a multitude infuriated and infatuated by the cup of error and wickedness."[13] They appeared merely as fanatics.

But even fanatics deserve a hearing. And a council of seventy bishops, however hotheaded, should never have been dismissed. Today we would say that they had a right to convene, to be consulted, and to receive a portion of the economic benefits granted by Constantine.[14] Had the Donatists known and asserted these rights, the controversy might have been resolved. The mere assertion of rights might have resulted in a deeper inquiry. It might have motivated the parties to repair the breach in trust, to develop fair policies of imperial fund distribution, and to build consensus. The Donatists might have sought redress rather than rupture.

The same is true in today's parish. Indeed, Bill Bonaducci had to remind Father Jack Manly of the school board's right to be heard when a minor tempest blew up over bingo. Manly and Marie Courtois disliked sponsoring weekly games of bingo to support the parochial school. They felt that it was a form of gambling, and so barely legal under civil law. Moreover, they believed that it preyed upon the elderly—who formed the majority of players—many of whom were on fixed incomes. Manly and Courtois had privately decided to raise the tuition and phase bingo out.

When the school board members (all of whom were parents of school pupils) heard about the decision, they were incensed. From their viewpoint, bingo income was an essential adjunct to tuition. It enabled the school to purchase "extras" such as new classroom projectors or science equipment. Many parochial schools, they knew, had successful bingo programs. Some school board members even felt that the pastor and the principal, by abolishing bingo and raising tuition, were trying to punish them.

Claiming Their Rights

In the face of this new crisis, Bonaducci persuaded Father Manly to discuss the matter with the school board. The pastor knew that he was entitled to decide policy, but grudgingly agreed to a meeting. Bonaducci knew that Manly could not very well refuse to meet with the board. By asking for the meeting, the board members were only claiming their right to present their opinions to the pastor.

During the meeting Father Manly came to realize that the matter of bingo had symbolic importance for the board. Bingo symbolized its share in responsibility for school finance. Although the pastor and the principal disliked the bingo program, they appreciated its financial significance, both to the school and to the parents of pupils. Manly and Courtois knew that, by making a concession to the board's desire to maintain the bingo program, they would be showing a willingness to honor its wishes. So they agreed to continue the program. This satisfied the board members. Their insistence on meeting with the pastor enabled them to effectively represent their views.

It is not enough for parishioners, like the St. Brigid School Board, to merely know their rights. They must also claim them. The pastor, who in canon law represents the parish in all juridic affairs, is pre-eminently entitled to make claims on the parish's behalf. But in addition to the pastor and his substitutes, others with a direct parish interest may also stake a claim. They may do so in a variety of ways, the most formal of which is due process in an ecclesiastical court. Well before taking that step, however, there are lesser means of recourse. Coriden[15] outlines three of them:

- By engaging in initiatives that affect the parish and there looking out for its interest;
- By personally appealing to those who threaten the parish's rights and inviting conciliation and mediation; and
- By requesting review of an administrative decision to the author of the decision or to that person's hierarchical superior.

By these means, the parish asserts its rights, stakes a claim to them, and sees that they are honored. The St. Brigid School Board did this more effectively than the Donatists.

The Donatist Church too quickly seized upon the most formal means of claiming its rights. Scholars of the controversy have noted that there were legitimate grounds for the Donatist claim against the consecration of Caecilian. Secundus of Tigisis, who convened the Council of Seventy, could have argued that he as Primate of Numidia had a right to consecrate the new Primate of Africa at Carthage. But there were other African traditions of consecration, and Secundus may not have prevailed.[16] We have no record of Secundus asserting his rights regarding the Bishop of Carthage before the death of Bishop Mensurius. Nor did Secundus engage in a personal appeal to Caecilian. Instead, he took it upon himself to consider Caecilian's election invalid, and he appointed an interim administrator (who was reportedly murdered by Caecilian's party).[17] Doubtless, Secundus invited Caecilian to attend the Council of Seventy, but he refused to appear. Instead, Caecilian invited Secundus himself to state his complaints at Caecilian's own church. Secundus declined, and the Council of Seventy issued its condemnation.

Had the parties to the dispute claimed their rights in an incremental fashion, starting with personal appeals and a search for mediators, things might have turned out differently. Today we would say that a local church first should try to solve its own problems by logical and deliberate steps. Bill Bonaducci took those steps when he persuaded his pastor to meet with the unhappy members of the school board. Canon law commends this incremental approach. Such an approach, coupled with the recognition of social principles, rights, and obligations implicit in canon law, enables parishes like St. Brigid to realize their true selves. It helps parishes to manifest their sacramental nature.

Conclusion

Bill Bonaducci knows implicitly that his local decisions have theological consequences. The decisions may concern parish budgets, personnel supervision, or even bingo, but at the deepest level they reflect his and the parish's relation to God. Parish managers may think that their work has nothing to do with theology. This conclusion is false. The Donatist controversy provides a warning to contemporary church leaders. Poor management of a crisis can lead to heresy and schism.

Our analysis of Donatism in Part I revealed how management failures reverberate in theology. When we viewed the Donatist controversy in the light of eight managerial disciplines, we saw how poor choices in North Africa led to theological disaster. Good managers like Bill Bonaducci have an instinct for the practical. They know implicitly that it reflects an understanding of God, an understanding that ought to shape parish decisions. Poor managers lack this instinct. When confronted with problems, they ignore their own theological resources and appeal to outside authorities, as did the Donatists.

What is the basis for understanding the parish as a locale for theology? It is the parochial principle that we outlined in Part II. The parish is a structure that emerged rather late in the history of the Church but it reflects something fundamental. It reflects the idea that people encounter the God of Jesus Christ where they live and among their own. That locale is not just an accidental occasion for a spiritual encounter that exists more purely elsewhere—in the local cathedral, let us say, or at St. Peter's in Rome. No, the parish is where the ideal becomes real. Bill Bonaducci is not just a representative of his pastor who woodenly observes canon law. No, he is himself a minister who should exercise his role in a pastoral manner. His parishioners know the Catholic Church primarily as the local community of St. Brigid where they share their faith.

Local theology is the best context for understanding church management. It emphasizes the theological importance of parish decisions. Some may argue that the only legitimate theological viewpoint is that of the universal Church and its authoritative spokesman, the Vatican. Local theologians reply that the fullness of the church exists in every local or diocesan church. Although most will agree that the universal Church exists both "in" the local church and "out of" or by means of it, nevertheless the application of this formula is not clear.[18] We believe that the parochial principle and the principle of subsidiarity, which undergird the idea of the local church, clarify its relation to the universal Church. They suggest that the universal becomes an event locally. There it becomes a sign and instrument of communion.

Canon law affirms the parish as a locus of the Church. This was the main idea in Part III. There we saw how canon law's social principles, its rights and obligations, and its means for claiming rights support the dignity of the parish. As a juridic person, the parish has a standing within law that the universal Church has pledged to defend. The St. Brigid School Board members are not just passive objects of the Church's law and teaching, but active subjects whose rights deserve to be known and claimed.

Management decisions at the local level deserve theological reflection. To be sure, the universal Church has a certain priority. It is a society founded by Christ, governed by law, and united under a single pontiff. It has an indefectibility in holiness and truth that local churches do not enjoy. But the particularity of the Church —its actuality in dioceses and parishes throughout the world—is also important. When pastors lead well and parishes thrive, people are drawn to the gospel and incorporated more deeply into Christ.

Bill Bonaducci, our paradigm for the good manager, knows this well. By his response to the St. Brigid School Board, he helped parishioners claim their rights to a well-governed parish in which they can express their opinions. Bonaducci was able to do things that the pastor (whom the board members resented) could not do. He helped the members to participate effectively and to look out for their interests. He would have done St. Brigid a disservice had he tried to solve parish problems with a brusque appeal to higher authorities, whether canon law or diocesan policy. Bonaducci did not limit himself to observing the law and obeying the pastor. Sensitive to the local situation, he helped to make the parish an instrument of true communion.

Notes

1. Robert J. Schreiter, *Constructing Local Theologies* (Maryknoll, NY: Orbis Books, 1985).

2. Maureen A. Tilley, "The Collapse of a Collegial Church: North African Christianity on the Eve of Islam," *Theological Studies* 62:1 (March 2001): 3-22, esp. pp. 9 and 21.

3. W. H. C. Frend, *The Donatist Church: A Movement of Protest in Roman North Africa* (Oxford: Clarendon Press, 1952), esp. pp. 12-24, 141-168. See also *The Catholic Encyclopedia*, 1909 Edition, *sub voce* "Donatists" by John Chapman; and Hans Lietzmann, *A History of the Early Church*, four volumes in two (I-II and III-IV), translated by Bertram Lee Woolf, vol. III: *From Constantine to Julian* (London: Lutterworth Press, 1961), pp. 82-93. The earliest records of the controversy are contained in Optatus of Milevis (ca. 387), *The Work of St. Optatus, Bishop of Milevis, Against the Donatists*, with an "Appendix" (containing numerous documents pertaining to the controversy), translated by O. R. Vassall-Phillips (London: Longmans, Green, and Co., 1917); and Eusebius (260? - ?340), *The Ecclesiastical History*, with an English translation by J. E. L. Oulton, taken from the edition published in conjunction with H. J. Lawlor, in two volumes

(Cambridge: Harvard University Press, and London: William Heinemann Ltd., 1980), vol. II, esp. Book X, Chapters v-vii.

4. Tertullian, "Scorpiace: Antidote for the Scorpion's Sting," translated by S. Thelwall, in *The Ante-Nicene Fathers: Translation of the Fathers down to A.D. 325*, American Reprint of the Edinburgh Edition (1885), Edited by Alexander Roberts and James Donaldson, 10 volumes (Grand Rapids: Eerdmans, 1986), in Vol. III: *Latin Christianity: Its Founder, Tertullian*, pp. 633-648.

5. St. Augustine, "Against the Letters of Petilian, the Donatist Bishop of Cirta," 1:6-7, translated by J. R. King, translation revised by Chester D. Hartranft, in Philip Schaff, Editor, *A Select Library of the Nicene and Post-Nicene Fathers of the Christian Church*, First Series, VI Volumes (Buffalo: The Christian Literature Company, 1887), Vol. IV: *St. Augustin: The Writings against the Manichaeans and against the Donatists*, pp. 519-628, esp. p. 521.

6. Peter Brown, *Augustine of Hippo: A Biography* (Berkeley, Los Angeles, and London: University of California Press, 1967), p. 335.

7. Ludwig Ott, *Fundamentals of Catholic Dogma* (1952), edited in English by James Bastible and translated from the German by Patrick Lynch, Fourth (Cork: Mercier, 1960) Edition (Rockford, IL: Tan Books and Publishers, 1974), p. 342.

8. Karl Rahner, "Peaceful Reflections on the Parochial Principle," in Rahner, *Theological Investigations*, vol. II: *Man in the Church* (1955), translated by Karl-H. Kruger (London: Darton, Longman and Todd; and New York: The Seabury Press, 1963), pp. 283-318, p. 290 cited here.

9. Karl Rahner, "Theology of the Parish," in Hugo Rahner, Editor, *The Parish: From Theology to Practice*, translated by Robert Kress (Westminster, MD: The Newman Press, 1958), pp. 23-35, p. 30 cited here.

10. Rahner, "Theology of the Parish, p. 26.

11. James A. Coriden, *The Parish in Catholic Tradition: History, Theology and Canon Law* (New York and Mahwah: Paulist Press, 1997), esp. Chapter 4, "The Parish and the Church's Social Teaching," pp. 52-58.

12. Coriden, *The Parish in Catholic Tradition*, Chapter 6, "Parish Rights and Obligations," pp. 71-81. The law grants rights and obligations primarily to Christian individuals, wrote Coriden (p. 71), and extends them to parishes by implication.

13. Augustine, "Letter 43," chapter 5, no. 14, translated by J. G. Cunningham, in Schaff, Editor, *A Select Library of the Nicene and Post-Nicene Fathers*, First Series, Vol. I: *The Confessions and Letters of St. Augustin*, p. 280.

14. For an elaboration of the rights and freedoms pertaining to Christians, see Edward G. Pfnausch, Editor, *Code, Community, Ministry: Selected Studies for the Parish Minister Introducing the Code of Canon Law*, Second Revised Edition (Washington, D.C.: Canon Law Society of America at the Catholic University of America, 1992), especially Bertram F. Griffin, "A Bill of Rights and Freedoms" (pp. 62-64) and Richard C. Cunningham, "The Laity in the Revised Code" (pp. 65-70).

15. Coriden, *The Parish in Catholic Tradition*, pp. 86-90.

16. Frend notes (pp. 16-17) that some African bishops of the province might have claimed the right to consecrate, and the Bishop of Ostia might also have made that claim.

17. Augustine, "Letter 44," chapter 4, no. 8, in Schaff, Editor, Vol. I, pp. 287-288.

18. Kilian McDonnell, "The Ratzinger/Kasper Debate: The Universal Church and Local Churches," *Theological Studies* 63:2 (June 2002): 227-250. Both parties to the debate grant that "the universal Church exists 'in and from' the local church, and the local churches exist 'in and from' the universal Church" (p. 247). An emphasis on the universal Church tends to abstract from the historical reality, however, and may obscure the theological consequences of managerial decisions. An emphasis on the empirical church tends to reduce ecclesiology to sociology, so the counterargument runs, and may blur the line between merely local practice and the teaching of the universal Church.

2

PASTORAL COUNCILS
AND PARISH MANAGEMENT

Mark F. Fischer

In 1969, a young Ph.D. named Arthur X. Deegan published a book entitled *The Priest as Manager*.[1] The book did not enjoy large sales, Deegan later recalled, because of its title. "Priest as manager," Deegan said, suggested to many that a pastor is a kind of corporate executive. The image seemed to connote a cool and distant leader who makes decisions on behalf of others without knowing what they need or want. Book sales taught Deegan that the image of the priest as manager did not resonate with most Catholics.

Yet Deegan's image undoubtedly makes sense. The size of Catholic parishes in the U.S. has always been much larger than the typical Protestant congregation, and it has grown by 64 percent in the last half century. Today the average size of a Catholic parish is 3,085 members. One in eight parishes has more than 5,000 registered Catholics.[2] With congregations this large, a good pastor needs to be a good manager.

In addition to high numbers of parishioners, today's U.S. parish has a large number of lay staff members. Between 1992 and 1999, the number of laypersons (including vowed religious) working full- or part-time in formal pastoral roles grew 35 percent.[3] These 29,000 laypersons outnumber the 27,000 religious and diocesan priests now active in U.S. parishes.[4] To update Deegan's *The Priest as Manager*, we would have to speak of today's priest as (among other things) a personnel manager.

Art Deegan retired in 1997 as Executive Director of the Conference for Pastoral Planning and Council Development. One could argue that the growth of the

CPPCD, the only national organization dedicated to the promotion of pastoral planning, especially by councils, vindicated Deegan's views of 1969. The priest continues to be a manager, as Deegan wrote in his Introduction more than thirty years ago, and "shares with managers and all other leaders of men the duties and prerogatives of that profession."

Catholics do not usually speak of their priests, however, as managers. Nor do they educate them to manage. The Code of Canon Law states that seminarians are to be instructed in the "administration" of a parish, but there is no word about "management." References to the priest as parish manager are absent from the Church's official documents about priestly formation.[5] Seminaries prepare candidates to proclaim the word, to celebrate the sacraments, and to lead prayer, but do not usually offer a course in managing a parish.

Management does not come smoothly off the Catholic tongue because the word connotes a relationship of control. The verb "to manage" comes from the Latin *mano* or hand. Webster's first definition of the verb is "to handle or control." To manage is also "to make and keep submissive." Predicating this of the parish is repugnant. The congregation is more than a system, and pastoral leadership is more than handling or controlling it.[6] We Catholics do not relish the prospect of ordained leaders making decisions on our behalf without consulting us.

To say this is not to confess a kind of American individualism. Catholics expect to be consulted by their pastor not because they have repudiated the Church's hierarchical vision and embraced an Enlightenment ideal of the sovereignty of the people. No, ecclesial consultation is rooted, as we shall see below, in classical philosophy and the Judaeo-Christian tradition. The good pastor consults his people, not because he is subservient, but because he seeks their wisdom and wants to be one with them.

Vatican II proposed an instrument, the pastoral council, precisely for this reason. Pastors consult these councils because they seek knowledge and sound advice. Councils can offer the kind of practical wisdom and prudence that leads to good decisions, decisions that unify the parish. Thorough consultation persuades parishioners that they are not being "managed" in the derogatory sense of the term, that is, made and kept submissive. Rather, the pastor who sincerely consults a pastoral council seeks the truth that the parish may find wholeness in the truth (John 17:17).

My argument is that the search for wisdom and prudence is the main reason for pastoral councils and hence their primary contribution to parish management. This is not management in a negative sense, but rather in Webster's second sense, namely, "to achieve one's purpose." Councils help pastors achieve the purpose of the parish by studying the pastoral situation, reflecting on it, and recommending what to do about it.

Not everyone will affirm, however, that this is the main purpose of the pastoral council. Some will argue that councils exist to foster participation, or to promote lay leadership, or to lighten the pastor's administrative load. I disagree. While a good council may achieve these purposes, they are not its reason for being. In this chapter I hope to show that:

1. The main purpose of the council is pastoral planning.
2. Councillors should be popularly elected to serve this main purpose.
3. Pastors should cultivate a spirituality of consultation in search of truth.

Wherever pastoral councils exist—and they exist in more than 75 percent of 19,000 U.S. parishes[7]—their best contribution is to help pastors manage the parish by offering the wise and prudent knowledge residing within the community.

Pastoral councils help the priest avoid being the cool and distant leader who makes decisions on behalf of others without knowing what they need or want. Instead, they enable him to know his people and realize their purpose. The pastoral council lets him be the kind of manager that Art Deegan envisioned, the priest-manager who is committed to responsible leadership. No priest need be ashamed of that title when he embraces a management style built on thorough consultation with a pastoral council.

The Purpose of Councils

Is the pastoral council's main contribution to parish management really the practical wisdom and prudence that emerges in planning? Some may well doubt this assertion. Indeed, the doubters could marshal impressive arguments against it. Vatican II, they could say, did not use the term pastoral planning and was ambiguous about the role of local councils. Furthermore, pastoral planning was not seen as the main job of parish councils in the years immediately after Vatican II. And even after the 1983 Code of Canon Law dubbed parish councils as "pastoral," some tried to declare parish administration off-limits to councils, thus hindering their ability to plan. We have to answer these objections in order to maintain that pastoral planning is the primary contribution by councils to parish management.

Vatican II and Pastoral Councils

Vatican II is the origin, however indirect, of the parish pastoral council. If we want to know how the Church regards the contribution of such councils to parish planning and management, we have to start there. But Vatican II did not speak of pastoral planning. So how can we claim that it is the main contribution of councils to parish management? To answer, let us begin with a confession: the Vatican II origins of the parish pastoral council are obscure. The reasons for the obscurity have been probed a number of times, but the probes remain less than a complete success.[8] This complicates every effort to describe the role in parish planning and management that councils are supposed to play.

The fact is that Vatican II never recommended the establishment of parish pastoral councils. It did, however, lay their foundation. The Decree on the Pastoral Office of Bishops recommended "pastoral" councils at the diocesan level. The Decree on the Apostolate of Lay People recommended "apostolic" councils at a variety of levels, including the parish.[9] But when the bishops recommended "pastoral" councils, they envisioned them for the local Church (i.e., the diocese), and not for parochial churches. And when they spoke of parish councils, they used the word "apostolic" and not "pastoral." Without any clear reference to parish pastoral councils, Vatican II left them (and their contribution to parish planning and management) in obscurity.

The illuminating moment occurred in 1973, eight years after the Vatican Council. At that time, the Vatican's Sacred Congregation for the Clergy published a "Circular Letter" to the bishops of the world on the subject of pastoral councils.[10] It was (and is) the only Vatican publication entirely devoted to such councils. There, in the context of a discussion of diocesan pastoral councils, the document states that "there is nothing to prevent" the institution of pastoral councils at the parish level. This is the first official reference to parish pastoral councils. It suggests that they are councils of the "pastoral" type at the parish level.

This is the key to discerning the foundations of the parish pastoral council. The name pastoral suggests that the Vatican II Decree on Bishops (which first recommended "pastoral" councils) is their primary source. Pastoral councils, recommended in this decree at the diocesan level, have a specific planning purpose. Their function is "to investigate and consider matters relating to pastoral activity and to formulate practical conclusions concerning them" (par. 27). We can say that the same planning purpose (investigate, consider, formulate) belongs to parish pastoral councils as well.

To be sure, we cannot entirely dismiss the Decree on the Laity in regard to parish pastoral councils. After all, the Laity Decree is the only Vatican II document to recommend councils at the parish level, even if it called them "apostolic" councils. They "should be set up to assist the Church's apostolic work," the decree stated, and "can take care of the mutual coordination of the various lay associations and undertakings" associated with that work (par. 26). This is the way that the council fathers foresaw councils at the parish level. It would be rash to say that pastoral councils have no role in coordination. But that differs from their main work, the threefold task of study, reflection, and recommendation.

Councils before the New Code

The earliest councils, however, did not call themselves "pastoral." They were simply "parish" councils. Because they arose in the late 1960s, before the 1973 publication of the Circular Letter, they looked to the Decree on the Laity as their inspiration, not the Decree on Bishops. The Laity Decree said that they were to assist the Church's apostolic work. So they took upon themselves a wide variety of tasks:

- to "advise the pastor" and "initiate programs";
- to "create, inspire, and demonstrate leadership";
- to foster "cooperation and apostolic work";
- to engage in "dialogue, mutual listening…shared responsibility and care";
- to "participate in parish administration."[11]

All of these are ways of assisting the Church's "apostolic" work, but they are not the threefold task of the "pastoral" council. The earliest councils did not see their main task as investigating, reflecting, and recommending.

Indeed, if any one task of early councils was more important than others, it was the task of coordinating committees. This was how early councils often interpreted the phrase in the Laity Decree about "the mutual coordination of the various lay associations and undertakings" (par. 26). To this day, numerous councils view the coordination of ministerial committees as their primary work. There is even a name for this kind of council, the "council of ministries."[12] Such a council regards itself as a coordinator of the ministries of the parish.

If this is commonly the case, then how can we assert that pastoral planning (more than the coordination of ministerial committees) is the principal contribution of councils to parish management? The answer hinges on the transformation of "parish" councils into "pastoral" councils.

The New Code

Even after the publication of the Circular Letter in 1973, parish councils rarely described themselves as "pastoral" councils. That began to happen with frequency only after 1983, when the revised code of canon law was published. The term "pastoral council" became popular once Catholics began to reflect on canon 536. It stated:

§1. After the diocesan bishop has listened to the presbyteral council and if he judges it opportune, a pastoral council is to be established in each parish; the pastor presides over it, and through it the Christian faithful along with those who share in the pastoral care of the parish in virtue of their office give their help in fostering pastoral activity.

§2. This pastoral council possesses a consultative vote only and is governed by norms determined by the diocesan bishop.

Canon 536 is the sole reference in the code to the parish pastoral council. It makes deliberate use of the "pastoral" council idea taken from the Vatican II Decree on Bishops. It does not refer to the "apostolic" councils mentioned in the Laity Decree. As a result, the apostolic terminology fell into disuse. From the 1983 publication of the code, parish councils began to call themselves pastoral.

But what is a parish pastoral council in the new code? Canon 536 said that such councils "give their help in fostering pastoral activity." This statement of purpose is so bland that it could apply to every member of the Christian faithful. In the aftermath of the publication of the code, two kinds of attempts were made to sharpen the focus of the parish pastoral council. The first was an effort to limit the subject matter of councils. Some canonists argued that a focus on pastoral matters was meant to exclude temporal matters, parish administration, and the coordination of committees.[13] The second attempt was to refine the methodology of councils. Many popular writers said that "pastoral" means that a council should have a spiritual focus and be consensus-oriented.[14] The vague purpose that Canon 536 assigned to councils was supposed to be clarified by limiting their scope and improving their method.

Those who sought to limit the scope or refine the method of the parish pastoral council, however, were not altogether successful in clarifying its purpose. Their efforts hinged on definitions of the word pastoral, the very word used in the Vatican II Decree on Bishops. There we see that pastoral is not the antonym of temporal or administrative. Vatican II made it clear that pastoral councils have a role in everything that pertains to pastoral work, including administration.[15] Even the coordination of ministerial committees, while not the primary work of pastoral councils, lies within their ambit. We cannot discover the nature of a pastoral council by excluding the practical realm.

Nor is the word pastoral a synonym for a style of meeting. The popular writers who argue that a pastoral council ought to reach decisions by consensus, banning parliamentary procedure as a means for decision making, are confusing style with substance. A pastoral council is pastoral not because of its style, it is pastoral because it advises the pastor who consults it.[16] This emphasis on the role of the pastor is consistent with Vatican II and with canon 536's insistence that the pastoral council "possesses a consultative vote only." Pastors consult councils because they want sound advice about the parish. Once they accept the council's advice, pastors may want to implement it through the council, but this is a distinctly secondary initiative. Developing sound advice is primary. This advice emerges from the council's threefold task of investigating, reflecting on, and drawing conclusions about pastoral matters.¹⁷ These include the practical matters of parish administration.

Let us summarize what we have said about the purpose of the parish pastoral council. Its main purpose and contribution to parish management is pastoral planning. To be sure, Vatican II did not speak of parish pastoral councils. But subsequent official documents have defined this council in terms of the pastoral type recommended in the Decree on Bishops. Undoubtedly the earliest parish councils did not see the matter this clearly. They avoided the "pastoral" terminology and took upon themselves a plethora of tasks, including the support of a parish committee superstructure. Coordinating parish committees is certainly within the purview of the pastoral council. But it is not its primary duty. Once the 1983 code canonized the word pastoral, parish councils had to be guided by the Vatican II Decree on Bishops. Henceforth they had the threefold task of investigating and reflecting on pastoral matters and recommending their conclusions to the pastor. This task can be called pastoral planning. It is the pastoral council's main duty.

The Selection of Councillors

Let us grant, then, that the main work of parish councils is pastoral planning, and move on to our second concern. This is the question of why councils (and not others) should do such planning. Why should a pastor go to the trouble of recruiting and consulting wise parishioners, parishioners who may have no formal training in ministry or administration? Should he not be content to plan with his parish staff? After all, a parish staff may well include experts in theology, religious education, ministry, and other pastoral disciplines. In an era of ever-larger and well-trained staffs, is not the pastoral council obsolete?

This one question is really two. The first is about what a volunteer council can offer that a paid staff cannot. The second question is about how to recruit and select such a wise council. The second question depends on the first. If a council possesses something essential that does not necessarily belong to the lay staff, then a pastor will want to select councillors for the qualities that make the council essential. The essence of the pastoral council, I have said, lies in its threefold purpose of investigating, reflecting, and recommending. It achieves this purpose by means of dialogue among representative parishioners. Dialogue is an ancient Greek idea, a way of getting at the truth by means of conversation. In order to present the distinctive contribution of the parish pastoral council, we must show how the knowledge it yields differs from the expert knowledge of the staff member. Then we can show how to select representative councillors who are good at dialogue.

The Council and Dialogue

Although official Vatican documents do not say how to conduct meetings of the parish pastoral council, nevertheless the Vatican II Laity Decree does speak about the way in which laity and priests should work together. In paragraph 10 it states:

> The laity should develop the habit of working in the parish in close union with their priests, of bringing before the ecclesial community their own problems, world problems, and questions regarding man's salvation, to examine them together and solve them by general discussion.

The phrase "by general discussion" translates the Latin word "*consiliis*," that is, council. The text suggests that laity and priests should "take counsel" together. In this way they can examine questions and solve them. Although this passage does not refer to councils *per se*, it intimates a conciliar method. In recent years, this passage has been cited as a source for parish councils.[18] Their "method," we conclude, is the common examination of questions in order to solve them. It is the method of dialogue.

This brings us to classical philosophy. Such philosophy sheds light on the distinctive contribution of the pastoral council in contrast to that of experts such as the parish staff and finance council. Aristotle[19] distinguished between the kind of knowledge about which one has a dialogue and the kind of knowledge that is best left to experts. "No one deliberates," Aristotle wrote in the *Nicomachean Ethics*, "about things that are invariable." These are the technical matters that Aristotle called theory or science. It would be fruitless for a pastor to ask councillors their opinion on, let us say, construction techniques, employment law, or accounting practices. In these technical fields, a pastor ought to defer to architects, lawyers, and finance councillors. He can fairly presume that they have mastered their disciplines. He should consult them as experts.

Apart from the technical knowledge of experts, however, there is a second realm of knowledge. Aristotle called it practical wisdom. It is the ability, he wrote in the *Ethics*, "to deliberate well about what is good and expedient." Practical wisdom does not proceed by demonstration or by deduction from scientific first principles. It seeks not the unchanging knowledge of the expert. Instead, it aims at the contingent knowledge residing in a community, the knowledge we call prudence.[20]

Practical wisdom depends on what is right for a certain people at a given moment in their history. Only those who know the community and are good at deliberation have such wisdom. It emerges in the give-and-take of dialogue.

Aristotle's distinction between theoretical science and practical wisdom helps us see why a good pastor seeks the advice of prudent parishioners as well as that of experts. Prudence is the knowledge of how best to act. Prudent parishioners know the community and can discern what it should do. Moreover, they have a gift for dialogue. They can listen patiently to others. They can express their own views honestly, without flattery and in charity. They have the ability to synthesize various points of view. Experts can advise a pastor about the many things that can be done in typical situations. But after he has spoken with experts, he needs the advice of his people. Councillors with practical wisdom can help him judge, from among the many things that are possible, what the parish should actually do in its particular situation.

A pastor should certainly plan with his parish staff, but he would be wise to plan with non-staff councillors as well. Non-staffers who know the parish and are good at dialogue can make an important contribution that staff members cannot. Their contribution is practical wisdom, the ability in dialogue to get at the truth of contingent parish matters. To be sure, many staff members reside within the parish boundaries, and so can be said to know the parish community. But staff members are usually hired for their expertise. They are experts in religious education, liturgy, or other pastoral fields. They may not have the gift of reaching the truth in dialogue. Moreover, as employees of the parish, they have a vested interest in it and may not be as free as a non-employee to express the common sentiments of parishioners. In a word, they may not be able to represent the parish as well as non-staff councillors.

Ecclesial Representation

Official documents of the Church apply the term "representative" to pastoral councils. Diocesan pastoral councils are said to represent the diocese and reflect its regions, social conditions, and professions. Parish pastoral councillors are commonly encouraged to mirror the demographic profile of the community, to reflect a range of opinions, and to include a variety of gifts.[21] The Church's documents agree that that pastoral councils should be representative.

It is not immediately clear, however, what representation means. To begin, the Church distinguishes its concept of representation from the political concept of representative democracies. Councils do not represent the sovereignty of the people. The pastoral council is not a legislature or parliament distinct from the pastor. Parishioners cannot appeal to the council over the pastor's head. For another thing, most council guidelines allow pastors to appoint a limited number of councillors who have not been popularly elected to the council. This provision expresses a conviction that pastors should hear the advice of important minorities within the parish. The Church's emphasis on representation does not mean that the majority should always prevail.

At the most basic level, the ecclesial meaning of representation is that councils represent the practical wisdom of the people of God. The Church wants its pastors to be guided by prudence. Pastors in turn want to know what is best for their parishes to do. Questions about parish action obviously cannot be decided in the abstract. They do not hinge on purely logical consequences of sound first principles. Instead, they depend on knowledge that is contingent. They depend on the changing needs of the community. Prudent councillors know how to deliberate well, how to take counsel, how to inquire, and how to judge shrewdly. In that way they represent or "make present" the practical wisdom of the people of God.

Discernment of Council Members

How does a parish select such councillors? Official Roman documents allow for a variety of selection methods, including both election and appointment. But most guidelines for pastoral councils in the U.S. recommend parish-wide elections.[22] When such elections are conducted in a discerning fashion, they yield the best councillors.

Father Michael Parise, a pastor in the Boston archdiocese, described a discerning election in a 1995 article in *The Priest*.[23] Father Parise's parish, a busy place with fifty projects and programs, used a process of discernment to select councillors. Father Parise announced a series of three Sunday evening meetings with the explicit purpose of choosing a pastoral council. All parishioners were invited, and Father Parise sent personal invitations to a number of parishioners whom he especially wanted to consider council membership. In the first meeting, he spoke about the purpose he envisioned for the council. In the second meeting, he invited small group discussions about Church, discipleship, and the personal formation of the pastoral councillor. The third meeting emphasized the councillor's formation in the Christian life. It also included a process of nomination, discernment, and balloting. Father Parise invited the participants into the sanctuary of the church. There, in a climate of prayer, he led them through a process of discernment, asking them to nominate and vote for council members.

The "discernment" of council members was a method developed in the 1970s and 1980s. It emerged in conjunction with a critique of parish council elections, which some observers felt were akin to popularity contests.[24] Critics said that nominees for pastoral council membership often had not reflected deeply on whether they were qualified for effective service on the council. Moreover, parishioners had scant knowledge of the pastoral council task and often cast their ballots on the basis of a superficial first impression. The process of discernment—including a more serious way of nominating and a more knowledgeable scrutiny on the part of electors—was meant to correct the problem.

Father Parise's 1995 article exemplified the practice of discernment. It generally includes four stages. Discernment begins with the sharing of information about the council. The discernment proper takes place in a series of open parish meetings. In these meetings, people are nominated, and the participants examine and weigh the nominations in dialogue. Finally, there is the act of selection, usually by ballot. Guidelines for pastoral councils published by U.S. dioceses often recommend this style of discernment in popular elections of councillors.[25] I believe that a discerning election is the best process for choosing councillors.

Well-conducted elections awaken interest in parish governance, educate parishioners, and enable them to participate in the choice of their representatives. They liberate pastors from the onus of having to explain that their hand-picked councillors are more than cronies. Above all, an election invites the help of the entire parish in discerning who has the gift of practical wisdom and prudence needed on the pastoral council. The main contribution of the pastoral council to parish management is parish planning. Such planning aims to manifest the wisdom of the community. It is best accomplished by councillors who are good at the threefold task of the pastoral council, the task of investigating, pondering in dialogue, and making appropriate recommendations about what the parish ought to do. A discerning election is invaluable to the pastor who wants to find qualified councillors.

The Spirituality of the Council

Our first two arguments (about the purpose of the council and the kind of councillors it seeks) lead us to a third and final argument. This argument has to do with the spirituality of the council. By spirituality I mean the way in which councillors assimilate the mission of Christ and the Church. Council spirituality should be linked to the council's purpose and the gifts of its members. If pastoral councils are a distinctive type of council, characterized by a threefold purpose, and if the primary criterion for council membership is the members' ability to accomplish that purpose, then we can speak with some precision about the mission of the council. It is a specific aspect of a wider mission. Councillors become partners with their pastor in understanding the parish and recommending responses to its needs. In doing this, they are not just accomplishing a threefold task. They are assimilating, in a way specific to council members, the mission of Christ.

Some readers may ask whether a discussion of spirituality ought to have any place in a book about parish management. Management, they might say, has little to do with the spiritual practices of pastoral council members. Spiritual practices—that is what many people ordinarily understand by spirituality. Earlier treatments of council spirituality, in fact, commonly referred to spiritual practices or to an explicitly spiritual (i.e., "pastoral") subject matter. Councillors were advised to incorporate prayer as a major part of meetings, to undertake annual retreats, to make decisions by spiritual discernment, to avoid squabbles about administration, and to limit the scope of the council to the spiritual mission of the parish.[26] While no one can gainsay prayer and retreats, they are no more important to the councillor than to any other member of the Christian faithful. The spirituality of the council cannot be reduced to a set of practices. Nor does it depend on a style of decision making or on a spiritual subject matter. It is rather the way in which pastors and councillors accept their specific mission, that of pastoral planning.

The achievement of a fruitful relationship between pastor and councillors enables us to speak of the spirituality of the pastoral council. This spirituality has two aspects. One aspect has to do with the obligations that exist between pastor and council. These obligations are implicit in the Church's teaching about councils. The second aspect of council spirituality is the freedom that belongs to every Christian and is exercised in the council meeting. It is the freedom to listen to God's Word, obey it, and pursue its truth. Let us look at each of these aspects in turn.

Spiritual Obligation in the Council

Consultation obligates a pastor to enter sincerely into a relationship of dialogue with the council. By consulting it, he invites the council to do what the Church intends for it to do—namely, to study a pastoral matter, ponder it, and draw sound conclusions. This is the proper function of councils. This function presupposes pastors with questions and parishioners who seek answers by means of dialogue. All are bound together by mutual expectations. Pastors are to consult sincerely and honestly. Councillors are to respond by investigating and reflecting. Each has an obligation to the other.

Pastors consult councils, as I have said, but are not bound by their advice. Vatican documents do not require pastors to consult their councils about any specific subject matter.[27] Moreover, pastors may reject the recommendations they receive. No pastor is obliged to accept bad advice, and most Catholics would affirm such a principle. So being a council member entails asceticism. Participating in the council is a religious discipline, we can say, in which councillors may have to deny themselves the satisfaction of always having their advice accepted. This calls for humility. The pastor may not find the council's recommendations persuasive.

But councillors do have a right to be consulted. That is constitutive of being a pastoral council member. The pastor is supposed to invite his council to study, reflect, and reach conclusions. Admittedly, councillors need not be consulted on every matter, and not even about every important matter. No pastor has enough time to consult everybody about everything. But consultation expresses a fundamental aspect of the councillors' relationship with him. If a pastor does not choose to discuss a matter that his councillors want to discuss, he should explain why. About matters before the council, councillors deserve a say. That is their proper function.

When council members encounter dysfunction, they are not without recourse. If pastors do not really consult them, or do so badly, councillors have the right and obligation to speak up. This is a canonical right of Catholics everywhere.[28] They have the right to state their beliefs, to talk with other parishioners, and to try to persuade the pastor—all within the bounds of charity. And if after that they still feel that they are being treated unfairly, they have the right to bring their concerns to the attention of diocesan officials—once again, within the bounds of charity. And even if they are not satisfied with diocesan officials, faithful Catholics still have recourse. As Father Richard C. Cunningham has written, "Ultimately they still possess the power of numbers, of finances, of public opinion, of *sensus fidelium*, of conscience, and the radical power of shaking the dust from their feet as they exit."

For the most part, however, the relationship between pastors and councillors is amicable. Dysfunctional pastors are the exception. The impressive growth of councils over the last thirty-five years suggests that pastors rely on the advice of councils, and that councillors make a significant contribution to parish governance. They share a relationship of mutual obligation. The pastor seeks the advice of councillors because he wants to lead them where God is calling the parish. Councillors try to provide him with the truth of practical wisdom, that truth that builds community. This mutual obligation is the bedrock and first aspect of council spirituality. Now let us look at the second aspect, that of freedom.

The Council's Spirituality of Freedom

The freedom of consultation does not mean simply that a pastor can take or leave the council's advice. If that were all, it would encourage pastors to be indifferent to their councils. While occasionally we find pastors who are indifferent, they are hardly the ideal. The freedom of consultation calls not for indifference but disinterestedness. The good pastor seeks practical wisdom, not for his own sake, but for that of the parish. He is disinterested in that he avoids narrow self-interest, both his own and that of the council. He seeks the truth, the true knowledge of the pastoral situation, the truth that will free the community to hear God's word and follow it.

A pastor ought to take the lead in consulting the council. He should give his councillors clear instructions. He should provide direction and define a focus. If he wants the council's help, he needs to explain how and why. At the same time, however, he must honor the councillors' freedom. He should free them to perform their own specific kind of service. In some ways, his spirituality in the council meeting is like that of Socrates, the philosopher who (in Plato's *Apology*) knew that he did not know everything. The good pastor raises questions, focusing the conversation, allowing the wisdom of the members to emerge. His leadership does not coerce a preordained end. It enables the truth to come out.

When council members undertake the investigation of a pastoral topic, they exercise a fundamental Christian freedom. It is the freedom to hear God's word and obey it. It is the freedom to study a matter thoroughly and discern its truth in conversation with others. By doing so, councillors strive to free themselves and the parish from misperceptions and illusions. They strive to free themselves from trivial preoccupations and to gain a deeper insight. Their goal is to discern what the parish ought to do. The act of discernment expresses their spiritual freedom.

A pastor should not accept the advice of his council, however, until he is confident that its advice is sound. This too manifests spiritual freedom. He needs to express his reservations and misgivings, share his doubts about the course recommended by the council, and invite further research and reflection. Who decides when enough consultation is enough? The pastor does. That is part of the freedom of consultation. Councillors cannot force the pastor to keep consulting. Forcing the pastor to follow the council's advice over his own better judgment would not serve that truth. The freedom of consultation implies that not even well-meaning councillors should constrain the search for practical wisdom. A good pastor ought to conclude the period of study and reflection when—and only when—there is enough knowledge for a good decision.

In short, the spirituality of the council hinges on the mutual obligations between pastor and councillor and on the freedom they enjoy to do what the Church intends them to do. The council is not a mere instrument of the pastor, but a group to which he turns for practical wisdom. He must be honest with them, explaining the kind of help he seeks and indicating when he is dissatisfied with their work. They in turn have an obligation to be honest with him and to faithfully represent the wisdom of the community. Although he is not bound by the council's advice, he should free the members to discover what is wise and prudent for the parish to do. And although they should not expect that their advice will always be taken, they have a freedom to speak the truth and to walk away from a dysfunctional situation.

Conclusion

The main contribution of the pastoral council to parish management is pastoral planning. Such planning is the shorthand term in the U.S. for the threefold task of the pastoral council as expressed in Roman documents, the task of investigating, pondering, and drawing conclusions about parish matters. Pastoral planning accords better with canon law's description of the consultative role of councils than do others assigned to councils, such as the coordination of parish committees or the implementation of council initiatives.

Representative councillors offer pastors a benefit that neither expert advisors nor even a pastoral staff can provide. This was our second argument. Councillors offer pastors the benefit of practical wisdom, defined as the prudent knowledge of what a parish ought to do in a given situation. Unlike the knowledge of the expert, which is independent of local variables, practical wisdom depends on knowledge of a specific community. It emerges in a dialogue among parishioners. And unlike the knowledge of the parish staff, the council's practical wisdom stems from members who are representatives. They do not represent a technical field or the parish administration, but the common sense of parishioners. They do not pursue knowledge in general, but the practical question of what the parish ought to do.

Our third argument is that the spirituality of councils flows from their purpose and representative nature. What pastors seek from councils is ultimately a spiritual good. It is the good of knowledge, of that practical wisdom about what is prudent for the community to do. It is not primarily about spiritual practices, a style of meeting, or a spiritual subject matter. Rather, council spirituality is best expressed in the way that council participants make the mission of the council their own. It consists in the mutual obligations that unite pastor and councillor, and in the freedom they enjoy to do what the Church wants them to do. This identifies the specific contribution to parish management of councils. They help the pastor plan a response to parish needs by representing, that is, making present, the wisdom of the community.

Notes

1. Arthur X. Deegan, II, *The Priest as Manager* (New York: The Bruce Publishing Company, 1969). In a private conversation Deegan linked the book's limited sales to its title.

2. Bryan T. Froehle and Mary L. Gautier of the Center for Applied Research in the Apostolate (CARA) of Georgetown University, *Catholicism USA: A Portrait of the Catholic Church in the United States*, vol. 1 of the series "The Catholic Church Today" (Maryknoll, NY: Orbis Books, 2000), pp. 48-49.

3. Philip J. Murnion and David DeLambo, *Parishes and Parish Ministers* (New York: National Pastoral Life Center), as cited by the National Conference of Catholic Bishops, Lay Ministry Subcommittee of the Committee on the Laity, "Lay Ecclesial Ministry: State of the Questions," *Origins* 29:31 (January 20, 2000): 497, 499-512, at p. 499.

4. National Conference of Catholic Bishops, "The Study of the Impact of Fewer Priests on the Pastoral Ministry," Supplementary Document "D," including research conducted for the U.S. bishops by the Center for Applied Research in the Apostolate, presented at the NCCB's Spring General Meeting, June 15-17, 2000 at Milwaukee, Wisconsin (Washington, DC: National Conference of Catholic Bishops [unpublished]); see the chart entitled "Active and Retired Priests in 1999."

5. See Pope John Paul II, *Code of Canon Law*, Latin-English Edition, Translation prepared under the auspices of the Canon Law Society of America (Washington, DC: CLSA, 1983), Canon 256 §1. The practical training of priests is treated in the Sacred Congregation for Catholic Education's document entitled *The Theological Formation of Future Priests* (1976), in a collection of the National (U.S.) Conference of Catholic Bishops, *Norms for Priestly Formation: A Compendium of Official Documents on Training Candidates for the Priesthood*, compiled by the Bishops' Committee on Priestly Formation, Bishop Thomas J. Murphy, Chairman (Washington, DC: United States Catholic Conference, 1982), pp. 61-95. It devotes five paragraphs to "pastoral theology" (pars. 102-106), and emphasizes that theology should guide the pastoral ministry, but the document does not use the word "manager." Pope John Paul II takes a similar tack in his Post-Synodal Apostolic Exhortation on the Formation of Priests in the Circumstances of the Present Day, *Pastores Dabo Vobis* (April 7, 1992), published in *Origins* 21:45 (April 16, 1992): 717, 719-759. He states that pastoral study and practical application should be mutually related (pars. 57-59), but pastoral study apparently does not include parish management. The National (U.S.) Conference of Catholic Bishops' *Program of Priestly Formation*, Fourth Edition of 1993 (Washington, DC: United States Catholic Conference, 1995), speaks of pastoral theology (par. 341). It offers little more explanation than that the seminarian should study counseling and the RCIA (par. 379), should take "other" unspecified courses with a pastoral orientation (pars. 339, 367), and should continue his education after ordination (par. 389). The term parish management is not used.

6. *Pace* those who speak of "the inner workings of the congregation as a system." See Norman Shawchuck and Roger Heuser, *Managing the Congregation: Building Effective Systems to Serve People* (Nashville: Abingdon Press, 1996), p. 14.

7. The statement that 75 percent of U.S. parishes have councils is the conservative estimate of David C. Leege, "Parish Life Among the Leaders," Report No. 9 of the *Notre Dame Study of Catholic Parish Life*, edited by David C. Leege and Joseph Gremillion (Notre Dame, IN:

University of Notre Dame, 1986), p. 6. The report's findings were also published as Jim Castelli and Joseph Gremillion, *The Emerging Parish: The Notre Dame Study of Catholic Life Since Vatican II* (San Francisco: Harper and Row, 1987), p. 61. A more recent study puts the figure at 82 percent. See Bryan T. Froehle and Mary L. Gautier, *National Parish Inventory Project Report* (Washington, DC: Center for Applied Research in the Apostolate, Georgetown University, October, 1999). The 1999 report first put the figure at 90 percent (p. 22). Data from the newest wave of the Inventory (based on preliminary results from 8,942 parishes and reported by Froehle and Gautier at the April 2-5, 2000 annual convention of the Conference for Pastoral Planning and Council Development in Orlando, FL) suggest that 82 percent of parishes have a pastoral council, for a total of 15,728 councils.

8. The earliest researcher of this theme was Roch Pagé, *The Diocesan Pastoral Council*, trans. by Bernard A. Prince (Paramus, NJ: Newman Press, 1970). The best source from a canonical perspective is John A. Renken, "Pastoral Councils: Pastoral Planning and Dialogue among the People of God," *The Jurist* 53 (1993): 132-154. More recently, see Mark F. Fischer, "What Was Vatican II's Intent Regarding Parish Councils?" *Studia Canonica* 33 (1999): 5-25.

9. Two conciliar documents recommend diocesan pastoral councils. See Vatican Council II, "Decree on the Pastoral Office of Bishops in the Church" (*Christus Dominus*, October 28, 1965), translation by Matthew Dillon, Edward O'Leary and Austin P. Flannery, at no. 27; and "Decree on the Church's Missionary Activity" (*Ad Gentes Divinitus*, December 7, 1965), translated by Redmond Fitzmaurice, at no. 30, all in *The Documents of Vatican II*, Austin P. Flannery, General Editor, Preface by John Cardinal Wright (New York: Pillar Books, 1975), pp. 564-590 and 813-856. Apostolic councils were recommended in Vatican II, "Decree on the Apostolate of Lay People" (*Apostolicam actuositatem*, November 18, 1965), no. 26, translated by Father Finnian, OCSO, in *The Documents of Vatican II*, pp. 766-798.

10. The Sacred Congregation for the Clergy's private letter to the bishops of the world was issued on January 25, 1973 and published in the United States as "Patterns in Local Pastoral Councils" (*Origins* 3:12 [Sept. 13, 1973]: 186-190), and also as "Pastoral Councils" in James I. O'Connor, Editor, *The Canon Law Digest*, vol. VIII: Officially Published Documents Affecting the Code of Canon Law 1973-1977 (Mundelein, IL: Chicago Province of the Society of Jesus, St. Mary of the Lake Seminary, 1978), pp. 280-288. The reference to pastoral councils at the parish level occurs in section 12. The complete text is available on the internet at http://www.west.net/~fischer/A42.htm.

11. These were the tasks of the parish council in, respectively, Robert C. Broderick, *The Parish Council Handbook: A Handbook to Bring the Power of Renewal to Your Parish* (Chicago: Franciscan Herald Press, 1968), p. 45; Bernard Lyons, *Parish Councils: Renewing the Christian Community* (Techny, Illinois: Divine Word Publications, 1967), p. 124; The National Council of Catholic Men, *Parish Councils: A Report on Principles, Purposes, Structures and Goals* (Washington, D.C.: NCCM, 1968), p. 2; David P. O'Neill, *The Sharing Community: Parish Councils and Their Meaning* (Dayton: Pflaum, 1968), p. 30; and Edward E. Ryan, *How to Establish a Parish Council: A Step-by-Step Program for Setting Up Parish Councils* (Chicago: Claretian Publications, 1968), p. 14.

12. "Council of Ministries" is the term of Thomas Sweetser and Carol Wisniewski Holden, *Leadership in a Successful Parish* (San Francisco: Harper and Row, 1987), p. 124. This type of council (though not described as such) is also the recommendation of William J. Rademacher

with Marliss Rogers, *The New Practical Guide for Parish Councils*, Foreword by Most Rev. Rembert G. Weakland, OSB (Mystic: Twenty-Third Publications, 1988).

13. John Keating ("Consultation in the Parish," Origins 14:17 [October 11, 1984]: 257, 259-266, esp. p. 264) stated that pastoral councils should not concern themselves with parish administration. Orville Griese ("The New Code of Canon Law and Parish Councils," *Homiletic and Pastoral Review* 85:4 [January 1985]: 47-53, esp. 47-48) called it a misinterpretation to say that parish councils should coordinate ministries.

14. Mary Ann Gubish and Susan Jenny, S.C., with Arlene McGannon (*Revisioning the Parish Pastoral Council: A Workbook* [New York and Mahwah: Paulist Press, 2001]) stated that the evolution from the "parish" to the "pastoral" council means embracing prayer and discernment, collaboration, and consensus (p. 10). John Heaps (*Parish Pastoral Councils: Co-responsibility and Leadership* [Newtown, NSW, Australia: E.J. Dwyer, 1993]) noted that the development of consensus would avoid polarizing council members (pp. 27-28). Robert J. Howes, by contrast (*Creating an Effective Parish Pastoral Council* [Collegeville, MN: Liturgical Press, 1991], argued that consensus "should be used by a council when dealing with relatively minor, non-controversial agenda items, Robert's Rules otherwise" (p. 50).

15. Pope Paul VI, Apostolic Letter, written *Motu Proprio*, on the Implementation of the Decrees Christus Dominus, Presbyterorum Ordinis and Perfectae Caritatis, *Ecclesiae Sanctae I* (August 6, 1966), par. 16, in *The Documents of Vatican II*, ed. Flannery, pp. 591-610, at p. 601. Referring to this passage, the Congregation for the Clergy's Circular Letter to the world's bishops on pastoral councils (see footnote 10 above) stated: "Nothing prevents the pastoral council, however, from considering questions requiring mandates of a jurisdictional act for execution and proposing suggestions regarding them" (no. 9).

16. This is the view of Roch Pagé and of James H. Provost. Pagé ("The Parish Pastoral Council," *Proceedings of the Canon Law Society of America* 43 [1982]: 45-61, at p. 48) wrote, "Everything depends on the pastor" in the realm of pastoral councils, including their "establishment, direction, resources, effectiveness and dynamism." Provost ("Canon Law and the Role of Consultation," *Origins* 18:47 [May 4, 1989]: 793, 795-99, at p. 798) wrote, "Nothing, therefore, escapes the category of *pastoral* if it truly pertains to the Church."

17. The threefold task, first described in the Vatican II Bishop's Decree at no. 27, has been assigned to pastoral councils ever since. Virtually identical language describes pastoral councils in Pope Paul VI's Apostolic Letter "*Ecclesiae Sanctae I*" at no. 16; in the 1971 document of the Synod of Bishops entitled "The Ministerial Priesthood" (Part 2, II, section 3, p. 364); in the 1973 *Directory on the Pastoral Ministry of Bishops* by the Sacred Congregation for Bishops (no. 204, p. 105); in the 1973 "Circular Letter on 'Pastoral Councils'" by the Sacred Congregation for Clergy (no. 9); and in Canon 511 of the 1983 *Code of Canon Law*. To be sure, these documents refer mainly to pastoral councils at the diocesan level. Only the 1973 "Circular Letter" explicitly extends the language about diocesan pastoral councils to parish pastoral councils. In my view, however, that is decisive. The consistent threefold description of the "pastoral" council in Vatican documents, and the application of this in the "Circular Letter" to the PPC, suggests that PPCs foster pastoral activity in the same threefold way as pastoral councils in general.

18. See John Paul II, "*Christifideles Laici*: Apostolic Exhortation on the Laity" (January 30, 1987), based on the 1987 World Synod of Bishops, *Origins* 18:35 (Feb. 9, 1989): 561, 653-595. It stated, "The [Second Vatican] council's mention of examining and solving pastoral problems 'by

general discussion' [footnote reference to *Apostolicam actuositatem*, no. 10] ought to find its adequate and structured development through a more convinced, extensive and decided appreciation for 'parish pastoral councils,' on which the synod fathers have rightly insisted" (no. 27, p. 574).

19. Aristotle, "Ethica Nicomachea," trans. W. D. Ross, in *Aristotle, The Basic Works of Aristotle*, edited and with an Introduction by Richard McKeon (New York: Random House, 1941): 927-1112. See Book VI, Chapter 5 (1140a).

20. Thomas Aquinas, *Summa Theologica*, first complete American edition in three volumes, translated by the Fathers of the English Dominican Province (New York et al.: Benziger Brothers, Inc., 1947). See the discussion of prudence in the Second Part of the Second Part, Question 47 (vol. II, pp. 1389-1399).

21. On representation of the diocese, see the Sacred Congregation for the Clergy, "Circular Letter," at no. 7. On reflecting the regions, conditions, and professions, See Canon 512 §2. Demographic representation of the parish by its pastoral council is endorsed in the diocesan guidelines for parish pastoral councils published, for example, by the dioceses of Hartford, Ogdensburg, Philadelphia, Baltimore, Nashville, Detroit, Green Bay, and Seattle.

22. A 1990 survey found that ten out of thirteen guidelines for parish pastoral councils published by U.S. dioceses (one from each of the 13 episcopal regions) recommended that the majority of councillors be elected either at-large or from parish organizations and standing committees. A 1995 survey found that nine out of a different thirteen guidelines called for elections as the primary means of choosing councillors. See Mark F. Fischer, *Pastoral Councils in Today's Catholic Parish* (Mystic, CT: Twenty-Third Publications, 2001), p. 58.

23. Michael Parise ("Forming Your Parish Pastoral Council," The Priest 51:7 [July 1995]: 43-47) describes his parish's voting on p. 45 and the evaluation of the 50 projects and programs on p. 46.

24. "While *election* may be a good word to describe an important aspect of democracy in action," wrote William J. Rademacher (*The Practical Guide for Parish Councils* [West Mystic, CT: Twenty-Third Publications, 1979], p. 118), "it's hardly the best word to describe that Spirit-inspired process whereby a Christian community discerns who is gifted with the ministry of the leadership for the parish council."

25. Mary Benet McKinney (*Sharing Wisdom: A Process for Group Decision-Making* [Allen, Texas: Tabor Publishing, 1987], reprint edition, Chicago: Thomas More Press, 1998) defines the four stages of discernment at p. 81 and in her Appendix I, pp. 140-143. Discernment is a necessary adjunct to elections in the pastoral council guidelines of Cincinnati, Fort Worth, and Greensburg. They are an option in the guidelines of Detroit and Green Bay.

26. On making prayer a major part of meetings, see Rademacher with Rogers, which affirms the recommendation of the Archdiocese of Milwaukee that councillors should spend at least one-half hour of every meeting in prayer and formation (p. 199). On retreats, see Marie Kevin Tighe, "Council Spirituality: Foundation for Mission," in Arthur X. Deegan II, *Developing a Vibrant Parish Pastoral Council* (New York and Mahwah: Paulist Press 1995), pp. 88-99, esp. p. 98, which states that days of retreat should be obligatory. On making decisions by spiritual discernment, see McKinney, esp. "Appendix II: Communal Discernment in the Tradition," pp. 155-162. On avoiding parish administration and focusing on "pastoral" matters, see John R. Keating, "Consultation in the Parish," *Origins* 14:17 (Oct. 11, 1984): 257, 259-266, esp. p. 260.

27. Guidelines for parish pastoral councils published by dioceses occasionally indicate, however, the areas in which they would like the pastor to consult the council. They do this (1) by specifying a certain number of committees of the council (education, social justice, liturgy, etc.) and (2) by specifying themes for planning (such as worship, service, stewardship, and so forth). See Fischer, *Pastoral Councils*, pp. 34, 174.

28. See Bertram F. Griffin, "A Bill of Rights and Freedoms" [based on canons 208 and 211-221], in Edward G. Pfnausch, Editor, *Code, Community, Ministry: Selected Studies for the Parish Minister Introducing the Code of Canon Law*, Second Revised Edition (Washington, D.C.: Canon Law Society of America, The Catholic University of America, 1992), pp. 62-64. The quote from Richard C. Cunningham is taken from his article "The Laity in the Revised Code," ibid., pp. 65-70, at p. 70.

3

PARISH IDENTITY:
THE SUM OF CHOICES MADE;
DECISION MAKING: A GOSPEL CHALLENGE

Janet Baker, RSM

Each parish, regardless of place or population, must answer a fundamental question: "Who are we as a parish, as a community, in communion with the universal Church?" A parish could describe itself as "an evangelizing parish," "a vital parish," "a Christ-like parish," or whatever descriptor best fit its set of core values, but the basic design is the same. A parish is intended to be an authentic replication of the gospel lived out in the twenty-first century. "A parish is a community of the Christian faithful..." says the *Catechism*, "who gather together in the celebration of the Eucharist, who teach [and embrace] Christ's saving doctrine and who practice the charity of the Lord in good works and brotherly love" (*Catechism of the Catholic Church #1279*).

Christ once posed a similar question to his disciples: "Who do people say that I am?" (Mark 8:29). The need to pose the question came from the significance and meaning of the "Who" to those who were beginning to form opinions about Jesus. When Peter answered Jesus, "You are the Messiah," Jesus predicted his passion, death, and resurrection. In other words, he was telling Peter that who he really was would be played out in how he fulfilled the Father's will for him.

A new neighbor or a curious co-worker might often ask a member of the parish, "What is your parish like?" A parishioner's answer to this question may reveal to the questioner just how genuinely the parish functions in the name of Christ.

We don't often think much about this, but it makes a difference to many persons as they enter a new parish. Even if they don't realize it, these persons are, in fact, searching for Christ, and they want to see him and know him in almost the same way that they would know a neighbor or relative. That is why the identifying characteristics of a parish are so significant and why it is important for the parish community to recognize its role in being attractive to incoming individuals and families, especially those who will be involved beyond the Sunday obligation. It is also important that the parish embodies qualities that will sustain each member of the parish who seeks a personal commitment to Christ.

Because a parish personifies a manifestation of Christ's values, words, and actions, the way in which a parish makes its choices is very important. Just as an individual's character is the sum total of his or her choices, the overriding description of a parish is also characterized by choices. While the pastor has ultimate responsibility for the parish choices, decisions are also influenced by the associates, the staff, the parish council, the organizations of the community, and the individuals who make up the parish community as a whole. Group decisions, or at least consultation from a group, are common in parish settings—not the only way, but an ordinary means for taking action. This chapter will attempt to address the power of the decision-making process in shaping the very life of the parish.

Parish: A People Called Together by God
Just as individual people shape their lives by the decisions they make, so, too, as members of a parish, every person in that parish shapes the life of the parish community, with differing roles and responsibilities.

We often visualize a parish at worship as the major parish activity of the week, but many decisions made within the parish structures keep alive the mission of the gospel on a day-to-day basis. On a good day the pastor and priests, the staff and the parish council are investing time in setting goals, choosing priorities, designing organizations, planning events and activities, and shaping the future. On an ordinary day the same people are probably solving crises.

No matter what engages their time they are making important choices. Notice how many of those choices are made by groups of persons working with the persons in the leadership roles. This does not mean that all decisions must be made in a group but it does point out the reason why parish members who function in some parish group need an understanding of the dynamics that support good decision making, especially when working with others.

We have all experienced, in our life and in our parish, some effective decision making and some that is not so effective. This leads to some questions: "Are there better ways of making decisions than what we do by mere instinct? Has research been able to identify some ways of doing business that insure better outcomes than what we might call our best hunches?"

A parish community that takes the time to examine its decision-making norms and is willing to explore some creative ways of finding a good set of practices to support good decision making will discover that what they do together holds great potential for good. The whole is greater than the sum of its parts—this bit of common wisdom is a rich reality waiting to be discovered.

In the past fifty years research in social sciences, particularly in organizational management, has produced a wide range of ideas on group decision-making processes. This research acknowledges the complexity of decision making, embedded as it is in many other personal skills, such as communication, leadership, conflict resolution, and problem solving. However, decision-making methodologies do offer some helpful structures that can assist groups as they take action on their ideas. Much research has also been done to examine the defining behaviors of persons who work together in groups. This research reveals some of the reasons why some people divide a group and others assist in integrating diverse people, and why good people often shun group work.

Taking a look at some of the ideas suggested by the social sciences would be appropriate for any parish leader whose role it is to develop and monitor the many groups that function in a parish community. It would be impossible for everyone who belongs to a parish group to become an expert in the field of group process before any effective group work could be done, but some awareness of a few basic ideas could make a difference.

If we examine ourselves first as individual members of a group we might want to remember that all groups are composed of individuals who bring multiple perspectives to a conversation. These perspectives have more of an exponential impact than an additive one on the work of the whole. Few people think alike, and it is this rich diversity that makes group work both challenging and frustrating. If a group follows a few basic principles it is amazing how the work will shift more toward being challenging and away from being frustrating.

Using Resources Well

Effective groups use the resources of the group members effectively. These include the talents, the time, and the experience of the people in the group. It is crucial to be conscious of the value of people's talent and time. When people gather to make decisions they want to know that their gifts are needed and that their time is valued. They may not say this in so many words but at some level they sense the reality. Asking people to attend a meeting that is not well planned or that is not directed toward significant decisions is a good way to cut future attendance.

Since most people in a parish work on a volunteer basis they can choose rather easily whether to attend a meeting or not. Most people will continue to attend meetings that have a clear purpose and have meaningful outcomes that make good use of their gifts and time. As people leave a meeting they usually say to themselves, "That was time well spent," or, "That was a waste of time." Either message imbeds in the memory a signal that will tell the person to take their attendance seriously the next time or to shrug it off.

Putting resources to good use also means asking the "right people" to attend a meeting. If the group is bogged down because a significant perspective or experience is missing they can defer action forever. Getting the right people together is an art. It involves knowing what information and experience you will need as well as knowing the people in the parish and what gifts they have to bring.

Building Group Interdependence
In effective groups, the members have respect for the dynamics of people working together and appreciate the worthwhile additive value of working through problems and coming to decisions that draw on multiple perspectives. A positive interdependence can enhance the quality of a decision and support the important step of implementation. But interdependence does not happen overnight. The group builds this type of cohesion by active listening and genuine dialogue. The aim of such a group is not dividing into winners and losers but finding common shared agreement about those goals that will bring about the mission of the parish.

Individuals working within a diverse group of people find pluses and minuses. Keeping a group to a reasonable size (at least six and fewer than twelve) diminishes some of the challenges. Having a leader who keeps the members on task and on time also keeps the energy of the group from dissipating. Nevertheless the group is only as good as the balance they can achieve between the benefits and the liabilities of working in a group.

No group will ever eliminate its potential for conflicts or its personality dysfunctions but every group can make efforts to allow certain norms to be established that can neutralize some of our inherent misbehavior. The following table illustrates the benefits and liabilities of group work.

Table 3-1 Benefits and Liabilities of Group Action	
BENEFITS	LIABILITIES
Groups can have a more accurate memory of what happens from meeting to meeting.	Complex tasks take a good bit of time and can reduce the group's productivity.
Group interaction results in the generation of multiple ideas and insights.	Groups can polarize if the members do not practice good listening habits.
Members of groups who have invested in the building of a decision add to the commitment to implement the decision.	Group's members are often too self-conscious about the other person's opinions of them and withhold ideas for fear of being rejected.
Involvement in the group work facilitates understanding and the necessary behavior changes that future work and implementation might require.	Group members sometimes form coalitions within the group or outside the group as back-up for a single opinion, and this can bias the outcome if it overpowers the ideas of one member who has the insight to see the best choice.
Group members learn about their ability to work with others and can improve their leadership/membership skills	Group members can compete with the designated leader to "get control," and this competition becomes the goal in place of the real goal. (Johnson and Johnson 2002)

These realities would be present in any dynamic group but the potential for error may actually discourage people from working in groups. It is for this reason that when we do work in groups we need to select a decision-making model that will at least neutralize the human side of group interaction.

Selecting The Right Decision-Making Method: Choosing How to Choose
Not all decisions made in any organization require the same method of choosing. Finding the right fit between the decision process and the hoped-for outcomes is a very significant choice that requires wisdom and experience. David Johnson and Frank Johnson (2002) in their text on group process, *Joining Together,* identify certain decision methods appropriate for certain outcomes, and their range seems to cover most of what is decided on a parish level.

Again all methods have advantages and disadvantages.

Table 3-2 **Decision-Making Methods**

METHOD	ADVANTAGES	DISADVANTAGES
1. Decision by authority without discussion	Major responsibility lies with the leader; he/she needs to act immediately.	Risk of resentment by those impacted; the decision can appear arbitrary.
2. Decision by expert	Competency of expert is necessary and appropriate. Credibility of the expert is key for the members' acceptance of the input.	There may be suspicion about the one designated as "expert" if he or she is not well known by the group.
3. Average of members' opinions	Useful when decision is urgent and member commitment not necessary.	If used too soon in the process it may leave unresolved conflict and confusion about implementation
4. Decision by authority after discussion	Resources of the group are valued.	Does not develop the level of commitment of the group that might be desired; sometimes it divides the group as people try to impress the designated leader.
5. Majority Control	Can be used when time is at a premium; brings closure when the group commitment is not so necessary.	Usually leaves an alienated minority, which can damage future group effectiveness.
6. Minority Control	Can be used for routine decisions when group support is not necessary; when only a few members have the resources to make the decision.	Does not utilize resources of the group; does not encourage commitment and can induce unresolved conflict.
7. Consensus	Produces innovative, creative, and high-quality decisions; brings about some commitment for the subsequent implementation; builds group's skills.	Takes a great deal of time, group skills, and psychological energy.

Once the leader has decided on the decision method, he or she has a choice of decision models, all of which have been tested and proven to be effective in complex human situations. Parish communities possess many good ideas, good intentions, and goals that could achieve good results; but not all good things can be done given limited resources and limited time. Thus the need to make wise choices requires a bit of work on the part of the people making choices. It also requires the wisdom to set priorities.

Some of the decision-making work is influenced by personal status and attitudinal bias; some of the work requires common sense especially when idealism is high and harsh realities are evident. Without a reasonable amount of logic and interior balance among differing peoples no decision-making method is better than another.

When the parish members are engaged in meeting as small groups they may have to select a decision method that is usually somewhere between a majority vote and consensus. Let's look a little more carefully at both of these situations.

Majority Vote

The use of a majority vote is consistent with our political experience. We propose certain actions, take a poll of the group, and move with the majority position. This works with some efficiency if not always with effectiveness. As a rule, when the group is limited in the time it can give to a discussion and decision, the choice of this method is acceptable. At the same time, however, because it produces "winners" and "losers," the majority vote model is not ideal for building community, which is the underlying goal of a parish. When the majority vote is used there are two cautions that can mitigate the sense of win/lose. In the first place the leader of the group needs to give the minority position an opportunity to express its perspective. There are probably some good ideas imbedded in the position. Second, it would be important to implement such a decision with care, evaluating it regularly, and correcting any strategies when necessary.

Consensus

The other method of group decision making that appears ideal for a community is the process of developing "consensus." This action is not one that will come with the speed often required by busy people. It takes patience, discipline, and maturity. It would be well to search for consensus for the "big ideas"; for example, the parish mission statement, the major goals of the strategic plan, and the ongoing policies for the use of resources.

Many writers have defined consensus. Zaleznik and Moment (1964) propose that "consensus lies in the degree of personal commitment the members feel toward the group decision after it is reached." Johnson and Johnson (2000) describe the consensus process as one characterized by certain member satisfaction: "members understand the decision and are prepared to support it, each believes he or she had a chance to influence the decision through discussion, even members who have doubts about the decision are willing to support it publicly and are willing to give it a try for a period of time."

Dialogue vs. Discussion

The basic tools of all group work are the means by which people exchange ideas. Often a group will have a history of conflict that is difficult to overcome, especially when new people come on board. The ordinary exchange of ideas can involve a debate searching for the "right idea." Some people convinced of the rightness of their idea lose sight of the goal and merely enjoy the debate. The group divides, and certain people feel "out," while others feel "in." The decision becomes secondary to the sport of discussion. The new person in the group is not likely to question the method or to raise doubts about the operating assumptions.

David Bohm (1989), in his description of Dialogue, argues that flawed decisions often result from flawed operating assumptions, and a group that avoids examining its assumptions can become mired in unspoken agenda. He encourages open listening, good inquiry (questions without judgments), and a search for shared meaning as essential to valid choices. Coming to a group with a tight hold on one's own argument does not augur well for discovering shared meaning. Stereotyping, false generalizations from limited input or experience, insufficient or inaccurate knowledge, and negative attitudes about people, in general, can often result in muddled thinking.

Bohm argues that every person working in a group must take responsibility for his or her own perspective and remain open to the possibility of learning from others (rather than a posture of convincing others of one's own "truth"). This can be a first step in making healthy and honest choices.

If a group lacks the skill to dialogue, the next-best method to dissipate untested assumptions is to at least come to some common agreement about how decisions will be made against specific criteria. The criteria for parish decisions normally flow from the mission statement of the parish as well as the authentic teaching of the Church. When the parish leadership (pastor, associate priests, and staff) have to make decisions and produce a well-publicized plan for the parish, it should be clear that the ways and means by which the parish came to a decision and carries out its plan remain faithful to its mission-based criteria.

For example if the parish is committed to encouraging leadership among the young and has written this into the plan as a priority, the youth minister seeking opportunities to do this would address some point of the criteria: "*This action will better serve the youth of our parish.*" If there is a range of ideas proposed for future action, the one that best fits the criteria becomes the obvious choice.

Other examples would demonstrate that one individual responsible for any of the parish's major goals should be able to function with the implicit approval of the community who developed the criteria. A plan based on good decision-making practices and criteria rooted in mission will provide the community with a challenging future based on the wise stewardship of resources.

Problem Solving and Strategic Planning

In special cases of decision making, such as problem solving and strategic planning, the issues are usually large and complex. Whatever method is chosen as the means to come to action, the people involved in this type of work need time to move from being an aggregate of persons to a high functioning group who can engage in the most productive decision making.

The primary variable to look at first is leadership. Leadership is an art, a mystery, a gift, a blessing, and many parishes will have strong leadership from among its clergy and laity. It would require another book to address all the leadership issues that impact decision making, but in this chapter let's look primarily at the critical activities of leadership in bringing about an effective problem-solving and planning group. One of the things a leader can employ to assist the group is the practice of dialogue, as described earlier, and the discipline of spiritual discernment.

Dialogue and Discernment

David Bohm's (1989) description of the Dialogue involves certain stages and acts of personal discipline. His idea of dialogue begins with an open-minded group of persons who are willing to take certain steps in addressing their ideas to one another. In the first place he recommends that, at least for the time of uncovering initial ideas and developing a range of options, the members of the group will want to:

1) suspend personal judgment as they listen with attention to the perspective of others;

2) follow the initial listening stage with a stage of "inquiry," which is the period of time when the members of the group invite the other speakers to elaborate on their original idea by asking them honest, open questions, e.g., "I like what you said about (*whatever the topic is*), and I would like to hear more about (*some specific idea that the speaker shared*)";

3) when inquiry has been exhausted the members of the group reflect on "what they heard" that created a group idea and answers the question: "What was the common thread"?

These steps produce a collage of ideas. This dialogue process is quite different from a group sitting wondering; "Did anybody hear what I said?" "Did anybody care?" "Can I get another shot at selling my idea?"

Once the group has determined the common shared meaning they then ask themselves about what assumptions are being held. This is the cleansing part of the thinking. In this part of the dialogue the members recognize what, as individuals, the members assume to be true, what others assume differently, and why members are not always even talking about the same thing. This needs to be resolved before any action is taken. Only when the members begin to recognize that their assumptions are only those things that they *think* they know, can they move ahead to clarity about what really is and, from that, to what can be. At this stage the group must plug in accurate and up-to-date information.

As the members share their diverse assumptions, imbedded in the current, accurate information, they will discover new and creative ways to think about an issue. In doing this they can then reframe disagreement and experience apparent conflict as an opportunity for growth and learning.

This leads to another very important step in group work. The group is enriched by the number of alternative solutions they can generate before they even begin to make choices. Having more than one route to travel, they can engage in true *discernment,* which weighs the pros and cons of alternatives and measures them against the spiritual criteria that guide the work.

Because spiritual values and material values impact our choices and often don't mix well, a wise group will use a simple device to determine the group's consensus or degrees of agreement about their alternative ideas. If each person in the group selects his or her top three alternatives (giving each a rank of 1, 2 or 3) the whole group begins to see preferences. This method allows for the group to find a weighted vote for each alternative based on the ranking each person gave the options. Again this avoids a notion that some choices are rejected and others espoused. Because some good probably can be found in each possible alternative, the weighted vote simply indicates a relative judgment of those present in the group that, we hope, also has the guidance of the Spirit. The conclusion is that the direction chosen is the best one, at least for now, given what we know, and is faithful to the spiritual values held as the deciding criteria.

Dialogue and discernment are best used when the group is seeking direction and is setting priorities. It presupposes a certain flexibility in thinking and choosing. It is not a substitute for learning the theological canons basic to parish life. When the Church is clear about a specific direction the greater need is to educate parish members about the teaching of the Church. Dialogue and discernment are applied to situations where the norms or strategies for implementation of values and activities can be decided locally and the teachings of the Church on the subject are already clear as the set of guiding principles. Opinions and ideas are shared in the dialogue, but the group remains grounded in the faith.

Frequently Asked Questions

Many questions arise whenever the topic of decision making is addressed by parish groups. Here are some of the most common.

1) Do we need a facilitator to assist us in decision making? The benefit of a facilitator is primarily in the objectivity they bring to the discussion. If the facilitator is well trained they can also point out some of the obstacles that keep the group from moving ahead. Because facilitators are free from vested interests they can also address conflict and encourage the members on both sides of a question to determine the critical difference in points of view and come to some resolution, without bias. If an outside person is not available, a member of the group can take the role of facilitator and provide a basic skill: keeping the group *on task* and *on time and allowing for each person having equal time.* The role can be rotated within the group from meeting to meeting. Some people become quite skilled by the experience.

2) How can we make meetings more productive? Be prepared. The answer may appear simplistic, but it is essential. Persons attending any meeting need to know what they are meeting about. This requires a prior agenda so people can come to the meeting with whatever information will be required. The group would also benefit from a clear sense of the meeting's expected outcomes. Everybody appreciates a meeting that begins and ends on time. Introduction of the dialogic process is helpful but needs direction, and people need to respect the ability of this process to allow everyone a chance to contribute to the outcome.

3) How do we keep the meeting moving? People always appreciate knowing that what they said had some importance. This is the one good reason to use a flip chart and record input as you go, especially if you are brainstorming or generating alternative options of activity. This can also be used to post "who is responsible to do what" without needing to repeat this at the end of the meeting. If ideas are not collected as they are given, they tend to be repeated, and this wastes valuable time.

4) Where is it best to meet? People also appreciate a setting that is conducive to working. A meeting room that is inadequate can be quite irritating. Too cold, too hot, too small, too close to outside interference, too dark can all contribute to a loss of motivation. Decisions are not all intellectual; sensory things will evoke emotional responses and influence people's behavior.

5) Can decision making really be improved? Yes, if a bit of attention is given to how a group is functioning and how it could be functioning. Unfortunately we are so accustomed to making decisions at every crossroad of life that people sometimes think they are expert at doing it and just want to "get it done," hoping for the best. Since parish decision making can affect a large number of people and have reverberations across many years and many subsequent events, it seems that we should spend sometime learning to do it right.

6) What do we do when we need to engage a very large number of people in a decision? This may mean that several large groups within a parish need to join together to set goals or it could mean that several parishes are working together to set priorities. In any case this is a good time to engage a professional who is familiar with the many options for large group decision making. This person can provide options and can listen to your expected gains from the large group gathering and offer the method most appropriate for the occasion.

One compilation of such models can be found in the work of Barbara Benedict Bunker and Billie Alban titled *Large Group Interventions: Engaging the Whole System for Rapid Change* (1997).

7) How do we know if we made a decision of high quality? The test of quality decision making is not only in the process chosen but in the plans for implementation of decisions that are designed concurrent with the decision-making process. There is always the danger that because a decision was reached those making the decision assume that action will follow. It is the same as if someone read all about good decision making and never applied what they had read.

Can you pick up from here and make a difference in your next meeting?

References

Bohm, David. 1964. *On Dialogue.* David Bohm Seminar November 6, 1989. Ojai, CA.

Bunker, Barbara Benedict and Billie Alban. 1997. *Large Group Interventions: Engaging the Whole System for Rapid Change.* San Francisco: Jossey-Bass.

Johnson, David and Frank Johnson. 2002. *Joining Together.* Boston: Allyn & Bacon.

Zaleznik, A. and D. Moment. 1964. *The Dynamics of Interpersonal Behavior.* New York: Wiley & Sons.

4

ENHANCING AND SUPPORTING
THE PEOPLE WHO WORK IN PARISHES

Robert Miller

The Challenge of Human Resource Management
in a Pastoral Setting

Today, the Catholic parish's ability to carry out its mission increasingly depends on the know-how, knowledge, skills, and abilities of the lay parish staff and parishioners who work with the pastor in ministerial roles and in providing services. Priests and religious who are active in parish ministry are aging, and their numbers are becoming smaller. There is a growing need to identify, train, develop, and support a new skilled and flexible lay workforce to complement the ordained clergy in the parishes of the twenty-first century. Parish leaders also need to consider the importance of excellent human resource management in the context of Catholic teaching regarding work, a full understanding of the vocation of ordained and lay persons, and trends in the workforce and geographic distribution of people. This chapter presents concepts of human resource management and volunteer management within the context of Church teaching and current trends in the U.S. workforce. It describes the human resource functions of planning, staffing, training and development, appraisal, and career planning in a parish setting. Particular issues of working with volunteers are also identified.

Catholic Teaching

Catholic parishes have a responsibility to live the gospel message. The Church's social teachings and the principles of good stewardship are specific and consistent in providing guidance regarding work and the relationship of employer and employee. The parish is an ideal setting to put these teachings into action. As Pope

John Paul II reminds us in his encyclical *Laborem Exercens* (On human work),

> The knowledge that by means of work, man shares in the work of creation constitutes the most profound motive for undertaking it in various sectors. "The faithful, therefore," we read in the Constitution *Lumen Gentium*, "must learn the deepest meaning and the value of all creation, and its orientation to the praise of God. Even by their secular activity they must assist one another to live holier lives. In this way the world will be permeated by the spirit of Christ and more effectively achieve its purpose in justice, charity and peace...Therefore, by their competence in secular fields and by their personal activity, elevated from within by the grace of Christ, let them work vigorously so that by human labor, technical skill, and civil culture created goods may be perfected according to the design of the Creator and the light of his Word." (LE, 25.6)

Speaking on the relationship between the worker and the direct employer the Holy Father states,

> Just remuneration for the work of an adult who is responsible for a family means remuneration which will suffice for establishing and properly maintaining a family and for providing security for its future. Such remuneration can be given either through what is called a family wage—that is, a single salary given to the head of the family for his work, sufficient for the needs of the family without the other spouse having to take up gainful employment outside the home—or through other social measures such as family allowances...(LE 19.3)

> Besides wages, various social benefits intended to ensure the life and health of workers and their families play a part here. The expenses involved in health care, especially in the case of accidents at work, demand that medical assistance should be easily available for workers, and that as far as possible it should be cheap or even free of charge... Another sector regarding benefits is the sector associated with the right to rest.... A third sector concerns the right to a pension and to insurance for old age...(LE 19.6)

In a pastoral letter entitled "Economic Justice for All" the U.S. bishops identify the "Church as an Economic Actor" and acknowledge that, "On the parish and diocesan level, through its agencies and institutions, the Church employs many people; it has investments; it has extensive properties for worship and mission. All the moral principles that govern the just operation of any economic endeavor apply to the Church and its agencies and institutions; indeed the Church should be exemplary" (347-358). Several important areas identified for special reflection include wages and salaries, rights of employees, and voluntary service.

The bishops identified the principle that those who serve the Church should receive a sufficient livelihood and the social benefits provided by responsible employers in our nation (351). They also caution to be particularly alert to inequities of salaries between women and men and to the concentration of women in jobs in the lower end of the wage scale. They call on all church institutions to fully recognize the rights of employees to organize but they also challenge the parishes and other church institutions to adopt new fruitful modes of cooperation (353). They recognize the importance of voluntary service to the life and vitality of the Church and the need to expand voluntary service roles for retired persons and for young people (352).

Stewardship involves stewardship of creation, vocation, and the Church. Stewardship of creation involves doing everything that can be done to enhance human life and make it flourish; stewardship of vocation requires each person to understand their own role and to respond generously to this call from God to be stewards of their own personal vocation; stewardship of the Church requires that all the faithful support efforts to proclaim, teach, serve and sanctify (*Stewardship, A Disciple's Response*, 1992). All persons in leadership positions in parishes (pastors and other clergy, lay pastoral workers, business managers, and leaders of volunteers) have responsibilities as good stewards to develop and enhance the human resources of the Church.

The Vocation of the Ordained and the Lay
The major documents of the Second Vatican Council recaptured for the Church its central importance as sacramental, and membership in the Church as essentially "priestly, prophetic, and kingly"—a sharing of the threefold ministry of Jesus Christ. While all are called to holiness, each of us receives a personal call from God to a specific vocation, with a basis in baptism, through which we know, love, and serve God and our neighbor. The call to vocation includes holy orders, religious life, marriage, or single life. The faithful live out their vocations in a manner of communion. Each is oriented to support and complete the other: the ordained's ministry strengthens the laity's witness to the gospel in everyday life, while the laity's witness informs and directs the ministry of the ordained.

The laity's distinctive and primary character is its secularity: to bear witness to the gospel in the world through the evangelization and sanctification of the temporal order. This evangelization of the temporal order takes place in the family, through the exercise of moral integrity in the workplace, and in all aspects of society. A great creative effort in activities and works demonstrating a life in harmony with the gospel is expected of the laity (*Ecclesia in America*, 1981, 44).

The continuing expansion of parish work in the U.S. has created a need for properly trained lay men and women to promote positive cooperation in different activities within the Church, while avoiding any confusions with the ordained ministries and the activities proper to the sacrament of orders, so that the common priesthood of the faithful remains clearly distinguished from that of the ordained. This need will intensify as larger numbers of diversely prepared lay staff and volunteers enter the parish workplaces.

This complementary dynamic of ordained and lay working together in communion requires a special human resource management activity that employs the best learning and tools available from management science in service to the parish and the gospel. In order to accomplish this, people assuming roles in the parishes need to be educated and well formed in their appropriate vocational roles first, so that they are able to work constructively together with the priest to carry out the mission of the parish. This is particularly necessary as the roles of priests, religious, and laypersons in parishes evolve to meet the changing demands of carrying out the parish mission and to accommodate the increasing age and decreasing numbers of priests and religious.

Trends in the Workforce and Geographic Distribution of the People

In the United States today, there are fewer priests in active ministry than in previous years but more Catholics than ever before. Only 5% of active priests are under age 35, while those over 55 are half of the total. In recent years, enrollment in seminaries has remained relatively stable with an average year-to-year decline of 1%. Today, nearly 2,500 parishes have no resident pastor. Since 1965, the number of religious sisters declined by half or 90,000. In 2000, half of all religious sisters were over the age of 68 (Froehle and Gautier 2000). Given these numbers, it will be necessary to look to other sources of human resources in order to provide staff for parishes in the future.

As the U.S. population ages, a long-term problem that is expected to emerge is persistent labor shortages in some sectors of the economy. Even in downturns in the economy, some major service sectors are already chronically short-staffed. These include health care providers and schools. The decline in U.S. births after the boom in births between 1946 and 1964 is only one reason for a tight labor market in some areas. In addition to a shrinking young workforce since the early 1980s, more of these same young people are extending their education in college and graduate school and, as graduates, want jobs that pay more and provide opportunities for building a career. As a result of these circumstances, some experts feel two things will happen: the government will take action to permit greater immigration and normalization of the status of those already in this country, and there will be an upward pressure on wages.

These trends will not affect parishes in every part of the country in the same way, because the size of the Catholic populations and the workforce vary from region to region. The Catholic population doubled between 1950 and the end of the century. Catholics became much more dispersed as descendants of immigrants moved from the cities in the Northeast and Midwest to other parts of the country. The share of this larger pool of Catholics has become less concentrated in the Northeast and the Midwest and larger in the West and the South. Migration within the country will also result in greater needs and a larger pool of potential Church workers in areas (usually in the South and the West) experiencing large in-migration. There will be fewer demands on parishes in areas that are losing population (usually in the North and the East), but these older areas may also have fewer people willing or able to assume positions in the parish.

As the Catholic population expands in some areas and declines in others, dioceses have been faced with the need to establish new parishes in new areas, and close or combine parishes under the pastorate of one priest in others. The emerging parish structures are often large. Some are growing parishes of several thousand families with many groups and organizations. In other cases, groups of smaller parishes, each with their own parish organizations, share programs, staff positions, and priests. Frequently the pastor is responsible for providing leadership and direction in structures that are far more complex, with more professional lay employees, than parishes of the past.

These trends in the workforce and the Catholic population present opportunities and challenges for parishes as they seek to obtain and keep qualified workers. To qualify a parish workforce, the Church will need to make a greater effort not only to attract people to priestly and religious vocations where proper education and formation is provided, but also to recruit lay persons into parish work and provide continuing education, formation and training in theology, pastoral ministry, languages, and other knowledge required to carry out the work of the twenty-first-century parish. These educational requirements, as well as the need to provide living wages that are competitive enough to attract people to work for parishes, are expected to place an increasing demand on parish financial resources. Having well developed parish human resource policies and practices is essential if parishes are to maximize the benefits of this investment.

Pastoral Planning and Human Resource Functions

Change is a necessary part of any vital parish. Some changes are reactive, resulting when external forces have already had an effect on the life of the parish. Other changes are more proactive, being initiated by pastoral leaders to take advantage of opportunities or circumstances that support accomplishing the mission of the parish. Parishes are called to ongoing renewal, and the parishioners to ongoing conversion. Parish actions taken to bring about this ongoing renewal are proactive changes done with the intent of improving current practices. This is an important part of the work of the parish because, in addition to providing new programs, these changes can provide new opportunities for parish workers and parishioners to continue their conversion and to assist others in their faith journeys. As we have seen, changing demographics and available resources also drive parishes to reactive change.

Most people understand that the way things were done five or ten years ago is very different from how they are done today or will be done in five or ten years. Nevertheless, people often resist change because it requires them to modify or abandon ways of working that have been successful or familiar to them. To manage these changes, pastors and other parish leaders need to envision the future; communicate this vision to the parishioners and parish employees; set clear expectations for performance; build the capability to act by hiring, training, and organizing people; allocate assets; and listen to the ideas and concerns of the parish employees and parishioners. Pastoral planning helps parishes be proactive in considering the number and characteristics of parish staff that are required and the best way to employ staff already present. The pastoral plan identifies the work to be done in order to accomplish the parish mission and the particular jobs to be performed. People who work in these jobs are supported by the parish human resource policy and the functions of staffing, compensation, training, developing, supervising, and motivating.

Work Requirements and Job Descriptions

Staff is hired to carry out the work necessary to accomplish the parish's mission. If the mission is unclear, or the activities required to carry out the mission are unspecified, the people working in the parish may be the wrong people doing the wrong work. Having a clear sense of mission—and a well-described plan to accomplish it—is key to defining the number and type of human resources required. Everyone is not prepared to do every part of the work of parishes. It is necessary that pastors clearly describe the work to be done, identify the required education and experience necessary to perform the work, and provide the necessary space and tools required to carry out the work. With a clear understanding of what work needs to be done to accomplish the work of the parish, it is possible to write job descriptions.

Writing a job description is a process of obtaining information about jobs by determining what duties, tasks, and activities need to be performed by the people holding the jobs. Usually, the description is written by the person directly supervising the position but it can be written by the person holding the position subject to review by the supervisor. For an existing position, one gathers this information by observing or interviewing the people holding the position or asking them to keep a diary. New job descriptions are developed from a thoughtful consideration of the work that needs to be accomplished.

There are three broad work functions: working with data or information (e.g., writing homilies, copying, filling out forms, making budgets, planning liturgies), working with people (e.g., attending Mass, counseling, serving, supervising, attending planning meetings), or working with things (e.g., driving, operating the computer, fax, parish electrical or heating system). A job description identifies the different functions in each of these general areas and the amount of time spent on each function. It is very important to make a clear distinction between the person doing the work and the particular job that they are doing.

It is almost impossible to write a job description for a priest or a mother. Their vocations call them to perform many different jobs and to do the jobs with a particular attitude and orientation. On the other hand, the mother's (or father's) particular job of preparing a meal for a child, or the priest's job of taking communion to a person in a nursing home, must be described in order to delegate the work and manage time.

Pastors who write job descriptions for their own positions are sometimes disappointed to see the portion of time they spend processing forms and making budgets versus counseling parishioners and preparing homilies. The process of making a job description permits the pastor to see how he is spending his time and, if possible, to delegate some work to another position in order to free his time for the work he holds as a priority.

Written job descriptions usually contain the job title, job duties, requirements to hold the job (job specifications), and identifying information, such as the person to whom the position reports, and when the description was last revised. The description writer arranges job duties or essential functions in the order of importance and includes the responsibilities the duties entail, the amount of time required or the importance of each duty, and any required tools or equipment. Job specifications include education, experience, and any specialized training, personal traits or abilities, and manual dexterity that the job might require. It also includes physical requirements such as the amount of walking, standing, lifting, or talking that the job involves. Job descriptions should use clear, specific language and be updated regularly, and the specifications should be related to job success (e.g., being a woman is not a specification for a cook).

Research has shown that improved work performance, internal motivation, and lower absenteeism and turnover result when employees and volunteers experience meaningfulness in the work they perform, have personal responsibility for work outcomes, and have knowledge of the effects of the work they perform. The five job characteristics that produce these feelings are:

1. work that requires different skills and talents (skill variety);
2. having responsibility for the job from beginning to end (task identity);
3. the degree to which the work has an impact on others (task significance);
4. the degree to which the job provides freedom, independence, and discretion (autonomy), and
5. the worker receives direct and clear information about the effectiveness of her or his performance (feedback). (Sherman et al. 1998)

When possible the pastor should organize parish work into jobs with these characteristics.

Forming teams of workers or parishioners can also enable them to take on a greater role in parish work. They can be organized to take on a project, to solve or resolve a problem, or, as cross-functional groups, to bring people together with different strengths. Regardless of the purpose of the team or group, the following characteristics have been identified with successful teams:

• commitment to shared goals;
• consensus decision making;
• open and honest communication;
• shared leadership;
• climate of cooperation, collaboration, trust and support;

• valuing individuals for their differences, and
• recognition of conflict and its positive resolution.

Another way of improving job design is to alter the normal workweek. Though such arrangements are common in parishes, frequently they evolve from what was understood (either rightly or wrongly) to be a "regular" (8:30 to 4:30) Monday through Friday job. But parish jobs can be designed intentionally to use a compressed or an expanded workweek, affording the parish coverage when it most needs it and allowing employees free time for family responsibilities when they need it most. Flextime or flexible working hours permits the employees the option of choosing daily starting and quitting times, provided they work a certain number of hours per day or week. Job sharing permits two part-time employees to perform the job of one full-time person. Job sharers frequently work three days per week, creating an overlap day for extended face-to-face interaction. Some workers can work at home using personal computers and other communications technologies such as e-mail, fax, and telephone call forwarding. Parishes that are reasonably close together could share staff. Two or more parishes that have part-time work available, such as on the maintenance staff, could create a full-time position with benefits by coordinating the days and hours required in each parish. Such an arrangement provides professional growth opportunities for the staff person and permits each of the parishes to benefit from the wealth of experience provided to this employee.

Many of the strategies mentioned lend themselves well to a mixed workforce of paid staff and volunteers. Good stewardship and the appropriate role of the parish in helping parishioners to act on their baptismal call requires parish work that is organized for parishioner volunteers. On the other hand, while any one of these arrangements may be ideal to fully support the needs of the paid employees and the parishioner volunteers, justice requires that they not be used to create part-time positions—at reduced salaries and without benefits—that full-time employees would perform better.

Any parish working to build an effective program of parishioner volunteers need to remember that the type and variety of volunteer tasks enhance motivation (Fisher and Cole 1993, 72). The parish leaders responsible for developing volunteers need to clearly describe the different volunteer positions, the expected level of performance (including specific goals and performance objectives), the connection of the work to the parish mission, and the opportunity for moving into other volunteer positions in the parish. It is simply good practice to match the volunteer's skills, interests, and expectations with the position, and to adapt positions to make the best use of the volunteer. This reduces the risk of under placement or requiring capable people to perform trivial tasks (Saxon and Sawyer 1984, 39). Job characteristics found to be effective for volunteer positions include building in autonomy, setting challenging goals, and creating a sense of responsibility for the results of the volunteer's work.

Recruiting, and Selecting Parish Employees and Volunteers

Once parish leaders design jobs and write job descriptions, it is possible to look for someone who has the ability to perform in that work. If it is necessary to hire a new person, the person needs to have a clear idea of the work they are to perform. In addition to well-written job descriptions, effective recruiting will assist the hiring process. There are several sources for parish human resources, including contingent workers (temporaries), current staff and volunteers (recruiting from within), or a new staff person or volunteer (recruiting from outside).

In larger dioceses with compact geographic areas, it is common to obtain help from retired priests or priests in other ministries to cover Mass schedules and other sacraments. School principals also employ substitute teachers when the health or schedules of regular staff require it. These contingent workers, or "temporaries," are an important source of parish workers when the work is only periodic or where the nature of the work might be best performed by a specialist. Accounting services, printing and mailing services, and temporary secretarial staff are common examples of this type of work. Computing services, administrative support with specialized computing skills, and building services are also areas where work has shifted away from direct hire of permanent workers to contingent workers.

The advantage of this type of worker is that the parish only needs to pay for a limited amount of work to be completed. The parish obtains the worker or service without an employment relationship. The disadvantage is that typically parish workers do a wide range of activities for which temporary help are not prepared. The work frequently involves sensitive information requiring a level of confidentiality and trust that may not be possible with a temporary employee. Effective job design helps to identify parish work best done by temporary services.

Recruiting

While a systematic approach to recruiting and selecting parish staff may seem a bit extreme in a parish where simply attracting anyone to a position is considered a success, it is not foreign to admissions directors in seminaries and novitiates. The work that lay people are hired to do in parishes is very important, and settling for whomever is willing to do the work is not sufficient to insure that the parish will have workers who will perform well and meet the needs of the parishioners.

Recruitment is the process of locating and encouraging the best available applicants to apply for existing job openings. Most organizations try to follow a policy of filling job vacancies above entry level through promotions and transfers. An advantage to recruiting within an organization is that it helps to recover the investment in recruiting, selecting, training, and developing current employees. Promotion also serves as a reward for past performance and an incentive for others. It contributes to improving morale within organizations. While transfer lacks the motivational value of promotion, it can serve to protect employees from layoffs and to broaden their job experience.

Most parishes do not employ large numbers of people. This limits opportunities for employee promotion. Parishes are also independent employers. Transfer, at least in the traditional sense, is limited to transfer within a single parish. Even though the Catholic Church is a large institution (especially in large cities), many parishes frequently have no alternative to hiring entry-level people from outside the parish for every position. Parish hirers may overlook an experienced parish worker in a neighboring small parish who may be well prepared to supervise a much larger activity with additional staff in a larger parish. Parishes could use diocesan-level job posting or cooperative postings among parishes, centralized record systems, and internal newsletters to permit experienced parish employees to be recruited "from within." Besides placing this important tool of recruiting "from within" in the hands of parish hirers, such a system would provide career development support to parish workers who consider their work for the Church to be a part of their vocational "calling" and who also want to grow professionally.

Applicants hired from outside, particularly for certain technical (computer literate secretary) and managerial (business manager) positions can be a source of new ideas and may bring with them the latest knowledge acquired from their previous employer. But the parish has to compete for these workers in the local labor market. Advertising, public and private employment agencies, educational institutions, employee referrals, unsolicited applications and resumes, and other church organizations are the most common recruiting sources from outside the parish. The costs involved and the need to compete with many other employment offers require that parish staff plan well, develop a good job description, consult records of the source of currently effective employees, and maintain an active file of all applicants for a reasonable time for possible future consideration.

Eighty-five percent of parish workers identified in a recent study as "new parish ministers" are women (Murnion 1992). The share of parish staffs that are disabled, minorities, or older people are not known. Hiring persons who are not present in large numbers in the Church workforce should be a serious consideration for any recruiting activity. Parishes have a particular responsibility to act in support of the social teachings of the Church and to recruit and hire people of different ages, races, and nationalities who might be particularly suited to the work of the parish.

Understanding parishioners' motivations helps in recruiting volunteers. Research on volunteer behavior divides motivators into three categories: needs, reasons, and benefits. Needs common to most people are belonging and autonomy. Needs for achievement, affiliation, control, growth, fun, power, variety, and uniqueness also influence decisions to engage in an active volunteer role. Parish leadership also needs to attend to the particular needs that are dominant among those they seek to involve. Young unmarried men might be most interested in work involving young unmarried women. To attract disadvantaged groups, the parish must clearly describe how the position will satisfy the physiological and safety needs of the volunteers.

Reasons provided by volunteers focus on the tasks to be performed and the setting. Making the parish a better community, carrying out one's baptismal call, working with a particular group, repaying benefits received, socializing or making new acquaintances, and gaining experience are typical of reasons why parishioners volunteer.

Benefits that have been reported by volunteers include the opportunity to perform an important task, the relationships that can develop with others, the opportunity for volunteers to use their abilities and skills, recognition received, and the relationships with clergy, religious, and parish professional staff and the supervision and assistance they provide (Gidron 1983, 63).

Selecting

The actual process of selection is the act of choosing people who have the right qualifications to do the work required for the job. This action requires two pieces of information: the competencies required to do the job, and the characteristics of the candidates. Job specifications, included in every job description, provide the information about the individual competencies needed to do the job: the knowledge, skills, abilities, and other factors that lead to success.

Human resource recruiters use many sources to get information about the candidates. These include application forms, references, tests, and interviews.

Remember, the information gathered is intended to select the person most likely to succeed, given the individual competencies required for the job. The information that is most important to acquire is whether the candidate possesses the knowledge, skills, abilities, and other factors identified in the job description that lead to success in the job.

The National Association of Church Personnel Administrators (NACPA) recommends that hiring be done in a team environment by forming a search committee with persons who are most associated with the position invited to participate. The advantages to the search committee is that members have an opportunity to shape the job description based on their sense of the needs of the parish, and they are more likely to support the selনection decision. Several people divide the work of developing a job description, recruiting, interviewing, and selecting the candidate. The disadvantage is that this is a time-consuming activity and could tie up large amounts of staff and volunteer hours in search committees. Whether or not a search committee is used, those most associated with the position and the final candidate(s) should have an opportunity to meet with one another and to identify the important requirements of the position prior to the offer and acceptance.

Written applications serve several purposes. They provide information on whether the candidate has the experience, education, etc., needed for the job. They provide a basis for questions in the interview, and they provide sources for reference checks. The applicant should sign the application, indicating that the information given is accurate. Here are some suggestions for putting together an application form:

- *Application date.* The applicant should date the application. This helps the pastor know when the form was completed and gives him an idea of the time limit (for example, one year) that the form should be kept on file.

- *Educational background.* The applicant should also provide grade school, high school, college, and post-college attendance—but not the dates attended, since that can be connected with age.

- *Experience.* Virtually any questions that focus on work experience related to the job are permissible.

- *Arrests and criminal convictions.* Questions about arrests alone are not permissible. But questions about convictions are fine. However, the Rehabilitation of Offenders Act of 1974 allows that, for some crimes, the applicant has no duty to disclose the conviction to a prospective employer after a certain time period has passed. The law allows the applicant to act as if the crime never occurred. There are certain professions, such as teaching and nursing, that are exceptions to this rule.

Country of Citizenship. Such questions are not permitted. It is allowable to ask if the person is legally prevented from working in the United States.

References. It is both permissible and advisable that the names, addresses, and phone numbers of references be provided. As a legal protection, it is important to fill out forms permitting information to be solicited from former employers and other reference sources (Sherman 1998).

There are two types of employment tests. Aptitude tests measure a person's capacity to learn or acquire skills. Achievement tests measure what a person knows or can do right now. Tests need to be reliable (measure the knowledge, skill, and abilities required in the job) and valid (distinguish between people who can do the work and those who cannot). A standard typing test is an example of a reliable and valid achievement test for a job that requires typing. With the rise in the number of computerized systems in parishes, computer and specific software tests are probably needed.

Even though there is some concern about whether interviews can consistently and validly discriminate between applicants, interviews are an important part of selection because interviewers maintain great faith and confidence in their own judgments. Interviews also help the applicants determine whether the position is right for them by providing information about the specific job, the work of the parish, and their co-workers.

There are several kinds of interviews. Non-directive or unstructured interviews are the most common. The interviewer asks broad, open-ended questions such as, "Tell me about your work experience." Structured interviews have sets of standard questions, based on the job analysis, that are asked of every candidate. Structured interviews are more likely to provide information about candidates that can be compared in making a sound decision. In both types of interviews, questions of job knowledge, worker requirements, and situational questions (applicant is given a hypothetical situation and asked how she or he would respond) can be used. (See Table 4-1 for recommendations for interview questions).

Search committee or panel interviews involve the candidate meeting with (ideally) three to five interviewers, who take turns asking questions. Research has shown that this type of interview results in more valid decisions than a one-on-one interview. It also results in greater acceptance of the decision on the part of the panel.

The final decision on candidates usually follows one of two decision-making approaches. In the clinical approach, those making the decision review all the information on the candidates and then make their decision based on their understanding of the job and their knowledge of those who have been successful in the job. Different people come to different decisions based on different weights that they assign to the applicant's strengths and weaknesses. This approach frequently hides personal biases and stereotypes on which the decision is made.

A more objective approach combines scores or ratings from the interviews, tests, and other procedures and selects the candidate with the highest score. One approach lets high scores on one predictor of job success offset a low score on another, provided that some minimum competence is demonstrated. Another approach requires candidates to score a minimum on all predictors.

Table 4-1 **Appropriate and Inappropriate Interview Questions**

TOPIC	APPROPRIATE	INAPPROPRIATE
Age	Are you over 18?	How old are you? What is your date of birth?
Appearance	(Say nothing unless it is a bonafide occupational qualification)	How tall are you? How much do you weigh?
Citizenship	Are you legally able to work in the United States?	Are you a U.S. citizen?
Criminal record	Have you ever been convicted of a crime?	Have you ever been arrested?
Disabilities	Do you have any disabilities that may prevent or limit you from performing this work?	Do you have any physical defects? When was your last medical examination?
Education	What schools did you attend? Did you finish school?	Did you attend Catholic school? When did you graduate?
Experience	What is your prior work experience? Why did you leave? What is your salary history?	What are your hobbies?
Marital status	What is the name, address, and telephone number of a person we may contact in case of any emergency?	What is your marital status? Do you have any children? How old are your children?
Military record	Did you have any military education/experience that is related to this work?	What type of military discharge did you receive?
National Origin	What is your name? Have you ever worked under a different name? Do you speak any languages besides English that may be pertinent to this job?	What's the origin of your name? What is your ancestry? From your name and appearance, am I right in assuming you are Irish?
Race	(Say nothing)	What is your race?
Religion	If religion is a bonafide occupational question for the work in the parish, then religious preference can be asked. If religious practice, such as attendance at Mass, is a bonafide occupational qualification for the work in the parish, then questions about religious practice can be asked. (In every case, you may inform a person of the required work schedule.)	Do you have any religious affiliation? (Unless work related) Why don't I see you at Mass more frequently?

Managing Compensation and Benefits

The compensation offered is one of the important elements of extending an offer to a prospective employee. The goals of the compensation program should be specifically tied to the goals of the parish plan. The most common goals of compensation programs are to:

- reward employees' past performance;
- provide a living wage and remain competitive in the labor market;
- maintain salary equity among employees;
- connect an employee's future performance to accomplishing the parish goals;
- control the compensation budget;
- reduce unnecessary turnover.

At a minimum, the parish compensation policy should reflect the internal wage relationship among jobs and skill levels (higher pay for greater skill), experience and/or time in service, the parish's pay position relative to what competitors are paying, a policy for rewarding employee performance, and administrative decisions concerning elements of the pay system, such as overtime and payment periods. Sometimes dioceses provide guidelines for some of this policy.

There are several factors that contribute to the development of the wage mix in a parish. These include internal factors, such as the compensation policy of the parish, the worth of the job, the employee's relative worth, and the parish's ability to pay. External factors that influence the wage rate include the availability of qualified workers, the average wage rates for comparable jobs in the area, and the cost of living.

Employers compensate most staff on an hourly basis. They are normally paid only for the time they work. Salaried or professional employees generally get paid the same for each pay period regardless of the amount of time they work. Salaried employees frequently receive other benefits not given to hourly employees. Under the Fair Labor Standards Act (FLSA), most hourly employees are considered non-exempt employees. Under the act, non-exempt employees are covered by the act and must be paid 1.5 times their regular pay rate for time worked in excess of forty hours in their workweek. Managers, supervisors, and other "white collar" employees who have a high degree of independent judgment in their job and meet the narrow definition of exempt employee, as determined by the Department of Labor, are exempt from this provision of the FLSA.

Benefits constitute an indirect form of compensation intended to improve the quality of the work lives and the personal lives of employees. The major objectives of most benefits programs are to improve employee satisfaction, to meet employee health and security requirements, to attract and motivate employees, to reduce turnover, and to attract new workers. Controlling costs of benefits is an important consideration for the parish in any decision that is made.

To avoid unnecessary expense, many employers enlist the cooperation of employees in evaluating the importance of particular benefits. Benefits normally required by law include Social Security, unemployment insurance, workers' compensation insurance, and state disability insurance. Under the Family and Medical Leave Act, most employers grant leaves of absence to employees for personal reasons. Employees usually take these leaves without pay, but seniority and benefits are not changed.

Because of the high cost of health care, the health care *benefit* is very important to employees. At the same time, the high *cost* of the health care benefit is of considerable concern to the employer. Today health insurance plans cover medical, surgical, hospital expenses, prescription drugs, dental, optical, and mental health care. In order to control the cost of these programs, employees often have the option to elect to take them, and for the employee as well as the employer to contribute to their costs. Use of preferred provider organizations usually help to contain the cost of health care while increasing preventive care benefits and reducing paperwork.

Paid holidays, holy days, sick leave, and severance pay when employers terminate employees are also commonly paid benefits. The number of weeks of vacation and severance pay are usually tied to the number of years the employee has worked. Employers frequently finance additional benefits such as life insurance, disability insurance, and retirement programs.

Every parish can offer some opportunity for employees to augment their social security with a private retirement plan. Whether or not a parish (or diocese) has a "defined benefit" pension plan, under a tax deferred savings plan (403.B plan), all employees can make voluntary contributions to their retirement plan. The tax on the contribution and any earnings will not be taxed until the employee retires. If the diocese does not offer this type of plan, it is available through insurance companies and mutual funds. These are not a defined benefit plan and guarantee nothing. The return depends entirely on how much money goes into the plan and the rate of return on the investment.

One of the most important benefits for parish workers is the opportunity to participate in an annual retreat. This is an important part of the ongoing faith formation of all employees, particularly those lay employees with less experience and less opportunity for other kinds of faith formation. The parish provides paid time off and, in some instances, either part or all of the financial expenses of participation. In addition to motivating and improving employee satisfaction, this benefit directly enhances the spiritual life of the parish.

The parish also needs to provide parishioner volunteers with opportunities for personal and spiritual growth and development. Important ways to do this are through retreats, times of formation and prayer, and learning activities such as formal training events and access to the pastor and other parish and diocesan professional staff for advice and direction.

Developing People Who Work in the Parish

Frequently people are hired because they have most but not all of the background necessary to perform in the job that we have designed. This is where training and coached on-the-job experience come in. Ongoing faith formation and work-related education enhance human life and are excellent ways to practice good stewardship of human resources. These tools of human resource development enable people who are not completely prepared to assume a position with the clear hope that they will be able to perform in the role. These are also critical tools for enabling people to deal with a changing work environment where new people, expectations, languages, information, equipment, or ways of doing the work need to be performed by people who were not originally trained to perform the work in the new way.

Need for Ongoing Formation and Training

All of us are called to a life of ongoing conversion to the gospel. This means that seeking to change for the better is part of the life of a Christian. In this context, well-thought-out training of parish workers can be an evangelizing effort of the parish. Training and religious formation enhance the worker's value to the parish, to the community, and to society in general, including in any future work they may find themselves.

Regardless of whether training is done formally or informally, it begins with analyzing all the duties that need to be performed in the job and the knowledge, skills, and aptitudes required to perform them. Managers then need to sit down with employees and determine what training will help them to do their job. While most parishes will not be developing their own training programs, supervisors should regularly plan for employee religious education, education in the role of the parish, and training in the particular requirements of the employee's job. Each employee needs an organized education plan each year designed to improve what the employee does. This could include sending the employee to classroom instruction, purchasing and making time for computer-based (on discs) or programmed (workbook) training, and instruction available on the Internet. But the most important component of the parish training is on-the-job training, where listening, observing, and reading can help the employee acquire skills and knowledge. Methods for providing on-the-job training include:

- *Mentoring or coaching* with a continuing flow of instructions, comments, and suggestions from the supervisor to the subordinate. It frequently includes personal and informal management development;

- *Understudy assignments* that groom an individual to take over another person's job by gaining experience in handling important functions of the job;

- *Job rotation,* which provides broadened knowledge and understanding, through a variety of different work experiences;

- *Special projects* that provide an opportunity for individuals to become involved in the study of a current parish issue and in planning and decision making;

- *Meetings of persons with similar positions in other parishes* that provide peer support and experienced persons to provide advice and counsel;

- *Staff meetings* that enable participants to become more familiar with problems and events occurring outside their immediate area of responsibility by exposing them to the ideas and thinking of others;

- *Planned career* progressions that use all these different methods to provide employees with the training and development necessary to progress through a series of jobs requiring higher levels of knowledge and skills.

In contrast to the vocational call of priests and religious who frequently find themselves working in a parish, laypersons who choose to work in a parish are making an occupational choice. This kind of choice is supported by a personal career plan. Because of the size of parishes and number of employees, not much has been done to develop logical and systematic career tracks in parish work, of the type that exist in other organizations. Research in other fields tells us that there are five predictable stages of career development.

Stages of Career Development

STAGE 1: PREPARATION FOR WORK

Typical age range: 0-25

Major tasks: Develop occupational self-image, assess alternative occupations, develop initial occupational choice, and pursue necessary education.

STAGE 2: ORGANIZATIONAL ENTRY

Typical age range: 18-25

Major tasks: Obtain job offer(s) from desired organization(s), select appropriate job based on accurate information.

STAGE 3: EARLY CAREER

Typical age range: 25-40
Major tasks: Learn job, learn organizational rules and norms, fit into chosen occupation and organization, increase competence, pursue goals.

STAGE 4: MID CAREER

Typical age range: 40-55
Major tasks: Reappraise early career and early adulthood, reaffirm or modify goals, make choices appropriate to middle adult years, remain productive in work.

STAGE 5: LATE CAREER

Typical age range:
55-retirement
Major tasks: Remain productive in work, maintain self-esteem, and prepare for effective retirement.
(Greenhaus 1994).

Parish employers need to work with each employee to recognize with them the stages of the employee's career and the ways in which work in the Church will be available in each stage. Only the largest and most complex parishes will have the means to create career paths for employees, but, working with the diocese or other parishes, it may be possible to retain well-trained and productive Church workers throughout their careers and compete with other employers for the best prepared employees.

The guidance and support the parish provides to its volunteers is also essential to their successful performance. Training of those in the parish who will be supervising volunteers is critical and needs to include:

- how to involve volunteers
- how to enhance the value of volunteers to paid staff
- how to include volunteers in program planning and decision making
- how to evaluate and provide performance feedback to volunteers
- how to hold volunteers accountable
- how to build effective teams of volunteers and paid staff
- how to create a climate in which volunteers will be most productive
  (Fisher and Cole 1993, 122)

Appraising and Improving Performance

A performance appraisal program can benefit both the parish and the employee whose performance is being appraised. It gives employees the opportunity to discuss performance and performance standards with their supervisor. It provides the supervisor with a means of identifying the strengths and limitations of an employee's performance and, when performance is linked to reward, it provides a basis for a salary change. In light of the need for people to be supported to grow professionally, and for every employer in the Church to contribute to the pool of qualified Church workers, the most important reason for appraisal is that it provides the supervisor with a format to recommend specific actions designed to help an employee improve performance.

The supervisor usually rates performance but self-appraisal should also be a part of the process. Appraisals need to rate performance that is clearly job related. The supervisor develops standards of performance through the job analysis. Appraisers need fairly precise standards and need to develop good observational skills, but the most important part of the appraisal is the feedback to the employee in the appraisal interview. Here are some guidelines for that interview.

1. *Ask for a self-assessment.* It is useful to have employees evaluate their own performance prior to the appraisal interview. Even if this information is not used formally, the self-appraisal starts the employee thinking about his or her accomplishments. Self-appraisal also ensures that the employee knows against what criteria he or she is being evaluated, thus eliminating any potential surprises. Recent research evidence suggests that employees are more satisfied and view the appraisal system as providing more *justice* when they have input into the process (Korsgaard and Roberson 1995).

2. *Invite participation.* The real purpose of a performance appraisal interview is to initiate a dialogue that will help an employee improve her or his performance. In addition, research evidence suggests that participation is strongly related to an employee's satisfaction with the appraisal feedback as well as her or his intention to improve performance (Kennedy 1995). As a rule of thumb, supervisors should spend only about one-third of the time talking. The rest of the time they should be listening.

3. *Express appreciation.* Praise is a powerful motivator, and in an appraisal interview employees are seeking positive feedback. Supervisors should start the appraisal interview by expressing appreciation for what the

employee has done well. In this way, he or she may be less defensive and more likely to talk about aspects of the job that are not going so well.

4. *Minimize criticism.* Employees can absorb only so much criticism before they start to get defensive. If an employee has many areas in need of improvement, the supervisor should focus on those few objective issues that are most problematic or most important to the job.

5. *Change the behavior, not the person.* When dealing with a problem area, remember that it is not the person who is bad, but the actions exhibited on the job. Avoid suggestions about personal traits to change; instead suggest more acceptable ways of performing. It is difficult for employees to change who they are; it is usually much easier for them to change how they act.

6. *Focus on solving problems.* Supervisor and employee should avoid blaming each other for why a situation has arisen. Frequently, solving problems requires an analysis of the causes, but the appraisal interview should be primarily directed at devising a solution to the problem.

7. *Be supportive.* One of the better techniques for engaging an employee in the problem-solving process is for the pastor or parish leader to ask, "What can I do to help?" By being open and supportive, the manager conveys to the employee that he will try to eliminate external roadblocks and work with the employee to achieve higher standards.

8. *Establish goals.* Since a major purpose of the appraisal interview is to make plans for improvement, it is important to focus the employee's attention on the future rather than the past. In setting goals with an employee, the supervisor should 1) emphasize strengths on which the employee can build, 2) concentrate on opportunities for growth that exist within the employee's present position, and 3) establish specific action plans that spell out how each goal will be achieved. These action plans may also include a list of resources, and timetables for follow-up.

9. *Follow up day to day.* Ideally, performance feedback should be an ongoing part of a supervisor's work. Feedback is most useful when it is immediate and specific to a particular situation. A good approach is to have informal talks periodically to follow-up on the issues raised in the appraisal interview.

Employee Rights and Discipline

Beyond what is required by law, gospel values need to guide the employment relationship. Respect for each individual and an appreciation that work should provide workers the opportunity to experience their full potential, should guide the relationship between the parish employer and employees and volunteers. In this section we are going to deal with three important areas: employee rights, disciplinary policies and procedures, and discharge.

Employee rights can be defined as the guarantees of fair treatment that employees expect in protection of their employment status. The employment relationship has traditionally followed the common law doctrine of "employment at will." This principle assumes that the employee has the right to end the employment relationship for a better job or other personal reasons. Likewise, employers are free to terminate the employment relationship at any time without notice for any reason, no reason, or even a bad reason. This relationship is set up when an employee agrees to work for an employer for an unspecified period of time. Some state courts recognize three important exceptions to the "employment at will" doctrine:

1. *Violation of public policy.* This exception occurs when employers terminate employees for refusing to commit a crime or for disclosing illegal, unethical, or unsafe practices of the employer.

2. *Implied contract.* This exception occurs when employers' discharge the employee despite the employer's expressed or implied promise of job security.

3. *Implied covenant.* This exception occurs where a lack of good faith or fair dealing by the employer has been suggested (Sherman 1998).

In order to avoid these exceptions, pastors and other parish supervisors should:

1. not imply contract benefits in conversations with employees;

2. include in offers of employment a statement that the employee may terminate employment with proper notice and the employer may dismiss the employee at any time for any reason, and

3. have written proof that employees have read and understood the employment at will disclaimer.

Information contained in an employee's personnel file is frequently very important. Laws in many states permit employees to inspect their own personnel file. The privacy rights involved in these cases include the right to know the existence of one's personnel file, the right to inspect one's personnel file, and the right to correct inaccurate data in the file.

Some parish employees and volunteers handle parish property and money. In order to combat white-collar crime parish employers need to have the right to search employees without violating an employee's right to privacy. Improper searches can lead to lawsuits charging the employer with invasion of privacy, defamation of character, and negligent infliction of emotional distress. Pastors need to establish a written policy limiting such searches to those based on a probable and compelling reason. The penalty for refusing to consent to a search should be specified. The employer should obtain the employee's consent prior to the search, and it should be conducted in a discreet manner to avoid inflicting emotional distress.

Another area of privacy concerns the use of computer files and e-mail. Parishes need to have a written policy for the use of e-mail and computer files. This is especially important if parish employees use computers connected to the Internet.

Effective policies and procedures defining justifiable reasons need to govern the use of disciplinary actions taken against an employee. Rules should be reasonable, written, known to employees, and consistently enforced. Parishes that want to take action against employees for off-duty misconduct need to clearly establish a relationship between the misconduct and its negative effect on other employees, parishioners, or the parish. Parish supervisors should investigate discipline problems and maintain written documentation that includes:

1. the date, time, and location of the incident;

2. the problem (e.g., the negative performance or behavior exhibited by the employee);

3. the consequences of that action or behavior on the employee's work and the operation of the parish;

4. prior discussions (if any) with the employee about the problem;

5. disciplinary action to be taken and specified improvement expected;

6. consequences if improvement is not made, and a follow-up date;

7. the employee's reaction to the supervisor's attempt to change behavior;

8. the names and witnesses to the incident (if appropriate).

It is best to record this information immediately while the memory of it is still fresh.

When employees fail to conform to the parish rules, the final disciplinary action in some cases is discharge. Since this has serious consequences for the employee and sometimes the parish, this should be undertaken only after a deliberate, thorough review of the case. Regardless of the reason for the discharge, it should be done with personal consideration for the employee. While there is no one right way to handle a discharge meeting, the following guidelines will help make the discussion better:

1. come to the point within the first two or three minutes, and list in order all the reasons for termination;

2. be straightforward and firm, yet tactful, and remain resolute in your decision;

3. make the discussion private, businesslike, and fairly brief;

4. avoid making accusations against the employee and injecting personal feelings in the discussion;

5. avoid bringing up any personality differences between you and the employee;

6. provide any information concerning severance pay and the status of benefits and coverage; and

7. explain how you will handle employment inquiries from future employers. (Sherman 1998)

Making Parishes Great Places to Work

Not only should parishes be great places to work, they *need* to be great places to work in order to obtain the commitment from excellent lay people to spend a part of their career working there. Everyone who works in the parish needs to appreciate the privileged place in which they work, and the impact that their work has on the lives of the parishioners and the larger community in which the parish exists. Prayer and listening skills modeled by the pastor and other parish leaders need to be an integral part of the life of the staff. Regular opportunities for the staff to be reminded of their mission, to reflect on it, and to pray together for the guidance of the Spirit in their work are essential.

Opportunities to share information and expertise are also necessary, not only to promote a sense of common good and unity among the staff, but for continuing staff development. In addition, some general principles identified for the pastoral ministry of bishops, are also helpful in making parishes great places to work. These include:

The Principle of Responsible Cooperation

All the faithful, both individually and in association, have the right and duty of cooperating in the mission of the Church according to each one's particular vocation and the gifts of the Holy Spirit (cf. *Lumen Gentium*, Dogmatic Constitution on the Church 30, 33; *Apostolicam Actuositatem*, Decree on the Apostolate of the Laity 2, 3). They also enjoy equitable liberty of thinking and of taking action in matters that are not necessary for the common good. The pastor and other parish leaders need to share willingly with others the sense of both individual and group responsibility by showing confidence in those who give their assistance in church offices and duties.

The Principle of Subsidiarity
The pastor and other parish leaders need to take care that they do not ordinarily take upon themselves what others can do well. Parish leaders need to carefully respect the legitimate competencies of others and also give co-workers the powers they need.

The Principle of Coordination
Like the bishop, the pastor needs to take responsibility not only to "stir up, encourage and increase the energies within his (parish), but also to weld them together so as to avoid harmful scattering and useless duplications as well as destructive dissensions, while at the same time always preserving the lawful rights and liberty of the faithful."

The Principle of Putting the Right People in the Right Places
In making use of the human resources of those who cooperate in the work of the Church, the pastor and other parish leaders need to be led by supernatural considerations and pursue above all the good of souls by preserving the dignity of persons, by employing their talents in as fitting and useful a way as possible for the service of the community, and by placing the right person in the right place.

In his book *Excellent Catholic Parishes*, Paul Wilkes (2001) provides common traits of excellent parish communities. Among these are their willingness to be innovative and to make some mistakes; their ability to apply rules intelligently, deriving authority from reflective, sensible, practice; their tendency to encourage people to go beyond the usual assigned tasks; their belief in quality and never forgetting that, "They provide first and foremost places where people can come to be close to God...." This chapter provides a glimpse at how parish human resource management contributes to forming excellent Catholic parishes. For more description of many of the human resource functions identified here, I recommend a publication of the National Association of Church Personnel Administration entitled *Parish Personnel Administration*, 4th edition, available through their web site at http://www.nacpa.org

References

____*The Directory on the Pastoral Ministry of Bishops.* 1974. Ottawa: Canadian Catholic Conference.

____*Stewardship, A Disciple's Response. A Pastoral Letter on Stewardship.* 1992. Washington, National Conference of Catholic Bishops.

____*Tenth Anniversary Edition of Economic Justice for All, Pastoral Letter on Catholic Social Teaching and the U.S. Economy.* 1997. Washington: U.S. Catholic Conference Inc.

Branagan, Colleen and Edward Pratt, eds. 2000. *Parish Personnel Administration*, 4th ed. Cincinnati: The National Association of Church Personnel Administrators.

Dailey, R.C. 1986. "Understanding Organization Commitment for Volunteers: Empirical and Managerial Implications," *Journal of Voluntary Action Research* 15(1), 19-31.

Fisher, James C. and Kathleen M. Cole. 1993. *Leadership and Management of Volunteer Programs: A Guide for Volunteer Administrators.* San Francisco, Jossey-Bass.

Froehle, Bryan T. and Mary L Gautier. 2000. *Catholicism USA: A Portrait of the Catholic Church in the United States.* New York: Orbis Books.

Greenhaus, Jeffrey H. 1994. *Career Management*, 2nd ed., Forth Worth: Dryden Press.

John Paul II. 1981. *Ecclesia in America* (The Church in America)

John Paul II. 1981. *Laborem Exercens* (On Human Work).

Kennedy, Jeffrey C. 1995. "Empowering Employees Through the Appraisal Performance Process," *International Journal of Public Administration* 18, no. 5.

Korsgaard, Audrey M. and Loriann Roberson. 1995. "Procedural Justice in Performance Evaluation: The Role of the Instrumental and Non Instrumental Voice in Performance Appraisal Discussions," *Journal of Management*, 21 no 4, pp. 657-69.

Lally, Ann et al. 2001. "Volunteers: Getting Them, Placing Them, Keeping Them" *Today's Parish Reprint*, Mystic: Twenty-Third Publications.

Murnion, Philip et al. 1992. *New Parish Ministers: Laity and Religious on Parish Staffs. A Study Conducted by the Committee on Pastoral Practices of the National Conference of Catholic Bishops.* New York: National Pastoral Life Center.

Saxon, J.P. and H.W. Sawyer. 1984. "A Systematic Approach for Volunteer Assignment and Retention," *Journal of Volunteer Administration*, 2(4), pp. 39-45.

Second Vatican Council. 1965. *Apostolicam Actuositatem*, Decree on the Apostolate of the Laity. November 18.

Second Vatican Council. 1964. *Lumen Gentium*, Dogmatic Constitution on the Church. November 21.

Sherman, Arthur et al. 1998. *Managing Human Resources.* Cincinnati, Southwestern Publishing.

Wilkes, Paul. 2001. *Excellent Catholic Parishes: A Guide to Best Places and Practices.* Mahwah: Paulist Press.

5

PARISH ADMINISTRATION AND CIVIL LAW

Mary Angela Shaughnessy, SCN, JD, PhD

Thirty years ago pastors and religious administrators did not worry about lawsuits. Very few were brought against the Church and most of the ones that were filed were quickly disposed of under the doctrine of *charitable immunity*, which held that persons cannot successfully sue a charity. That doctrine has been largely eroded, and today's church leaders find themselves worrying about lawsuits in a way that their predecessors would never have imagined. The competent parish administrator will understand that the ministry of administration is two-fold and encompasses civil law as well as canon law. Most administrators have at least some working knowledge of church law but may find themselves lacking when confronting issues of civil law. This chapter will discuss the "basics" of civil law as it impacts religious institutions.

Parish administrators are risk managers, and that is an important job. They are like the men in the gospel story to whom their master entrusted money. When he returned home, he expected to see that the money had grown. Growing assets enable Church ministry. Without assets, there will be no growth and a diminution of ministry.

It is thought that there have been more lawsuits brought against the Catholic Church since 1980 than in all the time preceding 1980. If it were ever true that people won't sue the Catholic Church, it is not true today. It is not uncommon to hear plaintiff's counsel say, "If this were anyone else but the Catholic Church, we would not bring this lawsuit. But the Church will settle." Unfortunately, the Catholic Church is sometimes viewed as a "dream defendant."

The law is a boundary around ministry. Persons can do anything they want inside the boundary, but once they move outside the boundary, they can lose everything inside the boundary. Parish administrators are the gatekeepers who keep employees, volunteers, and participants within the boundary. This chapter will identify legal issues that need pastoral attention if parishes are to keep within legal boundaries.

The history of the Catholic Church and litigation is not a long one. It has been a mere seventy-seven years since the Catholic Church established its right to operate Catholic schools. In 1925, Oregon, fearing the presence of foreigners, passed a law requiring all children between the ages of eight and sixteen to go to public schools. A religious community of women, the Sisters of the Holy Names of Jesus and Mary, to whom all Catholic educators everywhere are indebted, operated a school and challenged the law in the case *Pierce v. the Society of Sisters*. The United States Supreme Court found that religious institutions had a right to exist and offer religious and educational programs of their choosing.

Constitutional Rights in the Private Sector: Never had them, probably never will

The lack of constitutional protections in the private sector is a reality that many people do not seem to understand. Students and teachers in Catholic schools, as well as participants in various parish programs, do not have the same rights they would have if they were in public schools and programs.

Invariably, employees and parents encountering this reality for the first time find it hard to believe. The United States Constitution grants churches the right to exist but it says nothing about how those who administer churches are to treat their members. A simple example will illustrate. If a Catholic school principal or DRE is walking down the hall and encounters a student wearing a button that states, "Abortion is a woman's right," the adult will tell the young person to remove the button because it offends Catholic teaching. Yet, a student in a public school or a city-sponsored program could wear such a button. What is the difference? First Amendment freedom of expression does not exist in the Catholic setting. The Constitution, particularly the Bill of Rights, talks about what the government must do, not about what private persons must do. Thus, no one in the Catholic parish has constitutional rights that the parish is required to protect, and parish administrators are not required to recognize the constitutional rights of staff and participants in parish-sponsored programs. Parishes can prohibit behaviors that public institutions cannot.

In very early rulings, the doctrine of separation of church and state protected church-sponsored institutions from being sued successfully. The last twenty years have seen a rise in the number of cases brought against the Catholic Church. The reticence that once seemed to preclude a church member suing a church authority has largely disappeared. The primary law governing church relations with members and employees is contract law whereas in the public setting, it is constitutional law.

State Action

No court to date has ruled that religious institutions have to grant constitutional protections. Before churches can be required to grant constitutional protections, the substantial presence of the state, called state action, must be demonstrated: the court must determine that the state is significantly involved in a specific contested private action to such an extent that the action can fairly be said to be that of the state. One must look to Catholic school discipline cases alleging constitutional deprivations to find precedents for current disputes. One particularly interesting 1979 Ohio case, *Geraci v. St. Xavier High School,* illustrates this. In this case, a student named Geraci encouraged a student from another Catholic high school to come to St. Xavier during final exam week and throw a pie in the face of an unpopular teacher. The school responded by expelling Geraci, who then brought a lawsuit alleging both constitutional and contract violations. State action was alleged; the litigants claimed that the presence of state law governing some aspects of the Catholic school, such as teacher certification and length of school year, made the school subject to the same constitutional requirements as public schools. The court found that, even if state action were present, it would have to be so entwined with the contested activity (i.e., dismissal of the student), that a symbiotic relationship could be held to exist between the state and the school's dismissal of the student. If no such relationship could be established, state action is not present and constitutional protections do not apply.

Thus, aggrieved parties in the Catholic Church cannot avail themselves of constitutional arguments in civil proceedings. This author has heard of a case in which a man sued alleging that his son was denied his constitutional right to the sacrament of confirmation. Practicing judicial restraint, the court declined to intervene in a religious matter. This story is a sign of the times. Persons increasingly turn to courts to solve problems, and church officials can expect an increase in litigation.

Some states have attempted to pass laws that would grant constitutional protections to students in private schools. Such a maneuver, if successful, would have given students in Catholic schools constitutional rights, not because of the constitution but because of statutory law, which can bind us in the Catholic Church.

Contract Issues

Since constitutional arguments cannot be successfully advanced, persons generally raise breach of contract issues. The previously mentioned *Geraci* case also alleged breach of contract. The school, plaintiffs argued, breached its contract with the student and his parents when it expelled him, particularly in view of the fact that the student had never been in serious trouble, had paid the deposit for his senior year, and had received his senior ring. The school had a disciplinary code that prohibited, among other things, "immorality in talk or action" and "conduct detrimental to the reputation of the school." The court ruled that throwing a pie in the face of a teacher was "patently immoral" and, therefore, the student breached the contract when he consented to, and participated in, such activity.

Clauses such as, "immorality in talk or action" and "conduct detrimental to the reputation of the school or parish" can be particularly effective. Parish and school officials spend unnecessary time trying to think of everything a person should be forbidden to do, when a broad clause will encompass all that is needed. Parish administrators should encourage program directors and school principals to strive for breadth in policy and rule development, rather than stricture. Anyone who has ever dealt with children or adolescents knows that they can generally find some behavior that the rule doesn't mention.

What happens when an individual claims that he or she has been disciplined in violation of contract or policy? The court will scrutinize the governing documents. Any ambiguity is resolved in favor of the non-writing party. The 1982 New Hampshire case *Reardon v. LeMoyne* will illustrate. Four religious sisters were told that their contracts as principal and teachers in a New Hampshire parish school would not be renewed. At trial, the court examined the contract signed by the sisters. One part of the contract stated that employment was for one year only and would end on a certain date in June; however, another part of the contract stated that a person could expect to be rehired until the summer following his or her seventieth birthday—two very different realities. In effect, the document guaranteed a twenty-one-year-old person forty-nine years of employment. Applying the rule of construing the document against the party who wrote it, the court ruled that in effect, the clauses canceled each other out. The Sisters ultimately won the case but agreed to an out-of-court settlement.

Pastoral administrators should insist that contractual documents, and documents like handbooks that can be considered contractual, be examined critically by more persons than the ones who wrote them. A diocesan attorney or someone in the diocesan office with some legal knowledge might review the handbooks for clarity, inconsistencies, and potential legal problems. If there is no one who can review the documents at the central office level, parish administrators should encourage program administrators to exchange handbooks with peers and provide feedback.

Lawyers often use the term "due diligence." A good definition for "due diligence" is common sense. Due diligence demands that those who administer parishes take all appropriate care in their administration and not place persons or parish property at unreasonable risk.

Supervision and Evaluation of Personnel

Parish administrators often have questions about the best ways to supervise and evaluate personnel. Those who have little experience with such matters may have little confidence in themselves as supervisors and evaluators. Actually, the successful parish administrator is a minister and knows and recognizes good ministry skills and results. The parish administrator does not need to be an expert in all areas; rather, he or she needs to assess the job performance of those who are experts.

Although some may view ministry as a non-business type setting, in reality most ministries involve some oversight and administration. Parishes are not only ministry sites; they are also businesses. Someone has to pay the bills, oversee the plant, collect monies owed, hire employees, and supervise and evaluate them. Administration is a very real form of ministry. One of the most important responsibilities of any administrator is ensuring that the people who work in the ministry are competent individuals who can be trusted with the resources, lives, and souls of others.

Supervising administrators must make decisions about employee performance. Employees who do not leave voluntarily when found to be professionally deficient or lacking in job performance should not have their contracts renewed or their employment continued if remedies for improvement have been exhausted. Conversely, competent employees should find supervision and evaluation procedures to be protections for them.

Often administrators find themselves struggling with the ethical as well as the legal dimensions of situations. No one wants to end the employment of an individual whose family livelihood depends on it. Yet, justice demands that those who serve be competent ministers. In ministry, as in many settings, it is the administrator who must weigh the good of the individual against the good of the whole community and make a just decision. The most effective way of ensuring justice is by using documented, tried and true methods of supervision and evaluation.

Supervision and evaluation are not synonymous terms. Leadership theory teaches that supervision is a formative experience in which supervisor and employee dialogue, explore options, and agree on goals and targets for improvement. Evaluation is a summative experience and utilizes both the supervisory data and other data. Supervision involves observation in the ministerial setting. Evaluation also involves more intangible elements, such as loyalty to the Catholic Church and its teachings, support for authority, flexibility, compassion, and so on.

The parish administrator must ensure that all employees and volunteers are supervised. No one, no matter how old or how experienced, should be exempt from supervision. It is not fair to treat some employees differently from others. Certainly, the frequency of supervision can be decreased for the more experienced employee, but the employee should still be supervised.

Evaluation is summative: an administrator sums up all the available data and makes a decision regarding contract renewal or continued employment. The national trend appears to be moving away from contracts for church employees and towards the concept of "employment at will," which simply means that church administrators can hire and fire whom they want; the sole exception would be for an action that would "shock the conscience of the court," and even then the remedy would be payment of damages, rather than reinstatement in one's job.

The importance of individuals knowing what is expected of them cannot be underestimated. The staff handbook should contain a statement describing the supervision and evaluation methods used in the parish. For example: Who supervises? How often? What besides supervisory data will be used for evaluation?

Supervision and evaluation enable an administrator to make legally sound decisions about job continuation. Declining to renew a contract or terminating a person's employment may appear unethical if no processes for supervision and evaluation have been followed. Consistent, careful supervision ensures that persons are treated in appropriate legal and ethical ways.

Nonrenewal and Termination Decisions

If a decision is made not to renew a contract or to terminate employment, administrators need to be clear about the individual's employment status. There is virtually no right to reinstatement. At best, the court would view the situation as one of contract violation, the remedy for which is damages. In parishes that use contracts, the usual length of time for a contract is one year. With the exception of the few dioceses where Catholic schoolteachers are unionized, all who work in the Church must understand that there are no guarantees of lengthy or lifetime employment.

Unless a handbook or contract states otherwise, an employee does not have to be given the reasons for nonrenewal or termination. It would seem, however, that the appropriate ethical action would be to give the person the reasons so that the employee may learn from mistakes, move to a new situation, and be better equipped for the job. Problems can result, nevertheless, when an employee then attempts to prove in court that the reasons were neither true nor sufficient. Such a situation is one example of an ethical/legal dilemma in which parish administrators may find themselves. In a way, administrators are engaged in a kind of juggling act as they attempt to balance the *legal* dimensions of the parish's position with the *ethical* ones.

The following suggestions may help ensure legally sound supervision and evaluation practices:

- Develop a planned, orderly procedure for supervision;
- Publish and distribute the procedure to all employees and volunteers;
- Treat all fairly. Ensure that all are supervised;
- Keep written records of observations, supervision, and evaluation, while being careful to:

   Keep to the facts;

   Avoid speculation on motive or attitude;

   Say nothing that doesn't have to be said;

   Write in terms that are specific, behavioral, and verifiable;

   Write with the certainty that others will read what you have written.

Discipline

Employees and students tend to sue when faced with two realities—suspension or dismissal. In *Geraci* the court stated what the position of most courts would be:

   The disciplinary proceedings of a private school are not governed by the Fourteenth Amendment to the Constitution; nonetheless, under its broad equitable powers, a court will intervene when the procedures do not comport with fundamental fairness.

What is "fundamental fairness"? Unfortunately, that term is also used as a definition for constitutional due process. The *Geraci* court was talking about reasonableness, about treating people decently. Sometimes, much time can be spent asking, "Can I do this legally?" when a better question would be, "What should I do?" Just because an individual can do something legally doesn't mean that the action is the right one to take.

Pastoral administrators must be concerned with both written policies and procedures and with actual implementation of policy. All the policies in the world won't help if an administrator acts in a way that violates the rights of an individual or creates a public relations nightmare for the church. Too many parishes and programs have outdated, legally risky operating manuals and handbooks—or, perhaps worse—none at all. The time to write a policy is not when it is needed. I recommend a proactive approach that anticipates problems and possible solutions. It is better to write a policy that is never used than to try to construct one after the fact.

The following example illustrates the importance of good policy. Some years ago, two Catholic high school students killed a gay man. One student readily admitted his involvement, was arrested, and withdrew from school. The other young man denied involvement. The school did not have a policy or rule stating that murder was prohibited. Much administrative time was spent dealing with what to do about this young man who had been accused, but not convicted, of a crime. School officials did not want the student in school for a number of reasons, not the least of which was the distraction his presence presented. Eventually, the student was arrested on another charge and sent to jail to await trial, and the question of school attendance became moot. Had the Catholic school had a simple policy that allowed it to place a student accused of a serious wrong on a home-study program pending the outcome of a trial or investigation, school officials could have moved quickly to remove the student from the school without the arguments that resulted when no applicable policy was found to be in place.

Illegal Activity

A person who has committed an illegal act may certainly have employment or volunteer status terminated. One who is convicted of, or who admits commission of, a crime should be removed from professional or volunteer status. The harder question arises when a person has simply been accused of, or arrested on suspicion of, a crime. Pastors and other administrators may be sharply divided on the proper response to make in such a situation. There have been more than a few cases in which parish employees or volunteers have been arrested or accused of serious wrongdoing. Institutions should have policies that allow them to remove the individuals from service pending the resolution of the accusations. Some may wonder why removal is recommended when, in our country, an individual is presumed innocent until proven guilty—although, in the last decade or so, it seems that a person is presumed guilty until proven innocent. The presence of an accused individual is generally disruptive to the learning or faith-formation process—so a "cooling off" period is usually in everyone's best interests.

Every parish entity should have a policy in place that allows the pastor or other administrator to place the accused individual on a leave of absence pending the outcome of an investigation or an adjudication of guilt. The prudent administrator will have policy in place that anticipates such situations, as it is far easier to deal with established policy and procedure than to try to fashion policy after the fact.

Issues of Lifestyle and Belief

A specific area of concern in discipline of employees is lifestyle and belief. Catholic parish and school employees are representatives of the Church twenty-four hours a day, seven days a week. As Church representatives, employees can't take a vacation from living a life consistent with the teachings of the Church. What parish employees do publicly reflects on the Church. No administrator wants to function as the private morality police, but appearances are important. A parish administrator's first legal, contractual obligation is to be true to the teachings of the Catholic Church; parish ministries are extensions of those teachings. No one should apologize for being Catholic.

No person can sit in judgment on the state of another's soul. But if agents of the Church do something that is "detrimental to the reputation of the Church," ministerial effectiveness may be compromised. Persons may be confused. Dioceses in the United States differ in their approaches to this very real problem. Some dioceses take the position that if a person does something seriously against the teachings of the Church—contracts a second marriage without an annulment, has a child out of wedlock, openly states that he or she is "living with" a person who is not a spouse, or is sexually active with a person of the same sex, the individual has forfeited the right to work in Church ministry. Once an individual performs an act that is inconsistent with a position in Church ministry, that person may no longer be qualified to minister in a given situation at a given time. While such a reality may seem obvious, it is recommended that documents state the requirement of supporting the teachings of the Church.

Some other dioceses take the stand that positions will be lost only if what was done causes a public scandal. Consistency within the parishes and institutions of the diocese is important. If public knowledge of scandalous behavior is the norm, then it should be upheld. It is unfair, and may be legally dangerous, to dismiss one person who marries without an annulment and keep another in similar circumstances.

Negligence

Negligence is the most often-litigated tort. Sometimes, in the forest of litigation, persons only see a particular tree. Parish administrators are far more likely to be sued for negligence than for any other action; unfortunately, many parish administrators do not possess a basic understanding of negligence.

Negligence, at its core, is an absence of care. Negligence is the violation of a duty that proximately causes an injury. If a parish administrator is sued, there is a high degree of probability that the suit will be one alleging negligence. Even though negligence is the "fault" against which administrators must guard most constantly, it is also one of the most difficult types of case about which to predict an accurate judicial outcome. What may be considered negligence in one court may not be so considered in another. It is much better, obviously, to avoid being accused of negligence in the first place than to take one's chances on the outcome of a lawsuit. Negligence can be either acts of commission or "sins" of omission. The negligent individual either did something he should not have done or failed to do something she should have done.

There are four elements that must be present before legal negligence can exist. These elements, which have been defined by many legal writers, are: duty, violation of duty, proximate cause, and injury. If any one of the four elements is missing, no legal negligence can be found. Since negligence is the unintentional act that results in an injury, a person charged with negligence is generally not going to face criminal charges or spend time in prison.

An examination of each of the four elements necessary to constitute a finding of negligence should be helpful. First, the person charged with negligence must have had a *duty* in the situation. Employees, volunteers, and participants have a right to safety, and parish administrators have a responsibility to protect the safety of all entrusted to their care. Administrators should develop rules and regulations that foster safety. Persons will generally not be held responsible for injuries occurring at a place where, or at a time when, they had no responsibility. A parishioner, for example, injured on the way to the youth ministry program, normally will not be able to demonstrate that the parish administrator or youth minister had a duty to protect that individual prior to arrival on parish property.

Parish administrators, however, should be aware of the fact that courts may hold them responsible for behavior and its consequences occurring on parish property before or after activities. For example, the presence of students on school grounds before school opens or after the school day ends has been extremely problematic. In a 1967 New Jersey case, *Titus v. Lindberg*, a school principal was found liable for student injury occurring on school grounds before school because: he knew that students arrived on the grounds before the doors were opened; he was present on the campus when they were; he had established no rules for student conduct outside the building, and he had not provided for supervision of the students. The court found that the principal had a reasonable duty to provide such supervision when he knew that students were on the property at unauthorized times as a regular practice.

The *Titus* case illustrates the dilemma in which parish administrators may find themselves. If a parent drops a child off at the parish at 6:00 P.M. and the religious education program begins at 7:30 P.M., is the administrator responsible for the student? How does the administrator provide for supervision? Should supervision be provided? There are no easy answers to these problems of supervision of young people.

Courts will consider the reasonableness of the administrator's behavior. It may not be reasonable to expect that an administrator will provide for the supervision of persons on parish grounds no matter how early they arrive or how late they stay, but the possibility of presence at "unauthorized" times should be recognized and policy developed to govern such situations.

The second element involved in negligence is *violation of duty*. Negligence cannot exist if an individual has not violated a duty. Courts expect that accidents and spontaneous actions can occur. If a pre-school teacher is properly supervising a playground at recess, and one child picks up a rock and throws it and so injures another child, the teacher cannot be held liable. However, if a teacher who is responsible for the supervision of the playground were to allow rock throwing to continue without attempting to stop it and a student were injured, the teacher would probably be held liable.

The third requirement of negligence is that the violation of duty must be the *proximate cause* of the injury. In other words, would the injury have occurred if proper supervision had been present? The jury has to decide whether proper supervision could have prevented the injury and, in so deciding, has to look at the facts of each individual case.

The well-known 1982 case of *Smith v. Archbishop of St. Louis*, involving a Catholic school, illustrates the concept of proximate cause. A second-grade teacher kept a lighted candle on her desk during the month of May to honor the Blessed Mother. One day a student walked too close to the desk and her clothes caught fire. The child sustained severe disfigurement, and experts testified that she would likely experience a lifetime of psychological problems. The appellate court upheld an award for damages and a finding of negligent supervision against the archdiocese. This case demonstrates the liability that can accrue to parishes and dioceses because of the negligence of a supervising adult.

The *Smith* case also illustrates the concept of foreseeability. The plaintiff did not have to prove that the defendant could foresee that a particular injury (plaintiff's costume catching fire) had to occur; the plaintiff had to establish that a reasonable person would have foreseen that injuries could result from having an unattended lighted candle in a second-grade classroom when no safety instructions had been given to the students. Church administrators must help those who share ministry with them to become foreseers of possible risks and injuries. In the wake of the sexual abuse cases, one must be ever more vigilant in foreseeing the possible dangers of certain practices and procedures.

Thus, negligence is a complex concept. It is often difficult to predict what a court will consider proximate cause in any particular allegation of negligence.

The fourth element necessary for a finding of negligence is *injury.* No matter how irresponsible the behavior of a supervisor, there is no legal negligence if there is no injury. If an adult leaves twenty seven-year-olds unsupervised near a lake and no one is injured, there can be no finding of negligence. Any reasonable person, though, can see that no one in authority should take risks that may result in injury. In parishes, as in other institutions, administrators are also expected to see that equipment and property are maintained and that areas are kept free of unnecessary hazards.

The younger the child, the greater the supervisor's responsibility. It might be acceptable to leave a group of high-school seniors alone for ten minutes in a math class when it would not be acceptable to leave a group of first graders alone. It is reasonable to expect that fifteen-year-olds of average intelligence could observe traffic signals when they are crossing a street. It would not be reasonable to expect mentally disabled fifteen-year-olds to be responsible for crossing the street.

In developing and implementing policies for supervision of young people as well as adults, the administrator must keep in mind the reasonableness standard and ask, "Is this what one would expect a reasonable person in a similar situation to do?" No one expects an administrator to think of every possible situation that might occur. No one can foresee everything that might happen, but reasonable persons can assume that certain situations are potentially dangerous. The teacher in the *Smith* case, for example, should have foreseen that an open flame might cause injury to second graders.

The best defense for an administrator in a negligence suit is the development of reasonable policies and rules. The reasonable administrator is one who supervises employees and volunteers in their implementation of rules.

The prudent administrator must take an offensive approach with regard to the elimination of hazards. All activities should be carefully monitored. All staff, paid and volunteer, should receive thorough and ongoing orientation and instruction. The administrator who practices prevention by constantly striving to eliminate foreseeable risks will avoid both injuries and costly litigation.

In the wake of the school violence witnessed over the past few years, administrators should lead their staffs in imagining the worst things that could happen in the parish and then discuss how those things could be handled. From that conversation, the beginnings of a crisis plan should arise.

While the information regarding negligence may seem daunting, there is much a parish administrator can do to avoid being charged with negligence, or if charged, to avoid a finding of negligence. Some recommendations follow.

First, ensure that the parish has hiring and volunteer selection procedures that allow for thorough background investigation and assessment of fitness for the position. Is the person mentally and physically capable of providing appropriate supervision? These questions should be answered before other ministry qualifications are assessed because, if the person does not possess the mental and physical competencies, it will not matter what other qualifications are met. Care must be taken to avoid putting persons in positions simply because they want those positions. It may be difficult to deny individuals a position, but it is far cheaper than the expense of a lawsuit due to failure to exercise appropriate supervision.

Second, administrators should ensure that personnel and volunteer handbooks and manuals contain clear policies and procedures for supervision of both young persons and adults, but which pay special attention to situations involving children under the age of 18. Pastors, principals, directors of religious education, and youth ministers should be able to provide directives that will ensure appropriate supervision, as discussed below. Courts follow the principle, "the younger the child chronologically or mentally, the greater the standard of care." Thus, supervisors of younger children will be held to a higher standard than will supervisors of older children and adults.

Those who cannot demonstrate appropriate supervisory skills should be removed from responsibility for persons. There is an old myth that volunteers cannot be fired. Volunteers can be thanked politely and invited to serve in other ways or not at all. Courts will not look kindly upon incidents of negligence that could have been avoided if persons had been properly instructed or if incompetent persons are retained.

Third, the administrator should at least annually ensure that a safety audit, discussed elsewhere in this chapter, is conducted. All areas of the parish buildings and grounds should be inspected. Areas of danger should be noted, and plans for addressing needs should be documented. A buildings and grounds committee of the parish council or other board can be most helpful in this regard.

Fourth, the administrator must establish a crisis plan. Administrators cannot take refuge in the mistaken belief that "it will never happen here." Plans should be developed when they are not needed, so they will be available when they are needed.

Supervision

Everyone will agree that adults have the duty to supervise young people. In parishes, schools, and religious education programs, adults supervise the learning and the safety of young people. Schoolteachers, by and large, have had at least some basic instruction in the supervision of young people. Catechists, youth ministry volunteers, and school volunteers may have little or no instruction in supervision of young people. Legal experts report that classrooms and other instructional spaces are the places in which injuries are more likely to occur, because that is where young people spend most of their time.

A concept, which is relatively recent in case law, is that of mental supervision. Supervision is a mental as well as a physical act. It is not enough to be physically present; one has to be mentally present as well. How do administrators ensure mental presence? By talking to adult supervisors about it and by requiring administrators to supervise the adult supervisors. This topic is sometimes a sore one. No one likes to be told to pay attention. But, in effect, that is what administrators must do: pay attention to those they supervise.

Other Safety Issues

Parish administrators are concerned with the overall legal vulnerability of the church and are usually fairly familiar with the property and buildings, although other employees may have more detailed knowledge of safety conditions and hazards. Most dioceses now require a safety audit in which a designated group of persons "walk through" the premises and make notes concerning possible safety violations and needs. There are really two areas of concern here: actual physical problems and less than prudent practices. The actual physical problems are usually easier to spot than the less-than-prudent practices.

When conducting a safety audit, it is important to include at least one person who has some professional construction or similar experience and who is not a parish employee. In perhaps too many parishes the maintenance person conducts the safety audit and draws up the safety plan. There are at least two problems here: (1) he or she knows the building so well, it is easy to overlook problems, and (2) he or she will probably be the person who will have to expend some effort to correct the safety problems.

Crisis planning is another legal issue for parish administrators. Five years ago, perhaps 50% of parishes and schools had crisis plans. In 2002, in response to school violence, the number is probably closer to 80%. Diocesan and parish administrators have to be concerned about the 20% with no plan. Administrators also have to be concerned with those who have plans, but probably could not find them if asked or whose staff members either never received a copy or do not know where it is. At the least, crisis plans should be readily accessible in each room. Posting plans is a good idea. Each parish or school or program should have a code phrase that will signal personnel that there is a problem and that crisis procedures should be inaugurated.

Threats of Violence

What about those who threaten violence to others? Today administrators are urged to adopt a zero-tolerance stance, but the stance should be age-appropriate. A kindergartner who yells, "I'm going to kill you" to his classmate who took his blocks should not be expelled. At the same time, all threats must be taken seriously. The author was once retained as an expert witness in a case, subsequently settled out of court, in which a high-school student who had been expelled for threatening violence claimed he was not serious. There is no room for joking or for delay when safety is threatened. People's lives may depend on administrative response.

Sexual Harassment

When persons believe that the Church response to allegations of sexual harassment and sexual abuse has been inadequate, Church administrators may find themselves charged with negligence. A discussion of sexual harassment and abuse laws follows.

Virtually, everyone recognizes the term "sexual harassment." Providing a working definition and appropriate policies and procedures, however, is not easy. No longer is sexual harassment something that is found only between two adults or between an adult and a child. School children claim that peers have harassed them. What, then, is a parish administrator to do?

Parish boards, pastors, and other administrators should enact and implement policies prohibiting sexual harassment; federal and state law can assist with this process. Title VII of the Civil Rights Act of 1964 mandated that the workplace be free of harassment based on sex. Later federal legislation requires that educational programs receiving federal funding be free of sexual harassment. Both these titled laws are anti-discrimination statutes. Some states are now prohibiting discrimination based on gender; such a requirement would prohibit such statements as "Boys are better at math than are girls."

Federal anti-discrimination law can bind Catholic institutions. Most schools and parishes routinely file statements of compliance with discrimination laws with appropriate local, state, and national authorities. Anti-discrimination legislation can impact Catholic institutions because the government has a compelling interest in the equal treatment of all citizens. Compliance with statutory law can be required if there is no less burdensome way to meet the requirements of the law. Sexual harassment is one type of discrimination.

The Equal Employment Opportunities Commission has issued guidelines that define sexual harassment, forbidden by Title VII, as unwelcome sexual advances, requests for sexual favors, and other verbal or physical conduct of a sexual nature when:

- submission to such conduct by an individual is made explicitly or implicitly a term of employment;
- submission to, or rejection of, such conduct by an individual is used as the basis for an employment decision;
- and such conduct has the purpose or effect to interfere with an individual's work performance, or creates a hostile or intimidating environment.

The above definition concerns employment conditions; however, "education" or "ministry" can be substituted for "employment" in the definitions, and the basis for violations would be evident. Courts, including the U.S. Supreme Court, are vigorously supporting persons' rights to be free from sexual harassment.

Actions that can be "Harassment"

The following are examples of behaviors that could constitute sexual harassment: sexual propositions, off-color jokes, inappropriate physical contact, innuendoes, sexual offers, looks, and gestures. In a number of recent public school cases and religious education cases, female students alleged that male students made sexual statements to them, and school officials, after being informed, declined to take action. One director of religious education found herself in "hot water" when the following occurred. A male student and a female student, both approximately thirteen years of age, approached the pencil sharpener at roughly the same time in the religious education classroom. The boy sharpened his pencil and then blew the shavings onto the chest area of the girl's sweater. He then proceeded to say, "Here, let me help you," as he used his hand to remove the shavings from the sweater. The embarrassed girl went to the director of religious education, who told her that, "boys will be boys." The girl's parents were outraged and threatened legal action. Ultimately, a resolution was reached outside court; it is easy to imagine, however, how a court might have viewed the situation.

Although one can argue that the person who sexually harasses another should be liable and not the school or program or administrators, case law is suggesting that administrators who ignore such behavior or do not take it seriously can be held liable to the offended parties.

Suggested Policies

Policies defining sexual harassment and procedures for dealing with claims of sexual harassment should be clear and understandable to the average reader. Staff members must be required to implement the policies. The following is one suggestion of a policy statement based on federal law.

Definition:

Sexual harassment is defined as (1) threatening to impose adverse employment, academic or disciplinary or other sanctions on a person, unless favors are given; and/or (2) conduct, containing sexual matter or suggestions, which would be offensive to a reasonable person.

Sexual harassment includes, but is not limited to, the following behaviors:

1. verbal conduct such as epithets, derogatory jokes or comments, slurs or unwanted sexual advances, imitations, or comments;

2. visual contact such as derogatory and/or sexually oriented posters, photography, cartoons, drawings, or gestures;

3. physical contact such as assault, unwanted touching, blocking normal movements, or interfering with work, study, or play because of sex;

4. threats and demands to submit to sexual requests as a condition of continued employment or grades or other benefits or to avoid some other loss and offers of benefits in return for sexual favors; and

5. retaliation for having reported or threatened to report sexual harassment.

Procedures for reporting should then be given. These procedures should include a statement such as, "All allegations will be taken seriously and promptly investigated." Administrators should stress confidentiality and express concern for both the alleged victim and the alleged perpetrator. Procedures should include copies of the forms used in such cases.

Every employee and volunteer should be required to sign a statement that he or she has been given a copy of the policies relating to sexual harassment and other sexual misconduct, has read the material, and agrees to be bound by it. Parent/student handbooks should contain at least a general statement that sexual harassment is not condoned in a Christian atmosphere, and both parents and students should sign a statement that they agree to be governed by the handbook.

Prevention

It is far easier to prevent claims of sexual harassment than it is to defend against them. To that end, teachers, other ministers, and volunteers should participate in some kind of inservice training that raises awareness of sexual harassment and other gender issues. Staff members must understand what sorts of behaviors can be construed as sexual harassment.

Teachers and other ministers should discuss issues of fair treatment of others with their students, and should promptly correct individuals who demean others. Defenses such as, "I was only kidding," will not be accepted if the alleged victim states that the behavior was offensive and unwelcome, and a court finds that a reasonable person could find the behavior offensive and unwelcome. Finally, of course, sexual harassment and other forms of demeaning behavior have no place in Catholic parishes and schools. Guarding the dignity of each member of the parish community should be a priority for all involved in the ministries of the Catholic Church.

Child Abuse

Certainly no cause of action has brought greater pain than sexual abuse. Even though it is not the most often litigated claim, it is possibly the most tragic. No one can give a person back his or her innocence. Parish administrators must act swiftly, decisively, and appropriately with due care for both the victim and the alleged perpetrator. Every diocese has sexual abuse policies. It is imperative that parish administrators insist that proper procedures be followed and that administrators not decide to conduct investigations independent of the police and social service agencies. Obviously, some data has to be gathered. But administrators must realize that they cannot handle such accusations alone.

Often it is the parish administrator who receives the information that a person has been abused. The administrator is in a particularly sensitive position. Abused young persons often choose teachers or other ministers as confidants. Therefore, all employees and volunteers should be as prepared as possible to deal with the realities of abuse and neglect. The parish administrator should consider the adoption of a policy such as, "This parish or program abides by the child abuse reporting statutes of the state." Further, policy should require that administrators spend some time reviewing pertinent state law and parish/school/program policies and providing information and discussion on the topic in staff meetings, particularly at the beginning of the programmatic or school year. If a separate meeting is not provided for other employees and volunteers, the parish administrator should consider having them present for the appropriate portion of the staff meeting.

Statutory Considerations

All fifty states have laws requiring educators to report suspected child abuse or neglect. Statutes will ordinarily require that persons who supervise children or adolescents report suspected child abuse; some states require anyone with knowledge of possible abuse to report it. Compliance with these statutes may not be as easy as it first appears. What arouses suspicion in one adult may not in another. In such cases, courts have to determine whether each individual sincerely believed in the correctness of his or her perception. Despite the best of intentions and efforts, staff members may fail to report suspected child abuse. In that case, the parish administrator could be held liable for failing to report under the doctrine of *respondeat superior,* "let the superior answer." However, if an appropriate policy is in place and has been appropriately implemented, responsibility for failure to report should be that of the individual staff member who failed, not of the institution.

Statutes generally mandate reporting procedures. The reporting individual usually makes a phone report that is followed by a written report within a specified time period. Statutes usually provide protection for a person who makes a good faith report of child abuse that later is discovered to be unfounded. Such a good-faith reporter will not be liable to the alleged abuser for defamation of character. However, a person can be held liable for making what is referred to as a "malicious report," one that has no basis in fact and that was made by a person who knew that no factual basis existed. Conversely, statutes usually mandate that a person who knew of child abuse or neglect and failed to report it can be fined and/or charged with a misdemeanor or felony.

Defining Abuse

What is child abuse? This author once heard an attorney define it as "corporal punishment gone too far." Although that definition excludes sexual abuse, the definition has merit. However, it also poses questions: How far is too far? Who makes the final determination? Can what one person considers abuse be considered valid parental corporal punishment by another? Are there any allowances for differing cultural practices? It is difficult to give a precise definition that will cover all eventualities. Certainly, some situations are so extreme that there can be little argument that abuse has occurred.

The majority of cases will probably not be clear-cut, and an educator or minister may well wonder if a report should be made. Many law enforcement officials and some attorneys instruct staff members to report everything that students or others tell then that could possibly constitute abuse or negligence. They further caution that it is not the reporter's job to determine if abuse has occurred. The reporter has a responsibility to present information to the agency designated to receive reports. Appropriate officials will then determine whether the report should be investigated further or simply "screened out" as a well-intentioned report, perhaps, that does not appear to be in the category of abuse.

Who Should File the Abuse Report?

Many experts advise that the school or program administrator make all child abuse and neglect reports, so that the same person is reporting all situations in a given setting. However, individual state laws vary on this point. Some states clearly require the person with the suspicion to file the report. In such a case, the staff member must personally report abuse to the appropriate agency and notify the administrator. At all times, though, everyone must remember that the obligation to see that a report is filed belongs to the person who suspects the abuse.

Parish administrators should decide in advance how visits and requests from police or social workers will be handled. Many states now require that school and other personnel allow police and social work officials to examine and question young people without anyone else present. Parish administrators should seek legal counsel in determining the applicable law for a given state.

Appearances of Impropriety

Administrators must encourage all who work in the Catholic Church to avoid even the appearance of impropriety. Perception becomes reality. A male high-school teacher once told the writer, "I would never stay alone in a room with a girl unless the door was open or people could see in through a window." A reputation is a terrible thing to lose and is almost impossible to rebuild—persons often remember the accusation, but not the exoneration. Some public school officials, trying to avoid liability, have forbidden any physical contact between students and teachers. A better approach is to ask one's self, "If I saw someone else touching a student in this way, would I think it is all right?" When in doubt, of course, adults should not touch children.

Boundary Issues

There is a related issue raising legal concerns today—boundary issues. One example is alienation of the parent/child relationship. This alienation, generally not alleged to have any sexual overtones, results when a parent believes that an adult, generally a teacher or counselor, has so insinuated himself or herself into the child's life that there is no room left for the parent. In such situations, parents seek, and are generally successful in obtaining, restraining orders. It is important for all who work in ministry to young people to understand that the minister is not the parent, however much the minister and young person might wish otherwise.

There have to be boundaries in relationships. Sometimes, well-meaning persons get "too close" to others. People tell all and answer any question. Far from being open, they are destroying the boundary that the person being ministered to needs. Catechists and teachers, for example, do not have to answer questions such as, "Did you sleep with your husband before you were married?" Boundaries are healthy, and personal boundaries help keep persons within the legal boundaries that surround ministry.

Ministers must understand that they are professionals rendering a service. Volunteers, while perhaps not professionally trained, are entrusted with certain ministerial functions. Just as a counselor or psychiatrist is professionally bound to avoid emotional involvement with a client, a minister should strive to avoid becoming so emotionally involved with another that objectivity and fairness are compromised. Ministers must remember that they have many persons who need them and their attention. If a relationship with one person keeps a staff member from responding to other needs on a regular basis, the staff member should seriously examine the appropriateness of the relationship.

In the wake of the stunning number of allegations of sexual abuse by priests and other ministers, it is important to note that parish administrators must carefully monitor what happens in their parishes. If an administrator is disturbed by something, he or she should speak up immediately and discuss the situation with the parties involved. If one has a "funny feeling," one should not ignore it, but should ask questions. If something causes discomfort or doesn't feel right, there is probably cause for concern. One reason situations can escalate into serious, even tragic, outcomes is because those in authority are fearful of saying anything without proof. As in most other ministerial situations, approach is everything. If an administrator notices that a man and woman, each married to another, are in each other's company fairly constantly and others are beginning to talk, the administrator does not have to confront the two with an allegation of sexual misconduct. Rather, the administrator could gently point out that he or she has become aware of some talk that involves the two and wanted to make them aware. Ministers should be grateful that the administrator cares enough to monitor what goes on in the name of ministry in a given parish and to protect the legal rights and good name of all.

Confidentiality

Persons who work in Church ministry should not compromise confidentiality lightly. However, all who work in Church ministries must realize that there is no legal privilege in matters involving life and safety. There are only two privileges left in this country: priest/penitent, which is absolute, and attorney/client, which is not. If one tells an attorney that she has killed someone, the attorney cannot tell that. But if one tells an attorney that he is about to kill someone, the attorney must warn the potential victim and take all reasonable steps to ensure his or her safety. Persons who are in counseling positions sometimes chafe at being told to report confidential matters. Guidelines for professional organizations may direct persons to keep information received in counseling sessions confidential. But there is no legal protection for the retreat director, for example, who is told by a student that he or she is contemplating suicide and who fails to do anything with that knowledge.

One of the fastest growing areas of litigation in public schools is journal writing. For example, a student writes in his journal: "I'm so depressed, I think I'll kill myself." Teacher writes back, "Please don't. We'd miss you." Student kills self. Parents get journal and sue. In some such cases, teachers have been bound over for trial on negligent homicide or voluntary manslaughter charges. Schools, religious education, and youth ministry programs often use journals. All who may receive confidences should be instructed to tell confiding individuals, "I will keep your confidence so long as no one's health, life, or safety is involved. Once health, life or safety is involved, confidentiality is gone."

Volunteers

Virtually every ministerial program has volunteers, even depends on them. Under the doctrine of *respondeat superior*, the parish is responsible for the actions of its agents. Volunteers can be seen as agents. The 1997 Volunteer Protection Act was hailed as the federal government's way of ensuring volunteers in programs and institutions that needed them. What most people aren't aware of, however, is that the protection is not absolute. It requires that a volunteer be immune from civil liability for any act or omission resulting in damages or injury, if the person was acting in good faith and within the scope of his official functions and duties, unless such damage or injury was caused by the willful or wanton misconduct of the person.

It is easy to see that the protection contains a few holes—a litigant can always claim that the volunteer was acting in bad faith or that whatever was done was the result of misconduct. Even with liability possibilities, most parishes have a retinue of faithful volunteers. Because so many lawsuits today are alleging negligence on the part of volunteers, however, a few suggestions are in order.

(1) Understand what the Volunteer Protection Act and your state statutes protect and what they do not protect.

(2) Do not tell volunteers they cannot be sued or that there is a law that does not allow people to sue them.

(3) Follow reasonable procedures in the recruitment of volunteers. Be sure that all volunteers who work with children have undergone a criminal background check.

(4) If volunteers use their own vehicles in the performance of their duties, require that copies of their drivers' licenses and proofs of insurance be on file.

(5) Provide a thorough orientation to volunteers.

(6) Develop and disseminate a volunteer handbook.

(7) Know what the institution's insurance covers and what it does not.

(8) Remember—volunteers can be fired. It may be difficult, but sometimes it must be done for the greater good.

Conclusion

Parish administrators are expected to be moral, ethical, and lawful persons. Moral/ethical/legal dilemmas are often present. Perhaps the words of Jesus, "Render unto Caesar the things that are Caesar's and unto God the things that are God's" are appropriate. Jesus does not tell us that we can disregard the law of God or humans; rather, he asks us to give both their due. Parish administrators should pray for the wisdom to discern how to meet Jesus' directive, and so help to ensure appropriate treatment for all in their parishes.

References

Geraci v. St. Xavier High School, 13 Ohio Op. 3d 146 (Ohio, 1978).

Pierce v. the Society of Sisters, 268 U.S. 510 (1925).

Reardon v. LeMoyne, 454 A.2d 428 (N.H. 1982).

Smith v. the Archbishop of St. Louis, 633 S.W.2d 516 (Mo. Ct. App. 1982).

Title VII of the Civil Rights Acts of 1964.

Titus v. Lindberg, 228 A.2d 65 (N.J., 1967).

United States Constitution.

6

THE CONSEQUENCES OF PASTORAL LEADERSHIP

Michael Cieslak

It would be difficult to argue against someone who says that pastoral leadership may be the most important quality in determining whether a parish is perceived as "alive" or "dead." Certainly anecdotal evidence suggests that the typical Catholic sees the parish taking on the quality of the pastor's leadership, for better or worse.

This chapter examines the extent to which objective research supports this anecdotal evidence. It also attempts to answer the question "what are some consequences of pastoral leadership?" The first step is to examine some insights about leadership by both secular and church authors. Then three issues on pastoral leadership within Catholic parishes will be examined:

1. The importance of pastors: Does changing pastors lead to a change in parishioner commitment, such as financial contributions?
2. Pastoral leadership and parish vitality: Is pastoral leadership associated with parish vitality?
3. Pastoral leadership style and parish preferences: Do parishes differ on the type of pastoral leadership they prefer?

The three questions on pastoral leadership are answered in part with data from the Rockford Catholic diocese. This diocese in northern Illinois is made up of about 350,000 Catholics in 104 parishes. The diocese is a mixture of rural, small town, urban, and suburban parishes. While 14 parishes have more than 2,000 registered households, more than twice as many (33) have less than 300 registered households. Results from the Rockford diocese should not be generalized to other dioceses since this diocese may have unique characteristics—such as diocesan leadership or demographic composition. The results presented here are meant more to raise questions about pastoral leadership than to answer them.

A disclaimer: unless otherwise noted, the term "pastoral leadership" refers to the leadership provided by priests, chiefly pastors. This is not to deny the good pastoral leadership that is provided by permanent deacons, women religious, and other lay people assisting in parish ministry or serving as parish directors. Nor is it intended to minimize the pastoral leadership given by effective parish pastoral councils and finance councils. Much of the analysis within this report, however, makes use of existing diocesan data that centers on the role of the pastor. At the same time, lay leaders will recognize that most of the findings in this chapter are applicable to their situations as well.

What is Leadership?

Leadership is like beauty: difficult to define, but most people will recognize it when they see it. One can interpret leadership broadly and state that "…a leader is someone who touches another's future" (Champlin 1993, 24). With this interpretation, leaders are clearly recognizable as those who affect the direction a person or a group (e.g., parish) will take. Peter Senge, writing in *The Fifth Discipline Fieldbook,* concurs with this understanding and notes that it is easy to perceive both good leadership and the absence of good leadership. "You can always sense the presence or absence of leadership when you begin working in a new organization. In some cases, you get a sense that something is off-kilter, though everyone is saying the 'right' things. You also know that *they* know something's off-kilter…" (1994, 65)

In a chapter entitled "There Are No Leaders, There Is Only Leadership," Richard Farson states that leadership is less the property of a person than the property of a group. He notes the examples of leaders who successfully move from one organization to another even though they may not be experts in the second organization's business. They are able to do this because they call forth the skills and creativity of those already within the organization. He concludes that in " …a well-functioning group, the behavior of the leader is not all that different from the behavior of other responsible group members" (1996, 144-145).

Eric Law reminds us that leadership is perceived differently in various cultures. He astutely notes that "…how a person is expected to manage a group is dependent on the group members' perception of their own power. How do you lead a group of people who believe they are equal to you? How do you lead a group of people who defer to you for all the decision making because you are the authority figure? How do you lead a group of people whose perception of their power spreads from one end of the power perception continuum to the other" (1993, 30)? Leadership in a multicultural setting is considerably more complex than leadership in a culturally homogeneous group.

Characteristics of Good Leadership

It is useful to compare the thoughts of two experts—one writing from a secular viewpoint and the other writing from a religious perspective—as they list the characteristics that a good leader should have. Warren Bennis is a professor of business administration and a consultant to multinational companies and governments. He sees leaders as having five major characteristics.

- *A Guiding Vision.* The leader has a clear idea of what he or she wants to do—professionally and personally—and the strength to persist in the face of setbacks, even failures.
- *Passion.* The leader has an underlying passion for the promises of life, combined with a very particular passion for a vocation, a profession, a course of action. The leader loves what he or she does and loves doing it.
- *Integrity.* The leader has true integrity, which is composed of self-knowledge, candor, and maturity.
- *Trust.* Trust is not so much an ingredient of leadership as it is a product. It is the one quality that cannot be acquired, but must be earned.
- *Curiosity and Daring.* The leader wonders about everything, wants to learn as much as he or she can, is willing to take risks, experiments, and tries new things (1989, 39-41).

Loughlan Sofield, a brother of the Missionary Servants of the Most Holy Trinity, is an internationally recognized author and consultant on ministry and personal development. Donald Kuhn, a specialist in leadership development, serves as a retreat director, workshop leader, and group facilitator. In *The Collaborative Leader* Sofield and Kuhn list two dominant characteristics that true leaders have:

- *Intense integrity* accompanied by the courage necessary to pursue integrity.
- *Generativity* motivated by a concern for others (1995, 27).

While these writers come from different experiences and perspectives there is some commonality in characteristics. Both sets of authors explicitly list integrity. Bennis adds vision, passion, trust, and curiosity and daring while Sofield and Kuhn only add generativity. While not demanding that the two lists be congruent, one could perceive Bennis' additional characteristics as necessary qualities for Sofield and Kuhn's generativity to take place.

A Guiding Vision

Bennis explicitly lists a guiding vision as one of the characteristics of a good leader. This quality is identified again and again by authors writing about leadership. The religious researcher and pollster George Barna begins his guide for leaders by quoting Proverbs 29:18— "Where there is no vision, the people perish." He notes that unless people have a clear understanding of where they are headed, the probability of a successful journey is severely limited. "Unless you attend to His call upon your life and ministry, you are likely to experience confusion, weariness, dissipation and impotence" (1992, 11). This topic is so important to Barna that he wrote an entire book, *The Power of Vision*, on the importance of capturing and communicating a vision of leadership.

Sofield and Kuhn equate vision with an in-depth understanding of where a group is going. One might be tempted to think that vision would more important for the business world, where success is easily measured by financial profit, than for the Christian Church. But Sofield and Kuhn insist that "church organizations…are no different from any other—they languish when they fail to establish a vision which is shared, clear, realistic, and dynamic" (1995, 56). They decry how many Christian leaders focus on maintenance instead of mission and vision. These leaders may merely solve current problems instead of actively searching for future opportunities.

Joseph Champlin, an author known for his pastoral leadership, writes from the perspective of a Catholic priest. Champlin would agree with Bennis, Barna, and Sofield and Kuhn about the importance of a guiding vision. "Above all else," he says, "good leaders are visionaries. They see beyond what is to what might be, could be, ought to be. They imagine the possibilities, recognize the potential. But, more than that, they inspire others to dream along with them. Together, the leaders and their colleagues shape their individual hopes and aspirations into a single vision for tomorrow. Then, with the dream defined, the leader reinforces it again and again, urging and stimulating everyone to sustain the effort until the dream becomes a reality" (1993, 37).

Self-knowledge and Maturity

How does one go about creating a vision and then articulating it clearly so that others may appropriate it? While there are strategies that may be employed—several are mentioned below—the key task for a person who wishes to become a leader is to grow in self-knowledge and maturity. It is not clear whether vision precedes self-knowledge, follows it, or develops simultaneously with it. Most authors agree, however, that self-knowledge and maturity are essential. Without these qualities a person may serve in a leadership position but it will be readily apparent that he or she is not a true leader, and will not have the ability to move people's hearts and minds.

After conducting in-depth interviews with 29 people that he considered "outstanding leaders," Bennis summarizes two points of consensus among the leaders. First, leaders are made, not born. This means that these people needed to work hard to develop their insights and leadership ability, and to understand their lives within a larger context. Second, no person who is a leader actually had a goal of becoming a leader. Their goals were to express themselves fully and freely. That is, they had no interest in *proving* themselves but a great interest in *expressing* themselves. Bennis notes "the difference is crucial, for it's the difference between being driven, as too many people are today, and leading, as too few people do" (1989, 5). Self-knowledge and maturity are assumed to be present within each of Bennis's points.

In *The Fifth Discipline Fieldbook* Peter Senge writes about the construct of a field, an unseen pattern of structure that is real enough to influence behavior. He writes that the primary task of leadership is to develop a field that encourages learning. This may be the only way a leader can influence or inspire others. The need for self-knowledge and maturity becomes apparent when one realizes that a leader does not look first to bring other people on board, that is, to his or her vision. Instead the leader attends to appropriate details within one's sphere, and people eventually come on board by themselves (1994, 65).

John Engels writes that not only must the leader have self-knowledge and maturity but he or she must recognize that the very purpose of leadership is to promote the maturity and responsibility of everyone in the organization. Leaders do this by: 1) taking care of themselves emotionally and physically; 2) not being afraid to challenge others; and 3) resisting the role of over-functioner (doing for others what they could be doing for themselves) (1999, 4-5).

The Pastor as Leader

Canon law designates the pastor of the parish to be its prime leader. Though the pastoral care of a parish may be entrusted to others in cases of need (cc. 516.2, 517.2), the ordinary expectation is that a parish will be led by an ordained priest, designated as pastor (c. 515.1). The pastor is to "… reside within the parish (c. 533), share the lives of the families entrusted to their care, get to know them personally and advise, support and assist them, especially the poor and afflicted among them (c. 529.1). This personal relationship and rapport with the people is at the heart of good pastoral care" (Coriden 1997, 75-76). Sofield and Kuhn strongly affirm this last point. They state that the credibility of pastoral leadership rests on people's sensing deep, personal faith and commitment within their leaders (1995, 37). Cieslak showed that the more a pastor participates in civic and ecumenical affairs, the more likely it is that his parishioners will become involved in the life of the parish. He theorized that the pastor serves as a model for involvement by his activities outside the parish, also creating the necessary structures and atmosphere within the parish to encourage parishioner involvement (1983, 112).

While the diocesan bishop may designate a priest to be the parish leader (i.e., pastor), leadership requires some skills and attributes that do not necessarily come with ordination. This is especially true since the Second Vatican Council, which necessitated a large change in the role of the pastor. Veteran pastor Msgr. John Murphy noted that the parish priest "...trained before Vatican II was schooled quite deliberately to be 'in charge' of the parish. He would spend some years as an assistant, following the dictates of another, and then he would realize his dream and become a *pastor*, responsible only to God and bishop (not always in that order). Everyone else would be responsible to him...Vatican II and the innovations introduced after it produced a monumental change in the role of the priest as leader in the parish" (1995, 50). The pastor was expected to develop the skills and structures that invited open dialogue, shared decision making, and effective action. The goal of leadership, then, was not simply to provide service for the people of the parish, but to enable them to minister to one another and to bring their Christian commitment to everything they do (NCCB 1980, 16-17)

Though the role of the priest changed after the council, the importance of pastoral leadership did not change. Reflecting on more than 25 years of experience in helping parishes address leadership issues, Sweetser and McKinney expected the impact of the pastor to lessen with the new emphasis on shared leadership and collaborative ministry. This did not happen. "The style and tone may have changed, but the influence is still just as great" (1998, 2). Philip Murnion affirmed this viewpoint. At a symposium on the parish he related how "the NCCB Parish Project confirmed the view that nothing affects a parish more than its pastor" (Byers 1986, 58). And the National Conference of Catholic Bishops wrote that the foremost leader of the parish remains the pastor. The bishops called the pastor "... the point of unity between the worship of the parish and its activities, between the spiritual aspects of the parish and the organizational, between the specific character of the parish and the mission of the larger church" (1980, 16).

How have priests adapted to changing leadership roles? Murphy notes that recently ordained priests may lack good preparation for leading a parish, including management training and leadership skills. "Letting go of a past tradition where the pastor ruled in the parish, some of today's priests may lack the confidence and the ability to take up the new, firm, visionary, skilled leadership demanded by our times and, remembering our focus, the new structures of parish life" (1995, 52). Philip Murnion also raised this need for a new kind of skilled pastoral leadership. After noting that there have been "…serious changes in styles of leadership since Vatican II," he calls for a style of leadership that is collegial and consultative. He notes "…the dynamics of leadership deserve careful attention" (Byers 1986, 58).

It may be interesting to note that such a reinterpretation of "good pastoral leadership" has taken place not only in the Catholic Church but also in most Christian denominations. The driving force for a reinterpretation of leadership was not Vatican II, since the council was not applicable to non-Catholic denominations; the driving force was a change in societal expectations. Loren Mead explains that these changing leadership roles and loss of role clarity among many Christian clergy often lead to high stress and burnout. "Most clergy come to their vocations from a deep faith and commitment. Trained in institutions that were generated by the mind-set of Christendom and ordained into denominations and congregations predominately shaped by Christendom, they discover that the rules have been changed in the middle of the game. Instead of being front-line leaders and spokespersons for mission, they now feel they are being asked to take a back seat to newly awakened laity. The role they sought out and trained themselves for no longer fits what they have to do. Many are unsure how to give leadership in the new time" (Mead 1991, 34). Writing from the Catholic perspective, Sofield and Kuhn note that many priests are relatively comfortable with the concept of lay ministry, but there is not generally a corresponding acceptance of the concept of lay leadership. They advocate using the expertise of the laity, conveying a sense of their being valued, not perceiving offers of assistance and participation as intrusion, and empowering the laity to the maximum extent possible (1995, 105).

The Importance of Pastors

One of the most traumatic occurrences in the life of a parish is the changing of parish leadership. The change may be expected, as when a pastor moves from a parish at the end of a defined term, or the change may be sudden and unexpected, as when a pastor dies or is incapacitated. Sometimes the change may be seen as positive (e.g., when an unpopular priest moves) or negative (e.g., when the parish loses a very popular pastor). In all cases the change affects many people. Most affected is the staff, followed by lay parish leadership (e.g., pastoral council and finance council), followed by involved parishioners. Even people who worship occasionally at the parish are affected to some degree.

Many Protestant denominations understand the importance of a transition period between pastors. They spend a great deal of time and effort trying to help both the pastors and the parishes through the transition (Sweetser and McKinney 1998, 15). Sweetser and Forster outline a transition process to help Catholic parishes prepare for a new pastor. This process centers on the role of a transition committee that prepares a "state of the parish" report that is sent to the diocese. The report is meant to help prospective pastors understand basic parish facts as well as its character, customs, traditions and plans for the future (1993, 73).

A successful approach to the transition period is crucial to the development of good pastoral leadership. Sweetser and Forster report that Loren Mead said "…the six months before and after a change of pastor provided the most important opportunity for parish renewal. Once a pastor is appointed and settles in, not much substantial change will happen. Programs will come and go, liturgies shift focus, but the tone and overall direction will remain constant until there is another change in pastor" (1993, 70).

Helping Pastors Grow in Leadership

Due to maturity, experience, and personality, some priests make better leaders than others. Yet all priests can be helped to grow in leadership. Several ideas are presented here.

Developing a Vision. Bennis, Barna, Sofield and Kuhn, and Champlin stressed the importance of a guiding vision. In order to develop a vision, conceive powerful goals, communicate them to others, and gain enthusiastic acceptance, Champlin advocated a three-pronged approach.

1. Gather grass-roots input. Unless people buy into the dream it will not significantly motivate them.
2. Keep repeating the dream. Keep the people focused on the vision by repeating it again and again.
3. Express the vision in some captivating way. Use symbols and appeal to the senses (1993, 46-49).

Necessity of Strategic Thinking. Peter Senge advocates strategic thinking as a way to grow in leadership. He notes that it is crucial for a leader to articulate to himself or herself: what is truly essential and what is secondary? Good strategic thinking also addresses dilemmas that might otherwise go unnoticed. Such dilemmas arise from conflict among competing goals and norms:

- We want to distribute power and authority, but we also want to improve control and coordination.
- We want organizations to be more responsive to changes in their environment and yet more stable and coherent in their sense of identity, purpose, and vision.
- We want high productivity and high creativity (1994, 16-17).

Using the Parish Pastoral Council. A pastor who is not using the pastoral council to help create a parish vision is probably carrying too much of a burden. Dennis O'Leary reminds us "the primary responsibility of the parish pastoral council is to assist the pastor in directional and strategic planning. If planning in these two areas is done well, administrative and program planning by the pastor, staff, and program leaders will naturally follow and the result will be a more focused and integrated approach to ministry" (1995, 32).

Eileen Tabert focuses on the need for good pastoral council training and notes how successful organizations put a premium on training. She writes of a practical parish leadership with five components:

- Recruitment. Good recruitment skills are the beginning of leadership. Good people are needed to be members of a leadership team, which develops a parish vision and ultimately implements it.
- Affirmation. It is especially important to affirm new council members, as it sets the tone for all subsequent parish volunteer work.
- Training. Good training cannot be overemphasized. An investment in quality training guarantees a committed, effective, and productive leadership group.
- Empowerment. One council goal should be to involve as many people as possible in parish life. People who are uninvolved usually have not been asked properly to become involved or have been asked at the wrong time.
- Dismissal. It is difficult for lay parish leaders to remain enthusiastic, committed, and creative year after year. There should be a formal process to "dismiss with joy" (1995, 73-87).

Testing the Theories

The theories presented here about general leadership and pastoral leadership may seem valid to people involved in parish ministry. Yet the scientific method demands that theories be tested with objective research and data. Accordingly, the rest of this chapter examines concepts of leadership and pastoral leadership as they present themselves in three parish issues:

- the importance of pastors;
- pastoral leadership and parish vitality; and
- pastoral leadership style and parish preferences.

Issue 1: Changing Pastors[1]

Conventional wisdom among financial leaders of Catholic dioceses is that the pastor strongly affects a parish's financial viability. This opinion stems from observation and is supported by regular internal monitoring of parish financial reports. It is not rare for a parish's income to increase or decrease by 30% when a pastor of a particular leadership style is replaced by a pastor of a radically different style. This change indicates, in effect, a parish referendum on the pastor's leadership. While some limited research exists on the relationship of a pastor's leadership to the parish's income (Cieslak 1984; Greeley 1990), there has been no systematic study published of the change in parish income that accompanies a change in pastors. Most published studies are point-in-time studies that ignore possible effects of pastoral changes on giving. This is true for both national probability surveys such as the Gallup Poll, and studies of particular parishes (Davidson and Pyle 1994; Zaleski and Zech 1994).

The study I am reporting here attempted to help fill this knowledge gap by investigating the extent to which parish income changes in each of the 106 parishes of the Rockford diocese when pastors change. The methodology supporting this study is described in Appendix 6-A. The hypothesis is that changes in pastors are associated with changes in parish income. It was recognized that just analyzing differences in contribution means would be insufficient because a large increase in contributions in one parish when a "popular" priest is appointed pastor could be canceled by a large decrease in another parish when an "unpopular" priest is appointed. This would mask the contribution dynamics. More important in this study would be evidence of significant differences in the variability of contribution amounts. An increase in the variability of offertory income following the appointment of a new pastor would be a sign that changing a pastor is associated with a contribution change. This change, depending upon the specific situation, may be positive or negative.

Findings
Overall Results

Initial inspection of the contribution data was through error charts. An error chart shows the distributions of several variables at a glance. The marker in the center of the vertical line indicates the mean, while the horizontal lines at the top and bottom indicate the spread of financial contributions. If there were an increase in contribution variability after the appointment of a new pastor, as hypothesized, the vertical length of the last three lines should increase. Figure 6-1 shows this is what happens. These findings support the hypothesis that changes in pastors are associated with changes in parish income.

Demographic and other independent variables were examined to determine whether this "pastor change" was constant across all parish subgroups. Important differences were seen in the several groups.

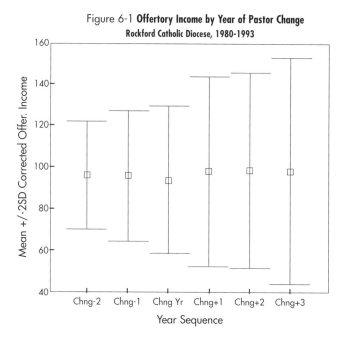

Figure 6-1 **Offertory Income by Year of Pastor Change**
Rockford Catholic Diocese, 1980-1993

Parish Location

Rexhausen and Cieslak (1994) classified parishes of the Archdiocese of Cincinnati into four geographical types and found that contributions to parishes differed by location. The geographical types were urban, suburban, small town, and rural. The same classifications were used in this study to investigate whether differences in contribution variability were associated with a change of pastors. Differences of contribution variability across the six-year time were found between suburban parishes and rural parishes.

Suburban parishes are generally the largest parishes in the Rockford diocese, with complex organizational structures, due to multiple ministries. Their parishioners are more likely to be people with high income and education. These factors suggest a new pastor faces both bewildering organizational tasks and high parishioner expectations. The increase in contribution variability may indicate a parish referendum on the new pastor. While this is true for all parishes, suburban parishes may show greater sensitivity to a pastor's leadership ability because of higher expectations.

In contrast to suburban parishes, rural parishes are generally the smallest parishes in the diocese. Their pastors are generally of two types: 1) older priests who are near retirement and value the lower demands of the rural parish; or 2) younger priests who are serving in their first or second pastorates. The latter priests often have youthful enthusiasm and a fresh look at matters of faith. The increase in contribution variability may reflect the varying experiences of rural parishes, depending upon which type of priest is assigned to them.

Parishioner Household Income

Parishes composed of middle-class or lower upper-class parishioners showed changes in contribution variability greater than the diocesan change. These effects may be due to higher expectations of people with higher incomes. They are the lawyers, small business owners, and mid-level managers who expect their pastor to show the same high level of management skills they find in their colleagues.

Tenure of the Previous Pastor

A priest in the Rockford diocese generally has been limited to a maximum of twelve years that he can serve consecutively as pastor at one parish. This can be extended for special circumstances, however, like when he is just a few years away from retirement, leading a crucial building campaign, or has a special relationship to a parish. Parishes that replaced a pastor present for more than twelve years showed a uniformly low variability during the last years of this pastor and a large increase in contribution variability during the new pastor's first year. This increase of 70% was the largest increase of any parish subgroup during a pastor's first year in this study.

It is likely that parishioners of a longtime pastor have become accustomed, years earlier, to his particular leadership style. Or, if they did not appreciate his style, it is likely they would have left for another parish/pastor more to their liking. For parishioners who stayed, there is little impetus to increase or decrease contributions during a pastor's last years.

Conclusion

Results of this study support the conventional wisdom of diocesan observers that a parish's income may change dramatically on the appointment of a new pastor. The greatest change typically takes place within a year after a new pastor is appointed. These dynamics were true for all parishes in the diocese and for various subgroups of parishes: suburban and rural parishes, parishes composed of wealthier parishioners, and parishes whose previous pastor had a tenure of more than twelve years.

Issue 2: Pastoral Leadership and Parish Vitality [2]

In February 1997 the Rockford Catholic diocese initiated a multi-year diocesan-wide planning process, *With a Heart Renewed: Parish Consultations Process*. The purpose of this process was renewal of the diocese's 105 parishes. It proposed to accomplish this through the following steps.

- Each parish identifies its needs through a survey of all parishioners and a qualitative analysis of strengths and weaknesses by leaders. The parish creates a pastoral plan that builds upon its strengths and addresses its weaknesses.
- Parishioners review the pastoral plan and comment upon it. The pastoral plan may be modified in light of parishioner observations.
- Each parish meets with other parishes in a geographical cluster, looking for ways to enhance overall parish ministry in the area. Options include sharing resources, devising new programs, and altering parish structures.
- Individual parish plans are modified in light of cluster discussions. The parishioners review the plan again, leading to final modifications.

Key to the process was the creation of a conceptual model of a vital parish. Using key church documents as resources, as well as models from other dioceses, the Rockford diocese created the Indicators of Parish Vitality. These indicators provided a vision of a modern Catholic parish that is attentive to both the needs of its parishioners and the needs of the greater society. By using this conceptual model, the diocese hoped to ground the parish needs analysis in the realm of objectivity and move beyond subjective contention. The Indicators of Parish Vitality appear as Appendix 6-B.

Measuring Parish Vitality

The Indicators of Parish Vitality are composed of four main sections (worship, community, service, and education/formation) and 17 subsections. To link this conceptual model with the experience of parishioners, a survey instrument was designed that included representative statements from each subsection. For example, representing the "Hospitality" subsection of the indicators were the following survey items.

- Our parish exhibits a spirit of warmth and hospitality at Mass and other services.
- Physically disabled people have access to parish facilities and activities.

A one-sheet questionnaire resulted with 34 items from the indicators and eight demographic questions. For each item from the indicators, parishioners were asked about both the theoretical importance of the item and its quality as experienced in a particular parish. Using the above item as an example, parishioners were thus asked how important it is that their parish exhibit a spirit of warmth and hospitality (importance) and how well this spirit is actually seen in their parish (quality). The questionnaire is available at http://www.cppcd.org/crf/rra_papers.htm.

The questionnaire was distributed to all people, age 16 and over, who were present at Masses in diocesan churches on September 13 or 14, 1997. More than 55,000 usable questionnaires were collected, processed, and analyzed. Each parish received a 200-page report, within which the parish data was presented in various ways.

Analysis

For statistical analysis, 16 indices of quality were created from the 34 items from the Indicators of Parish Vitality. The indices, shown within the four main sections, are:

Worship
    Celebration of Liturgy
    Celebration of Sacraments
    Spiritual Growth Programs
Community
    Hospitality
    Stewardship of Time, Talent and Treasure
    Stewardship of Facilities
    Evangelization
    Leadership
Service
    Within the Parish

To the Local Community
Beyond the Local Community
Education/Formation
Religious and Adult Education
Catholic Schools
Rite of Christian Initiation of Adults (RCIA)
Youth and Young Adult Ministry
Ecumenism

An index was also created for each major section (worship, community, service and education/formation). Finally an overall index of parish vitality was computed for each parish.

Correlation of Parish Size with Vitality

Analysis showed a strong correlation of parish size and vitality in 15 of the above 16 indices, three of the four major section indices, and the overall score of vitality. In all cases, the larger the parish the more likely it is that parishioners perceive it as vital. These results are summarized in Figure 6-2.

These findings are important. There is no inherent reason why smaller parishes should be rated relatively low on quality. The scores were not generated by "outside experts" who might observe that smaller parishes have fewer programs, fewer well-

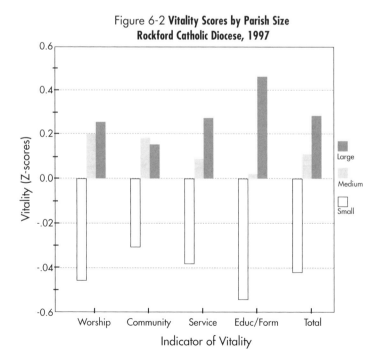

Figure 6-2 **Vitality Scores by Parish Size**
Rockford Catholic Diocese, 1997

trained leaders, etc., and therefore should receive lower scores. The scores represent the perceptions of parishioners who are living in the parish community and are in the pews on Sunday. Especially troublesome are relatively low scores in hospitality, evangelization, and stewardship of time, talent, and treasure—all areas in which one would expect small parishes to rate higher than larger parishes.

Best Predictor of Vitality

The analysis of the relationship of parish size and vitality continued: what was the best predictor of overall parish vitality? That is, which of the 16 indices correlates highest with overall parish vitality? While all indices correlate well with parish vitality, the single highest predictor is leadership. Parishes that are rated high in leadership by parishioners tend also to be rated high on overall vitality. There is no better predictor of parish vitality than the leadership index.

Next, parish size was measured against leadership scores for each of the 16 indices. As could be expected, in virtually all comparisons parishes with low leadership scores tended to have low vitality scores. This held for small, medium, and large parishes. Leadership scores, however, varied more in smaller parishes than larger parishes. In smaller parishes the difference in vitality scores among the leadership groups was greater than it was with medium and large parishes. These dynamics are seen in Figure 6-3, which uses box plots to compare the scores for the Leadership index across parish size. Each box plot shows the median (the heavy horizontal line), the quartiles (the shaded areas), and the extreme values (the light vertical lines).

All these results generally show that small parishes tend to be rated by parishioners as lower in leadership. The data also present a strong positive correlation between leadership and overall parish vitality. Thus, smaller parishes will generally score lower in overall vitality than medium and larger parishes.

Components of Leadership

The leadership index was calculated by taking the mean of scores to three questions in the parishioners' questionnaire:

23. There is sufficient qualified parish staff (paid and volunteer) to meet the parish's needs.

24. Parish leadership encourages many different kinds of people (young and old, women and men, etc.) to become involved in parish ministries.

25. Parish leadership is sensitive to the problems and concerns of the parish.

The most important of these three items, as measured by parishioners' perception of theoretical importance, is question 25. This question ranks as the 10th most important of the 34 items on the survey. The next important question is question 24, which ranks 15th. The least important question in this index is 23, which ranks 17th. The rankings varied very little across parish size.

While question 25 (on the sensitivity of parish leadership) is the highest ranked of the three questions on leadership, question 24 (on encouragement of diverse involvement in ministry) was the best predictor of parish vitality

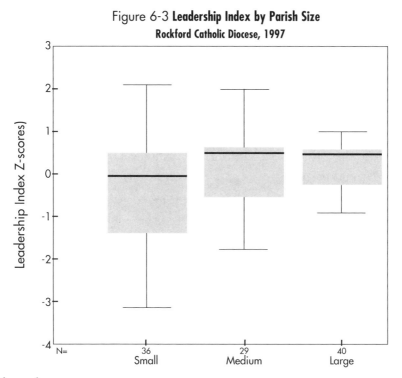

Figure 6-3 **Leadership Index by Parish Size**
Rockford Catholic Diocese, 1997

Discussion

The perceptions of 55,000 diocesan Catholics confirm in part what every diocesan leader suspects: pastoral leadership makes a difference. That is, parishes with good leadership are perceived as desirable, vibrant parishes. What is surprising is that the primary mechanism through which leadership is statistically linked with vitality is through encouragement of a diversity of people to become involved in parish ministries.

Conventional wisdom places great importance on the liturgy. By this way of thinking, a vital parish is one where the music is uplifting and the homilies are inspiring. This reasoning is encouraged through the high scores of importance given to liturgy

in general, and homilies in particular, in the parishioner survey. Yet without diminishing the importance of these liturgical items, they are not the best indicators of overall vitality. That honor is reserved for the variables that measure leadership, especially the one measuring encouragement for the laity to become involved.

The importance of Question 24, which asks about the extent to which the parish leadership encourages diverse involvement in ministry, probably lays in the assumptions behind it. In order for a parish to score high on this measure, two dynamics must be present: 1) the pastor, and other pastoral leaders, must be open to sharing responsibility with others; and 2) there must be various ministries in which people can become involved. The first condition requires parish leadership to be open to new experiences and at ease with diverse people. The second condition requires the presence of a certain minimum parish infrastructure for parish ministries, such as opportunities for training and recruitment of volunteers. When both these conditions are present, it is likely a parish will be perceived as vital.

Small parishes are often touted in church-related research as highly desirable. They are the places where people live out their faith with joy among their friends and neighbors. They are the places where people find it easy to give of themselves—their time, talent, and treasure. There is a type of nostalgia for the intimacy of the small parish. Yet this research has found that small parishes score lower than medium and large parishes in all measures of vitality. These results are stunning when one considers that it is the parishioners of the small parishes that are making these judgments.

I offer two explanations for these results. First, people in the small parish simply may have fewer experiences of organized parish ministry, other than that performed by a priest. This may be due to the pastor's skill level, or it may be their choice. That is, a young priest beginning his first pastorate at a small parish may have his "new ideas" of a broadened sense of ministry rejected by parishioners. Second, it may be that the diocesan questionnaire is unconsciously biased against a type of rural pastoral leadership that is not characterized by initiating large, complex programs.

In order to increase the vitality of all parishes, bishops may wish to consider placing emphasis on raising the skill level of all parish leaders, since this is the most important predictor of parish vitality. This is especially important for priests assigned to small parishes, be they young, new pastors or elderly priests approaching retirement. This training should emphasize "people skills" such as empathetic listening, conflict resolution, and understanding human psychological and faith development. Bishops may also wish to initiate a diocesan-wide emphasis on the development of quality parish pastoral councils, including the formation of council members. For many parishes the trained pastoral council could serve as the vehicle to enhance leadership communication. In some parishes the creation of a visible, active pastoral council would be a powerful symbol of a greater commitment to greater parish vitality.

Issue 3: Pastoral Leadership Style and Parish Preference[3]

In the past Catholics had little choice in their parish: most attended the parish within whose boundary they lived. If they belonged to an ethnic group that had a parish in the area, they were also free to register at that parish. While boundaries still officially exist, church officials generally have downplayed their importance during the last thirty years. Many Catholics choose their parish from among the Catholic parishes available in their area. In many ways the expectation of being able to choose one's own parish is taken for granted, like the expectation of being able to choose one's bank or physician.

Why do individual Catholics gravitate to particular parishes? The hypothesis presented here is that individual parishes have "corporate personalities" that can be conceptualized and quantified. One can get a sense of a parish's personality by analyzing what the parishioners of the parish consider important. This is possible in the Rockford, Illinois Catholic diocese because of the data collected in conjunction with a multi-year planning process.

Methodology

The methodology for this section follows the methodology of the previous section. In conjunction with a diocesan program of parish planning and renewal, a conceptual model of a vital parish was created—the Indicators of Parish Vitality. A one-sheet questionnaire resulted with 34 items from the indicators and eight demographic questions. For each item from the indicators, parishioners were asked about both the theoretical importance of the item and its quality as experienced in a particular parish. Questionnaires were distributed to all people, age 16 and over, who were present at Masses in diocesan churches on September 13 or 14, 1997.

The primary focus of this section is upon creating a system of categorizing parishes—a typology—from parishioner measures of importance. A parish's score for each of the 34 importance items was computed by taking the average of each item from parishioner questionnaires.

Findings

A statistical procedure—factor analysis—was the primary tool used in producing the typology. Factor analysis is a statistical procedure that shows how variables tend to cluster together, usually based upon preference scores. This analysis allows researchers to identify three overarching, theoretical principles about importance. These principles are not directly observable, nor do they appear as single survey items. (See the glossary in Appendix 6-C for more information about factor analysis.) Three factors emerged from the analysis.

Factor 1: "Catholic Schools"

The first factor was composed of two survey questions: 1) access to a Catholic elementary school; and 2) access to a Catholic high school. Catholics who expressed an opinion about the importance of one of these questions tended to express the same opinion about the second question. Note: factor analysis does not tell us what the opinion is (it could be pro-school or anti-school), only that the opinion was generally the same about both items.

Factor 2: "Horizontal Spirituality"

The second factor shows a distinct focus on the parish as community, or—to use a term from the Second Vatican Council—the "people of God." According to this principle, God is truly present within ordinary people in the Christian assembly. God is also present in a special way among the poor and dispossessed. The focus is upon God as "already present" within people instead of being perceived as "out there" and needing to be invited "down" to the human level. To capture this emphasis, the term "horizontal spirituality" was chosen as the name of the second factor.

Survey items most strongly linked in this factor are the following:

- the parish reaches out to the poor;
- parish leadership is sensitive to the problems and concerns of the parish;
- the parish exhibits a spirit of warmth and hospitality;
- the parish works with groups in the local community; and
- the parish promotes respect for human life.

Survey respondents who indicated high importance for any one item in this group generally also indicated high importance for the other items in this group. Conversely, respondents who indicated low importance for any one item in the group tended to indicate low importance for the other items.

Factor 3: "Vertical Spirituality"

The third factor focused upon sacraments and devotional services outside of Mass. There is also emphasis upon outward appearances, especially as it relates to the sacredness of the church and the reverence of liturgical ministers. This factor seems to be capturing the sense of God as transcendent, outside and above the human condition. One does not primarily find God in one's neighbor because he or she is also a sinful human; one primarily finds God in the sacraments, the Church, and Scripture. Because this spirituality focuses on God as "higher" and "above," the term "vertical spirituality" was chosen as the name of the third factor.[4]

The survey items most strongly linked in this factor are the following:

- there are sufficient opportunities to receive reconciliation;
- there are devotional services outside Mass;
- at Mass the liturgical ministers act reverently.

Like with the other two factors, survey respondents who indicated high importance for any one item in this group generally also indicated high importance for the other items in this group.

Describing Each Factor

The next analysis focused on understanding the three factors. This was done by using a statistical procedure (regression analysis—see the glossary in Appendix 6-C for more information on this subject) to select the demographic variables that are associated with the factor.

"Catholic Schools"

The participation of the parish in a Catholic elementary school—whether a parochial school or a consolidated school—is the best indicator of a parish's score on "Catholic schools." The location of the parish is also important. Parishes in urban or suburban areas are more likely to name Catholic schools as important than are parishes in small towns or rural areas. Since schools are more likely to be located in urban or suburban areas, this variable may be demonstrating the general familiarity of parishioners with Catholic schools, even if a particular parish does not have a school of its own. Or it may be demonstrating the personal experience of parishioners with Catholic schools in their youth.

"Horizontal Spirituality"

The demographic variable that best correlates with "horizontal spirituality" is the percentage of people who have been parishioners for two years or less. The higher the percentage of people in a parish who are relative newcomers, the greater the likelihood that "horizontal spirituality" is important to the parish. The survey variable might be a proxy or substitute for parishioners' transience rate, which is not directly measured in this study. The higher the transiency rate, the more important it might be for parishioners to quickly develop relationships within a particular community. There simply is not enough time to allow relationships to develop slowly because a relatively high percentage of parishioners may move within several years. This dynamic might present itself in the parish survey as a greater importance for community-centered activities.

Also correlating with "horizontal spirituality" is the location of the parish. Parishes in urban settings are more likely to hold "horizontal spirituality" in greater importance. The dynamics of this variable might be similar to the percentage of newcomers. People in urban settings might feel a greater need to become part of a community because of their neighborhoods, which might be perceived to be more impersonal than neighborhoods in suburban areas or small towns.

"Vertical Spirituality"

The most important indicator of "vertical spirituality" is large numbers of Hispanics in the parish. Traditional devotions and the emphasis on God's transcendence are a part of the Hispanic culture and spirituality, at least of the predominantly Mexican sub-culture found within the Rockford diocese. Interestingly, Hispanic parishes also were associated with high scores on "horizontal spirituality."

Parish leaders in the Rockford diocese have offered several explanations for this phenomenon. First, the majority of Hispanics in the ten Hispanic parishes in the diocese have relatively little education and may be unsophisticated in taking surveys. The high importance scores may reflect an inability to discriminate or confusion with survey terminology. If this were true, however, one would also expect Hispanic opinions about parish quality to be higher. This was not true; the Hispanic and non-Hispanic parish quality scores are very similar.

A second explanation for the higher Hispanic importance scores is based upon the theory that Hispanics fear losing the pastoral services they already have. Therefore they rate existing programs and services high so that they will retain them. This theory is not supported by the data, since, as mentioned above, Hispanic parishes do not rate the quality higher than non-Hispanic parishes.

The only explanation left is that Hispanics indeed value highly both the horizontal and vertical dimensions of spirituality. This is part of their religious experience and practice, and has implications for pastoral ministry. They will be discussed in the Implications section of this chapter.

Also correlating with "vertical spirituality" was the percentage of parishioners that report attending Mass at least every Sunday. In the survey parishioners were asked how often they attend Mass. The dynamics seem clear, as Mass attendance would be one of the clearest ways that vertical spirituality would be expressed.

Relationship of the Three Factors to Commitment

To further the understanding of the factors of importance, their relationships with four forms of commitment were analyzed. These include:

- the percentage of survey respondents who report they attend Mass at least every Sunday;
- the percentage of respondents who report they are very attached to the parish;
- the percentage of respondents who are defined as highly involved in the parish; and
- the estimated percentage of family income that is donated to the parish.

Mass

There is a moderately strong relationship between Mass attendance and "vertical spirituality." Parishes that are strong in "vertical spirituality" are likely to have a higher percentage of parishioners reporting that they attend Mass every Sunday.

Attachment to the Parish

Parishes in which parishioners describe Catholic schools as more important tend to have relatively fewer parishioners highly attached to the parish. There is also a strong relationship, however, between parish size and "Catholic Schools." Larger parishes, most of which participate in an elementary school, score higher on "Catholic Schools." When the effects of parish size are removed from the analysis, the relationship between "Catholic schools" and low attachment disappears. Thus one can make the case that there is an important negative relationship between size and attachment; that is, it is difficult for a large percentage of parishioners to feel very attached to larger parishes because of their impersonal nature. It just happens that larger parishes also tend to have Catholic schools and score higher on the factor "Catholic Schools."

Involvement in the Parish

There is a negative relationship between "Catholic Schools" and involvement in the parish. That is, parishes in which parishioners describe Catholic schools as more important tend to have a lower percentage of parishioners involved in the parish. This relationship stands even when taking into account the size of the parish. One possible explanation is that parishes that put much energy and resources into the school put relatively less energy and resources into other parish ministries. Thus there would be less opportunity for parishioners to become highly involved in the parish.

Family Income Donated to the Parish
No relationship was found between the percentage of family income donated to the parish and any of the three factors.

Relationship of the Three Factors of Importance to Quality

In addition to asking respondents to indicate the *importance* of various programs and services, the parishioner survey also presented opportunity to specify the *quality* of the same programs and services. Overall parish quality was assessed in two different ways: 1) externally defined norms; and 2) internally defined measures.

Externally defined Norms of Quality
The Rockford diocese set standards for parishes by developing the Indicators of Parish Vitality and creating a questionnaire based upon them. These norms of quality are externally based because there was no broad-based consultation about the constitutive elements of parish vitality. For this research, parish quality was defined as the average of the individual quality items on the survey.

There is a very strong relationship between "horizontal spirituality" and externally defined quality. Parishes with parishioners that indicate that a horizontal spirituality is important tend to be the parishes that score high on this type of quality. There is also a positive relationship, albeit weaker, between "Catholic schools" and externally defined quality.

This finding is important. It shows, in two of the three factors, that importance is not just theoretical. Importance is linked to quality, especially regarding the concept of "horizontal spirituality." Parishes with a high degree of community emphasis tend to be those parishes that have the highest quality. Different dynamics are seen in those parishes with a high "vertical spirituality." These parishes may be more likely to have parishioners attend Sunday Mass more frequently, but they are not likely to have high scores of overall quality.

Internally Defined Measures of Quality
There may be conceptual difficulties with the above relationship between "horizontal spirituality" and externally defined quality. Either the Indicators of Parish Vitality themselves or the particular subset of the indicators chosen for use in the questionnaire may be biased in some way toward a more contemporary spirituality, which in turn correlates well with "horizontal spirituality." The lack of correlation between "vertical spirituality" and externally defined quality may simply mean that another standard for quality is needed for this factor to present itself well.

A solution to this problem is to devise an alternative way of measuring parish quality. Since each parish identified its own items of importance through the survey, one option is to calculate quality ratings based upon only the most important items.[5] This method has its basis in the concept of "charism" or gift, which is found throughout Christian Scripture. Each person has certain attributes or gifts that are important to him or her and around which his or her life is built. In evaluating a person's life, the pertinent question is how well did he or she use these gifts? Did the nurse care for patients with both skill and compassion? Did the judge make wise decisions in balancing the needs of society and the rights of the individual?

Applying this concept to a parish, one asks whether more traditional parishes have good devotions? Are their liturgical ministers reverent? Quality in this sense was measured as the average score of the quality items that were associated with the top five items of importance. In other words, each parish was allowed to define its own components of quality, based upon what it considers most important.

Using internally defined quality, the relationship between quality and the factor "Catholic schools" drops out. As with externally defined norms of quality, however, there is a strong, positive relationship between "horizontal spirituality" and internally defined quality.

Implications and Conclusion
Importance of Catholic Schools
Catholics put a large amount of energy and resources into maintaining their parochial school system. The emergence of "Catholic schools" as a factor, therefore, is not surprising.

Analysis showed a negative relationship between "Catholic schools" and involvement in the parish. This correlation remained even after taking into account parish size. The implication is that parishes in which Catholic schools are very important may not be developing many opportunities for involvement in non-school ministries. When there are limitations of resources, parish leadership may tend to put the fewer resources into those areas that are seen as important by many people. The danger is that there will be fewer opportunities for adults without parochial school children to become involved in the parish outside of Sunday Mass. This issue is important and should be discussed by parish leaders.

There are also implications in the emergence of this factor for religious researchers. In much research on contributions and commitment, Catholics are compared to other denominations without acknowledging the presence of the Catholic school system and the commitment it receives. Given the importance of Catholic schools in the factor analysis and the degree to which Catholics use enormous resources in maintaining the school system, researchers minimally should note the possibility that commitment by Catholics may look different from commitment by other denominations.

Multi-dimensionality of Horizontal and Vertical Spiritualities

One may hear suggestions made in religious writings or conversation that suggest that a spirituality that emphasizes God's immanence (the horizontal dimension) is the opposite of one that emphasizes God's transcendence (the vertical dimension). The unspoken assumption is that there is one dimension to spirituality, with immanence found at one end and transcendence at the other. This research has shown that the two spiritualities actually compose two different dimensions. The opposite of high transcendence is low transcendence, not high immanence.

This multidimensionality raises several challenges for church leaders: understanding parish needs; promoting commitment; and assigning priests.

Understanding Parish Needs. The main issue revolves around parishes that score low on both "horizontal spirituality" and "vertical spirituality," i.e., what do they want? What services should the diocese provide? An inspection of the data suggests that parishes in this category tend to have a high percentage of parishioners who have been in the parish for at least 10 years. This category also seems to be made up of parishes that are predominantly rural and small. More research is needed in this area.

Promoting Commitment. Commitment was measured through four variables: Mass attendance, attachment to the parish (subjective measurement), involvement in the parish, and financial contributions to the parish. Only one positive relationship was found: between "vertical spirituality" and Mass attendance. While "horizontal spirituality" correlated highly with quality (both externally and internally-defined), this apparent satisfaction does not translate to greater commitment. Why do parishes with high "horizontal spirituality" not show greater commitment? Further research is needed about the relationship of parish typology to parish stewardship.

Assigning Pastors. This parish typology may find its greatest utility in assigning pastors to parishes. Pastor assignments should be made carefully so that pastoral leadership is sensitive to the natural yearnings of the people. A parish that scores high on one of the factors will not be a good fit for a priest who does not value that factor. It may be difficult, for example, for a parish that values horizontal spirituality to accept as its spiritual leader a priest who indicates he sees little value in this type of spirituality. It would also be difficult in this case for the priest to genuinely affirm the people.

On the other hand, a parish that scores low on a non-primary factor could benefit from a pastor who values this factor, *as long as he affirms parishioners' primary focus.* Take the case of a parish that scores high on the factor "Catholic schools" but low on "vertical spirituality." A good candidate for pastor would be a priest who values Catholic education but also sees the importance of a vertical spirituality. He could affirm the importance of Catholic schools—sharing this core value with his people—but also gently encourage them to appreciate traditional devotions.

Additional research is needed regarding the influence that a pastor actually has upon the parish. Does a "good pastor fit" depend more upon: 1) a shared core value between people and pastor or 2) the personality of the pastor? How does a pastor serve a parish that is low on all or most dimensions of importance?

Pastoral Care of Hispanic Parishes

Based upon the need to provide Spanish-language questionnaires, ten parishes in the Rockford diocese are defined as Hispanic. In order to provide good pastoral care to parishioners, priests and other pastoral care workers obviously need to be fluent in Spanish. This research points out another need—to be respectful of Hispanic culture. The parishes scoring highest on both "horizontal spirituality" and "vertical spirituality" are Hispanic. This suggests something about the uniqueness of Hispanic culture. While it is beyond the scope of this research to define the uniqueness, it does point out the need to better understand the culture.

Summary

Pastoral leadership is very important in determining what happens in a parish. While this statement may seem a "fine grasp of the obvious," there is a dearth of objective research on the issue. The data presented here are a first attempt to fill this gap, and several points were made.

A review of the literature about leadership leads one to the conclusion that the most important qualities that a good pastor needs are: 1) self-knowledge and maturity, and 2) a guiding vision. Also useful are passion, integrity, trust, and curiosity. These qualities cannot easily be mimicked. They are a part of a person's inner being and are soon apparent even to casual observers.

Leaders are made, not born. This does not mean, however, that they merely need to pick up tips and tricks to lead. Rather, true leaders work hard to develop their insights and leadership ability, and to understand their lives within a larger context. Warren Bennis offers the insight that no person who is a leader actually had a goal of becoming a leader. Their goals were to express themselves fully and freely (1989, 5) True leadership is the result of a gut-wrenching process of inner-knowledge.

Although "you can always sense the presence or absence of leadership . . ." (Senge 1994, 65), there is no direct way to measure pastoral leadership. Careful observation does allow one to see some indirect effects, however. One of the best indicators that Catholics in the pew are aware of a pastor's leadership is that a parish's income may change dramatically on the appointment of a new pastor. The greatest change typically takes place within a year after a new pastor is appointed. These dynamics were true for all parishes in the diocese and for numerous subgroups of parishes.

Other data confirm that pastoral leadership does make a difference within a parish. Parishes where the people rate the pastor high in leadership are perceived as desirable, vibrant parishes. A somewhat surprising finding is that leadership is correlated with encouraging a diversity of lay people to become involved in parish ministries. This quality is even more important in predicting overall parish vitality than the quality of the homily or the Sunday Liturgy. In encouraging lay involvement, perhaps a pastor is manifesting self-knowledge and maturity—both qualities of leadership.

Finally, data on constructing a parish typology shows the importance of matching a pastor to the corporate personality of a parish. It may be difficult, for example, for a parish that strongly values one type of spirituality to accept as its natural leader a priest who indicates he sees little value in this type of spirituality. It also could be difficult in this case for the priest to genuinely affirm the people. Leadership is always exercised within a context, and there may be too great of a gap between the people and their pastor for his leadership to be appreciated.

Notes

1. This section is a simplified version of a paper presented at the annual meeting of the Religious Research Association, November 5, 1994, as "Changing Pastors: Does it Lead to a Change in Financial Contributions?" The original paper is available at http://www.cppcd.org/crf/rra_papers.htm. Since this study was written, one parish of the Rockford diocese closed. Thus this section mentions 106 parishes and subsequent sections discuss the 105 diocesan parishes.

2. This section was presented as a paper at the annual meeting of the Religious Research Association, November 7, 1998 as "Parish Vitality and Pastoral Leadership." The paper is available in an abbreviated form at http://www.cppcd.org/crf/res_reviews1.htm.

3. This section is a simplified version of "Capturing the Spirit of Catholic Parishes: a Typology Based Upon Measures of Importance." This paper was presented at the annual meeting of the Religious Research Association, November 6, 1999. The paper is available at http://www.cppcd.org/crf/rra_papers.htm.

4. Both "horizontal spirituality" and "vertical spirituality" are authentic expressions of Catholic faith. The main issue is not one of legitimacy or orthodoxy but pastoral emphasis.

5. Thanks to Jeff Rexhausen for recommending such a creative approach.

References

Barna, George. 1992. *The Power of Vision.* Ventura, California: Regal Books.

Bennis, Warren. 1989. *On Becoming a Leader.* Reading, Massachusetts: Addison-Wesley.

Byers, David, ed. 1986. *The Parish in Transition.* Washington, D.C.: United States Catholic Conference.

Champlin, Joseph M., with Charles D. Champlin. 1993. *The Visionary Leader.* New York: Crossroad Publishing Company.

Cieslak, Michael J. 1984. "Parish Responsiveness and Parishioner Commitment," *Review of Religious Research* 26 (December), pp. 132-47.

Coriden, James A. 1997. *The Parish in Catholic Tradition.* Mahwah, New Jersey: Paulist Press.

Davidson, James D. and Ralph E. Pyle. 1994. "Passing the Plate in Affluent Churches: Why Some Members Give More Than Others," *Review of Religious Research* 36 (December), pp. 181-96.

Engels, John J. 1999. "Managing Relationships in Time of Change: What Churches Can Learn from Healthy Businesses," *Church Personnel Issues*, National Association of Church Personnel Administrators, April.

Farson, Richard. 1996. *Management of the Absurd*, New York: Simon & Schuster.

Greeley, Andrew. 1990. "Angry Catholics," *Chicago Sun-Times,* May 6-9.

Law, Eric H. F. 1993. *The Wolf Shall Dwell with the Lamb: A Spirituality for Leadership in a Multicultural Community*, St. Louis, Missouri: Chalice Press.

O'Leary, Dennis J. 1995. "Parish Pastoral Councils: Instruments of Visioning and Planning," in Arthur X. Deegan, ed. *Developing a Vibrant Parish Pastoral Council.* Mahwah, New Jersey: Paulist Press, pp. 19-35.

Mead, Loren B. 1991. *The Once and Future Church.* Washington, D.C.: The Alban Institute.

Murphy, John F. 1995. "A Pastor's View of How a Parish Pastoral Council Should Work," in Arthur X. Deegan, ed. *Developing a Vibrant Parish Pastoral Council,* pp. 51-60.

National Conference of Catholic Bishops. 1980. *The Parish: A People, A Mission, A Structure.* Washington, D.C.: United States Catholic Conference.

Rexhausen, Jeff and Michael J. Cieslak. 1994. "Relationship of Parish Characteristics to Sunday Giving among Catholics in the Archdiocese of Cincinnati," *Review of Religious Research* 36 (December), pp. 218-29.

Senge, Peter M., Charlotte Roberts, Richard B. Ross, Bryan J. Smith, and Art Kleiner. 1994. *The Fifth Discipline Fieldbook*, New York: Doubleday.

Sofield, Loughlan, and Donald H. Kuhn. 1995. *The Collaborative Leader*, Notre Dame, Indiana: Ave Maria Press.

Sweetser, Thomas P., and Patricia M. Forster. 1993. *Transforming the Parish: Models for the Future*, Kansas City: Sheed & Ward.

Sweetser, Thomas P., and Mary Benet McKinney. 1998. *Changing Pastors.* Kansas City: Sheed & Ward.

Tabert, Eileen (1995). "The Power in EmPOWERment," in Arthur X. Deegan, ed. *Developing a Vibrant Parish Pastoral Council*, pp. 71-87.

Zaleski, Peter A. and Charles E. Zech. 1994. "Economic and Attitudinal Factors in Religious Giving, *Review of Religious Research*, 36 (December), pp. 158-167.

Appendix 6-A

METHODOLOGY SUPPORTING STUDY OF IMPACT OF PASTORAL CHANGE ON PARISH FINANCIAL CONTRIBUTIONS

Parish giving was measured by ordinary income, which was defined as the income parishes receive in collections during Sundays and holy days. It does not include extraordinary contributions, such as a parish building campaign. While total parish income would show a fuller picture of parish financial income, data was not accessible for the full time period of this study. Ordinary income was judged to be sensitive enough to capture the dynamics of a change in contributions to parishes.

The focus of the study—called the dependent variable by researchers—was the ordinary income from the 106 parishes of the Rockford diocese between 1980 and 1993. Data was standardized in 1980 dollars to make comparisons across time meaningful. The unit of analysis was a "pastor change event." That is, each instance of a parish changing its pastor between 1980 and 1993 was a data record. The intention was to see if the changing of pastors was associated with a change in financial contributions. Contribution data was collected for two years before each pastor change, the pastor change year and three years after. The first three years show the contribution pattern under the former pastor while the last three years show the pattern under the new pastor. (The fact that the diocesan fiscal year ends in June, approximately the same time new pastors are installed, simplifies this comparison.) If there were overlapping pastor changes during these six years, only the most recent comparison was retained.

Analysis was primarily by examination of means and standard deviations (measuring the variability of contributions—see Appendix 6-C for more information) through error plots clustered by the year of pastor assignment. Several demographic variables—called independent variables—were included in the analysis: parish size; estimated parishioner household income; the ratio of infant baptisms to total funerals (a surrogate for parishioner age); financial participation in a parish elementary school; and geographical location of the parish. Other independent variables added include: the frequency of pastor change at the parish; the number of years the previous priest was pastor; and whether the priest was assigned as the pastor or whether he was designated the administrator (a more temporary assignment). Parishioner household income was estimated for each parish by using 1990 U.S. Census data to match parishioner addresses by zip code or census tract.

Of the 106 parishes in the diocese, there were 94 parishes with 146 pastor changes analyzed in this study. This resulted in data from 697 data years. Of the pastor changes, 43 parishes (45.7%) had no overlapping years (i.e., all six years of data were present). Twelve parishes were excluded from the study, seven of which had no pastor change between 1980 and 1993. Five parishes were excluded because their status changed significantly during these years, mainly opening or closing.

Aggregated diocesan offertory income in 1980 dollars increased between 1980 and 1993 by 32.6%. Diocesan financial leaders postulated that most of this increase was due to a diocesan-wide emphasis upon stewardship, with a diocesan-wide renewal program also helping by providing a positive environment. Control was needed for this general rise in offertory income due to extra-parochial dynamics, which would confound the analysis of a change in pastors. The dependent variable was then re-indexed to the diocesan aggregated offertory income.

Appendix 6-B

INDICATORS OF PARISH VITALITY
Rockford Catholic Diocese, April 1997

An essential part of the Parish Consultations Process asks the faithful to assess parish life and ministry. To guide the Parish Consultations Committee and the Parish Pastoral Council in their evaluative process the Diocesan Steering Committee has put forth the following "Indicators of a Vital Parish." These indicators strive to reflect a model of parish life that responds faithfully to both the nature of the Christian community presented in the New Testament, as well as to the particular needs of our Church today as set forth in the documents of Vatican II.

It is important to understand that these indicators are intended as a guideline to assist a parish in its self-evaluation. They are put forth as a point of departure in a parish's effort to affirm its strengths and to determine which needs deserve further attention. These indicators are not intended to judge the capabilities of an individual or to criticize any group. Nor are they put forth as rigid standards to be considered apart from the many variables that determine the unique identity of any given parish.

The "Ideal" Christian Community
In determining the basic expectation of parish life (here categorized under the key topic of worship, community, service and education) and subsequent signs of its vitality, the indicators suggested below flow from an understanding of the ideal Christian community initially presented in The Acts of the Apostles:

They devoted themselves to the teaching of the apostles and to the communal life, to the breaking of the bread and to the prayers. Awe came upon everyone, and many wonders and signs were done through the apostles. All who believed were together and had all things in common: they would sell their property and possessions and divide them among all according to each one's need. Acts 2:42–45

This image of Church is complemented by the Second Vatican Council's exhortation to be responsive to the ever-present "signs of the times":

The sacred Council has set out to impart an ever-increasing vigor to the Christian life of the faithful; to adapt more closely to the needs of our age those institutions which are subject to change; to foster whatever can promote union among all who believe in Christ; to strengthen whatever can call all mankind into the Church's fold. The Constitution on the Sacred Liturgy, #1

A parish faith community will always be so much more than what is listed below. These indicators simply serve as common reference points that allow analysis, planning, and creative renewal to begin.

I. Worship

As they prayed, the place where they gathered shook, and they were all filled with the holy Spirit and continued to speak the word of God with boldness. Acts 4:31

Mother Church earnestly desires that all the faithful should be led to that full, conscious, and active participation in liturgical celebrations which is demanded by the very nature of the liturgy... for it is the primary and indispensable source from which the faithful are to derive the true Christian spirit. The Constitution on the Sacred Liturgy #14

Celebration of the Liturgy

Some characteristics of good liturgy are:

- Eucharistic liturgies are celebrated in a prayerful and reverent manner.
- The liturgy is celebrated with music, competently led and sung, which invites the participation of the assembly.
- Homilies are instructive, challenging, well-prepared, and assist parishioners in applying the Scriptures and church teaching to their life experience.
- The physical environment (seating, art, sound system, etc.) is conducive to prayer and is capable of accommodating the rites of the church.
- The assembly is encouraged to participate in sung, spoken, and silent responses.
- The liturgical ministries (lectors, Eucharistic ministers, cantors, ushers, musicians, etc.) are a regular part of liturgies and are properly trained for their ministries.
- There is a worship committee, which meets regularly to plan liturgies.

Celebration of the Sacraments

Some dimensions of a vital sacramental life are:

- There is daily opportunity to participate in the Holy Sacrifice of the Mass and to receive the Holy Eucharist.
- There are adequate and regular opportunities for Sacraments of Reconciliation (individual absolution in both a communal and individual setting), and Anointing of the Sick (communal and individual).
- There is sufficient preparation for the Sacrament of Marriage in cooperation with the programs offered through the Diocesan Family Life Office.
- There is proper preparation for reception of the Sacraments, which includes family participation.
- There are various forms of devotional prayer offered and encouraged (e.g. Rosary, Adoration of the Eucharist, Benediction of the Most Blessed Sacrament, Stations of the Cross, etc.).
- There is Compassionate Ministry which assists in visitation to the homebound and sick, care for the grieving, and assists at funerals with compassion and understanding.
- The RCIA is being implemented and is part of the parish liturgical life.

Spiritual Growth Programs

Some ways to encourage spiritual growth are:

- Retreat/renewal programs that foster personal spiritual formation (parish missions, Cursillo, Christ Renews His Parish, Marriage Encounter, Life in the Spirit Seminars, etc.) are made available and encouraged.
- Prayer groups and small faith-sharing groups are explained and encouraged.
- Programs offered through the Diocese for spiritual enrichment (e.g. Millennium preparation, Life's Healing Journey, Family retreats, etc.) are utilized.

II. Community

Now you are Christ's body, and individually parts of it. 1 Cor 12:27

Hence that messianic people, ...is, however, a most sure seed of unity, hope and salvation for the whole human race. Established by Christ as a communion of life, love and truth, it is taken up by him also as the instrument for the salvation of all; as the light of the world and the salt of the earth it is sent forth into the whole world. Dogmatic Constitution on the Church, #9

The parish offers an outstanding example of community apostolate, for it gathers into a unity all the human diversities that are found there and inserts them into the universality of the Church. Decree on the Apostolate of Lay People, #10

Hospitality

Some illustrations of hospitality in the parish are:

- The integrity of Christian family life is fostered and respected in every parish undertaking.
- All parishioners are greeted with hospitality as they enter the weekly liturgy.
- An organized welcome program exists for new parish members.
- The elderly are invited to participate in parish life.
- Physically disabled members are included in all activities and have access to all facilities.
- Adolescents and young adults are made to feel a part of the parish community.

Stewardship

Some features of stewardship in the parish are:

- The parish has created a stewardship committee that promotes ongoing educational activities that instruct parish members about sharing their gifts as a faith response and as a way to meet the ministry needs of the parish and the local civic community.
- The parish conducts an annual stewardship renewal of time, treasure, and talent.
- The parish encourages a theology of stewardship that promotes sacrificial giving.
- The parish has a prepared budget and meets its ordinary expenses in timely fashion, including support of the pastor, liturgical worship, and assistance to the poor.
- The parish participates in the three combined appeals (national, international, and mission) at a level commensurate with its size.
- The parish regularly meets its target in the Diocesan Stewardship Appeal.
- The parish maintains its plant and facilities in good condition.
- The parish facilities are adequate for the present and future needs of its people and its programs.
- The parish works to retire any debt it has incurred and keeps up with

interest payments on a timely basis.
- Parish staff are paid just wages.
- The parish promotes the stewardship of assets and endowment awareness among parishioners for the long-term financial benefit of the parish, diocese, and universal Church.

Evangelization

Some aspects of an evangelizing parish are:
- The parish encourages all community members to ongoing spiritual conversion.
- The parish supports the mission activities of the Universal Church, e.g., Propagation of the Faith.
- Individual parishioners feel the responsibility and the freedom to invite others to join the community of faith.
- The parish, in some fashion, reaches out to the unchurched, alienated, non-practicing and marginal Catholics.

Leadership

Some characteristics of leadership in the parish are:
- Parish leadership identifies and encourages talents and interests of those in the community.
- Parish leadership seeks a wide diversity of people for involvement in activities and ministries.
- Parish leadership is able to identify the changing needs of the parishioners.
- The parish has sufficient qualified personnel as staff and for program leadership.
- The parish has an active Pastoral Council which meets regularly and advises the pastor.
- The parish has an active Finance Council which meets regularly and advises the pastor.
- The parish provides and encourages training and ongoing faith formation for all staff, as well as Pastoral and Finance Council members.

III. Service

If I, therefore, the master and teacher, have washed your feet, you ought to wash one another's feet. I have given you a model to follow, so that as I have done for you, you should do also. John 13:14–15

Christians can yearn for nothing more ardently than to serve [people] of this age with an ever growing generosity and success... It is the Father's will that we should recognize Christ our brother in the persons of all [people], and love them with an effective love, in words and in deeds, thus bearing witness to the truth; and it is his will that we should share with others the mystery of his heavenly love. Pastoral Constitution on the Church in the Modern World, #93

Within Parish

Some features of service within the parish are:

- Parishioners are instructed in their baptismal responsibility to serve in Jesus' name.
- Parishioners are made aware of the social teachings of the Catholic faith through homilies and various educational opportunities.
- The parish keeps contact with shut-ins and the ill, especially by means of Eucharistic visitations.
- Disadvantaged parishioners can get assistance with their material needs.

Local Community

Some ways the parish can be of service in the local community are:

- The parish welcomes beneficial community activities, such as: blood drives; food or clothing drives; various kinds of support groups such as A.A. and bereaved groups; Girl Scouts; and Boy Scouts.
- Parish groups reach out to local institutions: nursing homes, hospitals, prisons, etc.
- Parishioners are invited to participate in local soup kitchens, PADS, and other outreach programs in the local community.
- The parish contributes a portion of the Sunday collection to diocesan social ministries and worthy community and regional programs for the needy.

Beyond the Local Community

Some ways the parish can serve the needy throughout the world are:

- Parishioners are encouraged to respond generously to diocesan appeals for international aid to the poor and needy.
- Parishioners are encouraged to understand the Church's teaching on abortion and to protect every human's right to life.
- Parishioners are informed about the Church's missionary efforts and encouraged to support them with prayer and finances.

IV. Education/Formation

Go, therefore, and make disciples of all nations, baptizing them in the name of the Father, and of the Son, and of the Holy Spirit, teaching them to observe all that I have commanded you. Matthew 28:19–20

Quite early on, the name catechesis was given to the totality of the Church's efforts to make disciples, to help [people] believe that Jesus is the Son of God so that believing they might have life in his name, and to educate and instruct them in this life, thus building up the body of Christ. Catechism of the Catholic Church, #4 and Catechesi tradendae, #1,2

Before [one] can come to the liturgy [one] must be called to faith and conversion. Constitution on the Sacred Liturgy, #9

Total Parish Education Programs

Some concerns for every parish educational program are:

• Parish educational programs assist parents in understanding their primary role in the spiritual formation of their children.

• The parish looks for opportunities to educate the faithful concerning respect for life issues and sponsor pro-Life programs and activities.

• Parish educational programs foster an awareness of religious vocations.

Religious Education

Some features of effective Religious Education programs are:

• The parish offers complete programs of religious instruction for adults, youth, and children.

• The parish allots adequate funds, staff and space for effective catechesis.

• The parish has a qualified Director or Coordinator of Religious Education.

• The parish encourages and provides opportunities for training and educating for its catechists.

Catholic School (where applicable)

Some indicators for a vital Catholic School are:

• The parish provides Catholic elementary education.

• The parish supports students in obtaining a Catholic high school education.

• The parish employs a qualified Principal who encourages and oversees the Catholic identity of the school.

• The parish encourages and provides opportunities for training and educating for its teachers.

Adult Education

Some dimensions of Adult Education in the parish are:

- The parish offers a variety of opportunities for adult learning experiences (e.g. Bible study, speakers, discussions, etc.).
- The parish supports its lay ministers and volunteers with regular and ongoing in-service programs.
- The parish provides printed, audio and/or video materials for ongoing theological education.
- The parish provides occasional educational programs that address special needs such as single parenting, divorce, caring for the elderly or disabled, communication skills, etc.

RCIA

Some important aspects of the Adult Initiation process are:

- The parish implements the prescribed Rite for Adult Initiation, both liturgically and catechetically.
- The parish supports the training and ongoing formation of lay ministers who serve as catechists and team members for the RCIA.

Youth Ministry

Some features of Youth Ministry in the parish are:

- The parish encourages and provides young adults with opportunities to engage in activities that enhance their faith life.
- The parish has (or shares) a qualified Youth Ministry Coordinator.
- The parish has an active youth ministry program for adolescents and young adults.
- The parish encourages training and ongoing formation of lay ministers responsible as leaders in youth ministry.

Ecumenism

Some ways to encourage a spirit of Ecumenism in the parish are:

- The parish engages in education for Christian unity and in ecumenical activities.
- The parish fosters interfaith understanding by conducting and participating in ecumenical worship services.
- Parish leadership encourages interfaith dialogue and, when possible, participates in ecumenical worship services.

Appendix 6-C

GLOSSARY

Dependent Variable. The dependent variable is the main variable under scrutiny or being measured.

Factor Analysis. A factor analysis is a statistical procedure that shows how variables tend to cluster together, usually based upon preference scores. This analysis allows researchers to discover commonalities and hypothetical constructs among the variables. For example, let us say that a researcher took a survey of a group of people in which they were asked to rate their preference for various food items. After using factor analysis, the researcher discovered that cookies, cake, and graham crackers clustered together. That is, if someone likes cookies the odds are high that she will also like cake and graham crackers. And if someone else does not like cake, the odds are high he will not like cookies or graham crackers. The researcher has found a hypothetical construct, i.e., an explanatory principle about why these items are commonly liked or disliked. After inspecting the qualities of the items that cluster together, the researcher decides to name the hypothetical construct "sweetness." While this may seem obvious, with social science data the commonalities are more difficult to identify.

Independent Variable. Independent variables are variables, often demographic in nature, that may be associated with the dependent variable. For example, if someone is studying why people make financial contributions to their parishes, the dependent variable is probably the household's annual parish contribution. Independent variables may include: age, gender, secular education, religious education, income, and length of time in the parish.

Regression Analysis. Often one can make predictions about one quality of an entity (person, corporation, etc.) by knowing other qualities of the entity.

Knowing, for example, that a person graduated from Harvard with an MBA, one can predict in general what kind of attire he or she wears during the workday. Regression analysis is a statistical procedure that uses one or more variables (called independent variables) to predict a quality or score (called the dependent variable). In the physical sciences regression analysis is often very accurate but in the social sciences its accuracy is less. Simply put, it is difficult to predict people's behavior well.

Standard Deviation. The standard deviation is a measure of the variability or spread of scores. The larger the standard deviation, the more they spread out —both higher and lower—from the mean. The smaller the standard deviation, the more they are close to the mean. The standard deviation almost always is within the range –3 to +3. About two-thirds of all cases, however, are found within the range –1 to +1. A standard deviation of 0 means that there is no variation, i.e., that everyone has the same score.

7

DEVELOPING STEWARDS
IN A PARISH SETTING

Charles E. Zech

Catholics contribute less in financial support to their parishes than do members of nearly every other U.S. Church. This pattern was first discovered by Fr. Andrew Greeley in the 1980s and has been confirmed by every other study of religious giving since that time. In fact, the typical rule of thumb is that Catholics contribute to their parish at about half the rate of their Protestant neighbors. It has been estimated that if Catholics only gave at the same rate as Protestants, the U.S. Catholic Church would receive an additional $7.5 billion a year in contributions. It boggles the mind to think of what the Church could do with another $7.5 billion, ranging from addressing the deferred maintenance on our parish facilities, to paying a just salary to our parochial school teachers and other lay ministers, to enhanced outreach programs to the local community.

A number of theories have emerged to explain low Catholic giving. Father Greeley's own explanation was controversial, to say the least. He blamed low Catholic giving primarily on the fact that the Catholic laity was alienated from the Church hierarchy over the Church's teachings on sexual ethics issues, such as birth control. No other researcher has reached that conclusion.

In the early 1990s, the Lilly Endowment of Indianapolis, Indiana, concerned about religious giving across a variety of U.S. churches, undertook an initiative to study the problem. One outcome of this initiative was a nationwide study of religious giving that came to be known as The American Congregational Giving Study. A team of researchers was formed, led by Dean Hoge of Catholic University and including Michael Donahue of Search Institute, Patrick McNamara of the

University of New Mexico, and Charles Zech of Villanova University. Their findings were reported in the book *Money Matters: Personal Giving in American Churches* (1996). Later, Zech distilled the findings for just the Catholic Church and published them in *Why Catholics Don't Give...And What Can Be Done About It* (2000).

Their studies identified as the primary reason why Catholic giving lags behind Protestant giving the failure of the Catholic Church to educate its members on the meaning of stewardship. Developing parish stewards is the topic of the rest of this chapter. But they also pointed out that stewardship doesn't occur in a vacuum. In order for stewardship efforts to be successful, other concerns must also be addressed. These include parish decision-making processes, parish community building, and the need to remind parishioners that the Church needs their contributions.

Parish Decision-Making Processes

The Catholic Church is a hierarchical church, with a top-down ecclesiology and a top-down management structure. However, parishioners in the twenty-first century have an expectation that they will have an input into parish decision-making processes, especially those involving parish finances. If the parish wants their contributions, it had better be prepared to not only be accountable as to how those funds are spent, but also to ensure that parishioners have an input into both the development and approval of parish budgets.

Parish Community Building

Catholic parishes tend to be much larger than Protestant congregations. The large size of Catholic parishes relative to Protestant congregations is claimed to deter giving since large parishes tend to be impersonal and congested. Not all parishioners can fit in the parish church for a single Mass, for example, inhibiting the parish's ability to develop a sense of community. In addition, each member of the parish is tempted to believe that, with so many other parishioners contributing to support the parish, their individual contributions won't be missed. Naturally, when a large number of parishioners adopt that attitude, parish giving is stunted.

Large Catholic parishes deprive parishioners of a sense of community. Community is not only vital to religious contributions, but to parish life as a whole. Little can be done about the large size of Catholic parishes. In fact, with the growing priest shortage, the problem is likely to worsen. But the parish must make every effort to feel small. Developing small faith communities, getting parishioners involved in parish ministries, and devising programs that help parishioners find a niche in the parish are just some of the options available. If parishes want their members' financial contributions, they must find ways to make them feel that they are an important part of the parish.

Remind Parishioners That The Parish Needs Their Contributions

There is a healthy tension between stewardship advocates who preach, as is noted below, that parishioners must develop a "need to give," and more pragmatic fundraisers who are wont to encourage parishioners to "give to a need" to fund parish programs. The fact is that many Catholics, citing the Church's vast land holdings and other assets, and aware that the clergy is celibate, believe that the Church doesn't need their financial support. But it does, both to meet ongoing needs and to expand its ministries. In many ways, as is noted below, emphasizing giving to support the parish budget is contrary to the stewardship message. But it must be done, at least on occasion. Otherwise parishioners may choose to live out their stewardship by contributing to secular causes where they perceive the need to be greater.

The remainder of this chapter is devoted to the specifics of stewardship. First, we give a brief overview of the concept, followed by a consideration of its theological underpinnings. Then we analyze practical issues involved with introducing and promoting a parish-wide stewardship effort, including a discussion of the roles played by the key players. We end with "Ten Ways To Increase Parish Giving."

Stewardship

Stewardship: returning to God a portion of the bounty that God has given us in recognition that all we have is really a gift from God; developing in parishioners a need to give, as opposed to asking them to give to a need; sharing with parishioners the joy of giving; or, as one bishop has put it, teaching parishioners to be as reckless in their generosity to the Church as God has been in showering gifts upon them. The simple truth is that stewardship is a mission-driven approach to religious giving that works. Parishes that preach the message of stewardship receive larger contributions of time, talent, and treasure than do other parishes.

The Theological Basis of Stewardship

We're all familiar with the biblical notion of stewardship from the Christian Scriptures. The master has left on a trip, and the steward has been charged with overseeing the household in his absence. When the master returns, he asks for an accounting. The message, of course, is that God has entrusted all creation to humankind. In particular, each of us has been entrusted with a particular endowment of gifts. We are responsible for how these gifts are used and someday will be asked to give an accounting of them. This accounting will entail an examination of how well we used the allotment of our time, talent, and treasure in furthering God's kingdom on earth. Each of us has been given a different bundle of gifts, and we will be judged on the basis of what we have done with what we were given.

While not specifically using the term, the Code of Canon Law reinforces the theological underpinnings of stewardship. Book II of the code is entitled *The People of God.* In it, we are told that through our baptism we are called to fulfill the mission of the Church "in accord with the condition proper to each one" (canon 204). This message is repeated in canon 208, where we are told "all cooperate in the building up of the Body of Christ in accordance with each one's condition and function." Finally, canon 222 is even more specific. It tells us "The Christian faithful are obliged to assist with the needs of the Church so that the Church has what is necessary for divine worship, for apostolic works and works of charity and for the decent sustenance of ministers." Clearly, the implication is that *each* of us has a responsibility, and that responsibility extends beyond merely contributing our treasure.

The late Bishop Thomas J. Murphy (1997) has observed that, in their 1992 pastoral, *Stewardship: A Disciple's Response,* the U.S. Catholic bishops offered three convictions that serve to summarize the theology of stewardship:

1. To live as a Christian steward is an expression of mature discipleship. It is a conscious, firm decision carried out in action to be a follower of Jesus Christ despite the cost.

2. Being in conversion, a change of heart, this commitment to stewardship is not carried out in a single action or in a series of actions over a period of time but in one's entire way of life.

3. The practice of stewardship has the power to change how we understand our lives. Good stewards recognize God as the origin of life, the giver of freedom, and the source of all that they are and possess.

The Practical Theology of Stewardship

For many pastors and lay people, "stewardship" is the name given to the annual appeal in which the parish solicits members for their time, talent, and treasure. Typically employing secular fundraising methods, appeals are made to increase financial contributions with little or no parish interaction and with no attempt to provoke a change of parishioner heart or lifestyle. Although commonly used, this approach is not stewardship cultivation. The Center for Parish Development in Chicago (1996) has observed that it misses the mark in several ways:

1. It confuses "financing the church" with Christian stewardship, which is a faithful, wise, and responsible participation in the plan of God.

2. It makes stewardship something one does rather than who one is.

3. While it might raise limited funds and recruit some volunteers, it fails to cultivate a community of gratitude and generosity.

4. It is one-dimensional. Instead of helping people in their spiritual formation through prayerful processes of study and discernment, parish interaction, and an invitation to change one's heart and lifestyle, it only impacts people's checkbooks.

The process of cultivating Christian stewardship communities must be understood as a process leading to the conversion or evangelization of the church itself. What does it take to do this? Again, the Center for Parish Development offers some advice:

1) **An attitude of abundance, not of scarcity.** Forming a parish as a Christian stewardship community involves helping people develop an attitude of abundance. Both the Hebrew and the Christian Scriptures assume a world of plenty, where, when God's gracious righteousness reigns, there is more than enough for everyone. Embracing an attitude of abundance is not easy when one lives in a culture that assumes a world of scarcity, viewing material resources as limited or even fixed. Assuming a world of scarcity does dreadful things to people. They become afraid. They focus on their own survival. They become selfish, competitive, and protective of their own narrowly defined interests. These practices destroy community. The biblical traditions pose a radically different assumption: if we seek first the reign of God, all that we truly need will be provided. There was enough manna in the desert. A few loaves and fishes were enough for Jesus to feed the multitudes. By affirming the whole of life as a gracious gift and a sacred trust Christians assume abundance and exercise the gift of giving. This makes the sharing of time, talent, and treasure a primary part of Christian life rather than a secondary burden or good deed.

2) **A called people with a mission, not a vendor of religious goods and services.** Forming a parish as a stewardship community involves helping it learn to become mission-centered rather than need-centered. Most parishes struggle with this issue because a consumer model has taken such a firm hold in our culture. If unexamined and unmodified, a consumer orientation will change the rules so that rather than the "household of God," the church will become a mere vendor of religious goods and services. A vendor church caters to self-defined and unexamined needs and

wants of members. Self-interest replaces the common good. Stewardship parishes, on the other hand, establish standards for evaluating all of the parish's life and work so that all activities and programs are designed to help people understand and participate meaningfully in the parish's mission. They ask the following questions about every activity offered by their parish: 1) Does this activity equip people for life inside the household of God? 2) Does this activity enable the parish to demonstrate a redemptive way of life that shows the world an alternative way to be a society?

3) **What does it take to cultivate a stewardship community?** Most church stewardship programs fall short because they do not take the process seriously. They do not recognize the community-forming power of parish-wide processes of study, discovery, and growth. Quick-fix programs may raise more money than last year but they won't cultivate a stewardship community. Becoming a stewardship community involves a spiritual journey by the entire parish, clergy and laity together, as they begin to dream, think, and act in this way. When such conversion occurs, enormous energy is released. Time, talent, and treasure are shared generously. And people speak of "rediscovering" the excitement of the Catholic faith.

A reordering of priorities! That is what stewardship is really all about. Stewardship consists of each of us individually and collectively examining with prayer the blessings that have been bestowed upon us and comparing them with our existing stewardship as it stands today. After this examination we must decide what is most important to us and put the participation in our faith on the high level that it deserves.

Time and Talent versus Treasure

It is important to recognize that stewardship entails three equal components: time, talent, and treasure. All three are critical to a successful stewardship orientation. The analogy is a three-legged stool. It is tempting for a parish that is beset by financial difficulties (and what parish is not?) to consider circumventing the time and talent components and focus entirely on treasure. But this is not only bad theology, it is bad fundraising. Twisting the stewardship message to make it into just another fundraising campaign runs the risk of alienating parishioners. Plus, study after study has concluded that those parishioners who get involved in their parish through contributions of their time and talent, who feel a sense of commitment to the parish, contribute more financially as well. Money follows ministry.

Stewardship versus "What We're Already Doing"

Invariably, a pastor trying to introduce stewardship into his parish will run across the plea from current (often long-term) parishioners, "But we're already a generous parish. We're already supporting the parish financially, and a number of us are involved in volunteering our time to the parish." Other parishioners, who are comfortable with the current situation in the parish, will advise the pastor, "If it ain't broke, don't fix it." But wise pastors know that, no matter how generous parishioners are, asking them to examine their motives can be an exercise in spiritual growth. Stewardship, beyond its ability to generate parish resources, serves as an occasion to assist parishioners in the development of their spiritual life.

Table 7-1 lays out the difference between stewardship and "what we're already doing." While there's nothing wrong with the items listed in the table under the heading, "What We're Already Doing," the case can be made that the statements contained in the "Stewardship" column are more in line with Jesus' teachings and offer a greater opportunity for spiritual growth. In order for the ideal of stewardship to blossom in a parish, it is imperative that *every* parish organization evaluate its activities in light of the criteria set forth in the right-hand column of the table. Stewardship is not only theologically sound, it is a mission-driven means for enhancing parish resources.

Table 7-1 Stewardship versus What We're Already Doing

	WHAT WE'RE ALREADY DOING	STEWARDSHIP
Focus and Goals	To bring people into a relationship with our parish and with the work it does in a way that makes them want to support it.	To bring people into a closer relationship with God through the experiences of giving time, talent, and treasure that we help to create by offering occasions where this giving is consciously evoked as a spiritual act and practice.
Ideal Outcomes	Parishioners make a contribution to the parish in recognition that the parish needs resources if it is to continue its work (that is, parishioners give to a need).	Parishioners are more generous in their gifts to the parish of their time, talent, and treasure because every gift becomes an occasion for and a celebration of growth in faith (that is, parishioners develop a need to give).
Philosophical and Cultural Underpinnings	The philosophical and cultural root is philanthropy, "private action for public purposes." The intent is to encourage people to feel a commitment to the "common good of the parish," and voluntarily give of their resources—material goods that they feel they own—for the benefit of others.	The philosophical and cultural root of stewardship is a commitment to personal and collective behavior that recognizes and honors God's ultimate ownership of and profound generosity in all things. The intent is to encourage people to see all resources as gifts temporarily entrusted to us to be used and shared to promote the welfare of all God's creation.
Ultimate Objective	To provide financial (and other) support for our parish, so that it may carry out the godly work to which we believe it has been called.	To "build the household of God" so there will be more human and spiritual, as well as material, resources to carry out the work of building the kingdom, in whatever form that work may take.

Adapted from Thomas H. Jeavons and Rebekah Burch Basinger, *Growing Givers' Hearts*, 2000

Developing Stewardship in a Parish Setting — the Players

This section speaks to the roles of the key actors involved in introducing and expanding stewardship in a parish setting. While there is no one best way of introducing stewardship into a parish, the following are associated with successful stewardship parishes.

The Role of the Pastor

The leadership role of the pastor in introducing stewardship is essential. Pastors who are not convinced that stewardship can be successful, and who fail to lay out a vision of their parish as a stewardship parish, will doom the stewardship effort to failure before it begins. Pastors need to nurture stewardship across the variety of parish activities and ensure that it is a year-round theme of the parish.

But a pastor can't do it by himself. Patrick McNamara (1999) has described the successful stewardship pastor's role as "comfortably delegating." This involves a willingness to delegate combined with an appreciation that in order for stewardship to succeed over the long haul, more and more parishioners must be brought on board. The result is a pastor who is not only open to parishioners' suggestions, but also encourages and respects their initiatives while maintaining accountability in a supportive manner. According to McNamara, by giving parishioners the permission to use their individual gifts to improve the parish, pastors set a tone for the parishioners to flush out who they are and what God expects them to be.

What McNamara is calling for is a partnership model of pastoring, rather than a parenting model. Pastors need to escape from parishioners' dependency on them, and encourage parishioners to claim sovereignty with respect to their time, talent, and treasure. This is not to say that pastors shouldn't demand accountability from their parishioners as they pursue their stewardship. Rather, the accountability must be tempered by the pastor's willingness to relinquish total control.

A second role that pastors play is to recognize their own stewardship responsibilities with respect to the parish resources. If pastors want parishioners to contribute more of their time, talent, and treasure, they must convince their parishioners that these resources are being used wisely. Many pastors feel inadequately trained for this responsibility. If so, they need to recruit a staff that includes some members who can manage and supervise volunteers and others who can develop and oversee a budget. But in all cases, it is the pastor's responsibility to ensure that all parish financial dealings are open and transparent, that parishioners are given appropriate input, and that the parish is accountable in all matters, including parish finances.

A final important role that pastors play is a willingness to talk with their parishioners about the role of money in their lives. In order to achieve a stewardship outlook, parishioners need to have a balanced view of the gifts that God has given them. Most pastors are surprised to learn that Jesus preached on the themes of money and possessions far more frequently than he preached on any other subject, including love or the afterlife. This is because he knew that our attachment to our possessions presented a greater threat to our commitment to follow him than any other human quality. But many pastors feel awkward in talking to their parishioners about money. Perhaps it is their fear of offending their parishioners. Perhaps they feel inadequately trained in the subject. Maybe they are sensitive to the fact that their celibate lifestyle shields them from many of the financial issues that daily confront their parishioners. Or maybe they view their ministry as otherworldly, and fear getting bogged down in temporal discussions of possessions. Whatever the reason, pastors need to overcome any reluctance to talk about money and possessions so that they can assist parishioners in achieving their stewardship goals.

The Role of the Parish Pastoral Council

The parish pastoral council's role in stewardship is as a planning body. As Mark Fischer argues in this volume, council members are expected to use their experience and practical wisdom to advise the pastor on future courses of action that will carry forth the parish's mission. Since stewardship is a mission-driven approach, it is difficult to imagine a parish that doesn't have stewardship as a part of its pastoral plan. But this doesn't extend to actually implementing the stewardship plan by the pastoral council—that is the task of the parish stewardship committee. In addition to their advisory function, pastoral councils share with the pastor the stewardship responsibility of ensuring that all parish activities, including financial matters, are conducted in an open and transparent manner, with appropriate lay input, and with accountability to all parishioners.

The Role of the Parish Finance Committee

In many parishes there is a healthy tension between the parish finance committee and the parish stewardship committee. The finance committee recognizes that someone has to pay the bills if the parish is going to provide all the programs and services, both sacramental and non-sacramental, that parishioners believe are essential. They tend to focus on meeting the parish's needs, rather than developing a need to give among parishioners. While some parishes assign stewardship responsibilities to the parish finance committee, this practice is generally discouraged. <u>Stewardship is distinctly different from managing finances</u>. Stewardship stresses motivations for giving, not methods. Stewardship is a theological understanding of a total way of life, a means for lifting the discussion of money to a spiritual level. The parish finance committee is concerned with more pragmatic issues related to meeting the parish's budgetary requirements.

The Role of the Parish Stewardship Committee

In most parishes, the stewardship committee's <u>primary responsibility is to engage in stewardship formation and education</u>. They try to educate parishioners on the meaning of stewardship, educate them on parish opportunities to contribute time and talent, and educate them on the meaning of money in their lives and how their financial support can become an occasion for and a celebration of growth in faith (that is, help parishioners develop a need to give).

This educational task can take a variety of forms, including:

- preparing and keeping current a time and talent catalog of parish activities and organizations;
- organizing a parish ministry fair;
- sponsoring an annual appreciation dinner for all volunteers in the parish;
- publicizing stewardship thoughts weekly in the parish bulletin and, where applicable, in the parish newsletter;
- developing stewardship materials to be included in the packets distributed to new parishioners;
- ensuring that both parochial school children and those attending religious education classes are introduced to the concept of stewardship;
- recruiting individuals and/or couples to share their personal testimonials about stewardship with the parish.

Obviously, this list is not exhaustive. Some of these will be described in more detail below. But parish stewardship committees must search out ways and take advantage of every opportunity to educate parishioners on the meaning and importance of stewardship in their lives.

The Role of the Parish Staff

The primary stewardship function of the parish staff is to <u>work with the parish volunteers</u>. In many ways <u>volunteers are the lifeblood of the parish</u>. In this age of a shortage of priests, and with most parishes unable to afford a large paid staff, much of the work of the parish falls to volunteers. But even if the Church were flush with ordained priests, Vatican II tells us that, through their baptism, all of the faithful have a right and a responsibility to be involved in parish life. The parish staff's function is to ensure that the volunteer experience is a rewarding one for both the parish and the individual volunteer. Here are some of the important rules that the parish staff should follow in dealing with volunteers.

1. **Remember why people volunteer.** Parishioners volunteer for a variety of reasons, including a strong belief in the cause, because they have the desire to make a difference, or because they have an interest in a particular program. Others volunteer out of a sense of obligation, because they hope it will help them develop business contacts, or because they are lonely and desire social contact. The staff needs to meet the volunteers where they are, rather than where they *think* they should be.

2. **Treat volunteers as co-workers.** Delegate tasks to them and trust their decisions. In order to fully develop the time and talent aspects of stewardship, it is critical that staff members view their role as collaborators or enablers of parishioner talents, not as job supervisors. This includes listening to them and taking their suggestions seriously.

3. **Be organized.** Volunteer time is a scarce resource. It is both discouraging and an insult to them to waste their time. Make certain that volunteers have all the materials that they need and that the goals of their ministries are well defined.

4. **Train them.** Providing training for volunteers not only improves the quality of the ministry being supported, it also sends a signal to the volunteers that their efforts are important, and enhances their level of commitment.

5. **Affirm their work.** Volunteers need and want to be acknowledged for their effort. They must be made to feel that their contribution is important and appreciated. This means not only sponsoring an annual appreciation function for all parish volunteers, but also remembering to affirm individual volunteers and compliment them on a job well done whenever the opportunity presents itself.

6. **Require accountability.** Just as accountability is important in parish finances, so too, it is important in parish volunteer activities. Letting volunteers know that there is accountability sends them the message that their ministry is important, and deserves the best effort that they can provide. Make certain that volunteers know what their responsibilities are and what the parish expects of them, including the time commitment.

There are any number of excellent publications on the market that deal with the specific skills that parish staffs need to develop to attract and manage volunteers.

Specific Stewardship Activities

While stewardship should be emphasized year round, there are specific activities that have proven to be successful in many parishes.

Time and Talent Fairs

Many parishes sponsor an annual function to introduce parishioners to the various ministries and volunteer opportunities in the parish and to encourage them to commit their time and talent to one or more of them. This is the responsibility of the parish stewardship committee, supported by the parish staff and other committees and volunteers where appropriate. These functions typically provide mixed results: some are wildly successful, but far too many are disappointing. The most successful tend to be those that were the beneficiaries of extensive planning. Among the steps typically associated with successful time and talent fairs are:

- Well before the fair (at least 2-3 months in advance) the committee needs to begin preparing the printed materials, including a booklet describing each ministry (explained in detail below), cover letters for the mailings, and any banners or signage necessary for the logistics of the fair. At this time the parish ministries should all be contacted to alert them of the exact date of the fair and soliciting their cooperation in staffing information tables regarding their particular ministries. If the parish intends to use lay witnesses at each Mass on the day of the fair, these witnesses are recruited at this time.
- Two weeks before the fair, announcements concerning the fair should be inserted in the parish bulletin and read at every Mass.
- Ten-twelve days before the fair each parish household should receive a first mailing that includes both a cover letter from the pastor or chairperson of the stewardship committee summarizing the overall vision of stewardship, and a copy of the ministry description booklet described below.
- One week before the fair, a second announcement should be placed in the bulletin and read at Mass.
- In the week prior to the fair a second mailing is received by each parish household, reinforcing the importance of stewardship to both the parish and the parishioner.
- On the day of the fair, some combination of homily and lay witness presentation is used to promote the theological underpinnings of stewardship as well as the practical theology as it applies to this parish.
- At the Time and Talent Fair itself, refreshments are served while parishioners are encouraged to visit the table displays. Each is manned by a representative from that ministry who is there to answer questions.

• Immediately following the fair, ensure that every parishioner who expressed an interest in a ministry is contacted by that ministry within one week of the fair.

Many parishes invite stewardship committees from neighboring parishes to attend their fair as observers, both to share their creative ideas and to receive feedback on various aspects of the event.

The Parish Ministry Booklet

It has become common for parishes to develop a booklet describing each of its ongoing ministries. This booklet is distributed in conjunction with the Time and Talent Fair, but is also given to new registrants. Each ministry is allocated one page in the booklet, and should include at a minimum the following information:

- ministry name;
- purpose/responsibility (1-2 sentences);
- time commitment (includes time spent in meetings, preparation time, and time completing individual assignments);
- contact name and number.

For some ministries, it might be appropriate to include additional information, such as

- qualifications/skills needed;
- training/support provided;
- when ministry performed (time of day? seasonal? flexibility?);
- length of commitment;
- other information as appropriate.

These booklets should be updated annually.

Lay Witnesses

Many parishioners find lay witnesses to be more convincing advocates of stewardship, especially the treasure component, than celibate priests. C. Justin Clements (2000, 42-44) has written on the use of this potentially valuable stewardship tactic.

Who Should Witness?

Clements suggests that the best witness is someone known to the parish, preferably a married couple, who can relate a personal stewardship conversion story. But he recognizes that each parish has its own distinct personality and culture, and what works in one parish might not be successful in another. One issue to be considered is who would have more credibility, a fellow parishioner or a guest witness. Each parish must decide that for themselves. Some parishes choose to alternate the two.

Training and Preparation

Some dioceses sponsor a lay witness training program. Those that don't frequently provide appropriate training and support materials. In any event, Clements identifies some basic elements that should be a part of all lay witness talks:

- personal introduction;
- relationship to the parish;
- details of the witness's personal stewardship journey (including both successes and setbacks);
- what constitutes good stewardship;
- how the witness was introduced to stewardship;
- how the witness's life is different since beginning the stewardship journey;
- how the witness decides how much time, talent, and treasure to return to God;
- an invitation to the audience to join in the journey.

Most of all, witnesses are encouraged to just be themselves and speak openly. Clements doesn't take a stand on the point in the Mass where the lay witness' testimonial is most appropriate, recognizing that technically the homily is reserved for someone who is ordained, while a presentation made near the end of Mass can compromise the message or even alienate the attenders. He recommends that this decision be left to each parish. But in any event, it is common courtesy for a witness to provide the pastor with a copy of the talk a few days prior to presenting it.

Stewardship and Tithing

Some stewardship proponents advocate tithing, i.e., contributing one-tenth of household income to further God's work on earth. They can point to Scripture and verse in the Bible where tithing is mandated, and they often refer to it as "God's plan for giving." Some have even developed a formula for tithing: five percent of income to the parish, four percent to secular charities, and one percent to other Church causes.

But tithing is only biblically based if a person believes that the Bible ends with the Hebrew Scriptures. Jesus never once advocated tithing. In fact the only time he even mentions it is when he's mocking the Pharisees. Jesus promoted stewardship.

There's also a practical reason for not jumping on the tithing bandwagon. Studies have shown that a typical Catholic household contributes about one percent of its income to the Church (remember, Catholics lag well behind

Protestants). Asking a Catholic family to consider tithing can be so overwhelming that it may discourage them from increasing their giving at all.

A more productive approach is to teach proportionate giving. That is, ask parishioners to target a percent of their income (say, one percent if that's what they're currently giving) to contribute to the parish, and then try to increase that percentage by a reasonable amount (say, an extra one-half percent) each year. So a household might contribute one percent of their income to the parish this year, 1.5 percent next year, 2 percent the following year, etc. This accomplishes two things. It increases the household's percentage contribution, while that greater percent is based on a higher income. This approach, when supported by a stewardship message, is more fruitful than tithing because it is less daunting. And a household that pursues this strategy over time will approach the tithing standard eventually.

Pledging

Developing stewardship in a parish is not a casual undertaking. Parishioners must be challenged to seriously consider increasing their contributions of time, talent, and treasure. One approach is to challenge parishioners to make a commitment to themselves and to the parish in the form of an annual pledge.

All research supports the fact that parishioners who make annual pledges contribute more money. But pledging is not a popular concept among Catholic parishioners, many of whom associate it with a Protestant mindset. Others don't like the idea that giving is an obligation. Still others fear that unknown factors will prevent them from fulfilling their annual pledge, although almost no one teaches that a parish pledge is legally binding. Finally, there is the concern that an individual household's pledge won't remain confidential.

In addition to or in conjunction with their Time and Talent Fair, some parishes celebrate a variation of a Commitment Sunday, where parishioners deposit their annual pledge card at a point in the Mass, frequently the offertory. Some parishes ask their parishioners to make pledges of time and talent as well as treasure. In order to assure confidentiality, a parish might utilize a pledge card with a tear-off that physically separates the money portion of the commitment with the name and address portion. Other parishes, emphasizing that parishioners' pledges are really between them and God, publicly burn the sealed pledge cards.

Pledging tends to be least objectionable when it is part of an overall stewardship approach. Then it becomes an occasion for a transformation, an opportunity to consider all that God has done for us. Placed in this spiritual context, pledging becomes a sacred, rather than a secular, act of giving.

Summary: Ten Ways to Increase Parish Giving

A brief chapter such as this can't possibly cover all the possible issues surrounding a complicated matter like parish giving. We conclude with ten tips for parishes that wish to increase parishioner financial contributions.

1) Get the Pastor Actively on Board.

Many pastors are uncomfortable asking their parishioners for money. But it is almost impossible to implement an effective stewardship program without the pastor's leadership. If the pastor fails to communicate that giving is important, many parishioners will conclude that it is not. But the pastor's involvement needs to go beyond an annual stewardship homily; stewardship needs to be addressed throughout the year as the Sunday readings warrant. Pastors need to remember that stewardship is important both for the financial health of the parish and for the spiritual health of the parishioners.

2) Make the Connection Between Spirituality and Giving.

The best givers in any parish are those who give out of their relationship with God, not those who contribute out of a sense of guilt or obligation. It is important that parishioners not view stewardship as just another fundraising gimmick, but it is equally dangerous for them to view it in terms of anticipating a windfall in their temporal life. Stewardship must be presented as a holistic approach of spiritual renewal that challenges us to consider the role that possessions play in our life.

3) Emphasize the Mission of the Parish, Rather than its Budget.

It is easy for parishioners to get caught up in the complexities of the parish budget and to tie their giving to perceived budgetary needs. The parish leadership needs to divert attention away from the annual budget and the consumer mentality that it exemplifies and focus on the parish's mission, on the vision for where the parish is going and what it can become. Stewardship establishes standards for examining all of the parish's life and work. Parishioners who buy into the parish's mission and vision will be more generous in their support than those who are only concerned about contributing their share to fund this year's budget.

4) Stewardship Formation and Education Needs to Touch All Parishioners.

Not only must the parish stewardship effort be continued year-round, it must also have elements appropriate to each segment of the parish. Married couples need to hear a stewardship message tailored to their particular circumstance, but so do single, widowed, and divorced or separated parishioners as well as the children and youth. Each of these groups should be helped to understand the relationship between their faith and the resources that God has provided them.

5) Give Equal Emphasis to Time, Talent, and Treasure.

It is easy for a parish to emphasize the treasure component of stewardship over the other two. After all, even the wealthiest parish could find ways to improve if they had more money, and most parishes are living on the financial edge. But parishioners can see through this façade, and if all they hear is about the treasure component, they will regard stewardship as nothing more than another fundraising gimmick. The full benefits of stewardship, the transformed visions, changed attitudes, and altered lives, will not happen unless parishioners are challenged to evaluate the use of their time and talent as well as their treasure.

6) Encourage Proportionate Giving.

Many stewardship professionals teach tithing. But, as described above, tithing is not as biblically based as some would have us believe (Jesus never taught tithing). From a practical standpoint, it is unrealistic to think that we can turn low-giving Catholics (who typically contribute one percent of their income to their Church) into tithers. A more fruitful approach is to meet parishioners where they are at and form them into proportionate givers. Teach them to view their giving in terms of a percentage of their income, and then ask them to try to increase that percentage by a small amount (perhaps as little as one-half of a percent) each year. This approach will have much more credibility with the people in the pews.

7) Encourage Pledging.

A high percentage of Catholics (by one estimate, nearly 40 percent of our Sunday envelope users) base their giving each week on what they can afford that week. If they can afford little or nothing in a particular week, they contribute little or nothing. Catholics need to commit to their parish financially. If they are to take their stewardship seriously and make it a life-altering experience, they need to make a commitment to themselves and to their Church. Asking our parishioners to pledge is one way that we can help them actualize that commitment. To most parishioners, this is a foreign concept. They must be put at ease by understanding that no one will hound them about their pledge, that it is strictly between them and God. Asking them to pledge their time and talent, as well as their treasure, will help send the message that stewardship is not just a fund-raising scheme.

8) Support Special ("Second") Collections as a Part of Stewardship.

The U.S. bishops sponsor or support one special collection a month. These special collections sustain the heart of the Church's social ministry. They include funding for programs such as the American Bishops' Overseas Appeal (ABOA), the Campaign for Human Development (CHD), the Campaign for Latin America (CLA), and the collection for The National Religious Retirement Office (NRRO). These are large-scale programs. For example, the ABOA special collection generated nearly $17 million in the year 2001, and the NRRO raised nearly $33 million. It has been shown that those who belong to parishes that emphasize the message of stewardship as a guide for living their lives contribute more to the special collections. Apparently, that message carries over into other types of religious giving as well. Also, the discipline of pledging impacts giving to special collections. It has been shown that those who pledge not only contribute more to their parish, but they are also more generous in contributing to the special collections. Many pastors frankly resent the special collections because they're convinced that money contributed to the special collections comes at the expense of parish giving. This is a myth, backed only by anecdotal evidence. The data show that those who are more generous to their parish also contribute more to the special collections. Giving to parishes and giving to other causes are complementary activities, not substitutes for one another. Living out the message of stewardship doesn't stop at the parish boundaries.

9) Be Transparent and Accountable in all Parish Financial Matters.
Catholics recognize that through their baptism, they not only have a right but also a responsibility to participate in parish decision making, including those matters involving financial issues. This extends beyond merely being kept informed—they need to be consulted and have direct input. In many ways, shared parish decision-making is just an extension of stewardship. It would be difficult to develop a parish of stewards if all decision making was taken out of their hands. At best this would result in parishioners with an incomplete and immature sense of stewardship.

10) Remind Parishioners that Contributing through Estate Planning is Good Stewardship. Many parishioners have given sparingly during their lifetime, fearing that if they contribute too much they won't have enough left for their old age. Homilists frequently remind us "you can't take it with you." As part of their stewardship message, pastors should be helping parishioners to think about the values that they'd like to promote after they've died. There are a number of strategies that parishioners can use to demonstrate good stewardship through their estates. In addition to remembering the parish in their will, parishioners could make the parish a beneficiary of a life insurance policy, or establish a Charitable Remainder

Trust, which is a gift to a charity which allows the donors to use the property or income during their lifetime. In addition to benefiting the parish, some of these strategies offer significant tax advantages.

Stewardship is a long-term project. A parish starting from scratch should expect it to be a 5-7 year period before the concept takes hold. But the benefits to the parish, both spiritual and financial, make it well worth the effort.

References

Clements, C. Justin. 2000. *Stewardship: A Parish Handbook,* Ligouri, MO: Ligouri Publications.

Hoge, Dean R., Charles E. Zech, Patrick H. McNamara, and Michael J. Donahue. 1996. *Money Matters: Personal Giving in American Churches,* Louisville: Westminster/John Knox Press.

Jeavons, Thomas H. and Rebekah Burch Basinger. 2000. *Growing Givers' Hearts: Treating Fundraising as Ministry,* San Francisco: Jossey-Bass Publishers.

McNamara, Patrick H. 1999. *More Than Money: Portraits of Transfomative Stewardship,* Washington D.C. Alban Institute Press.

Murphy, Thomas J. 1997. "Giving From the Heart: Stewardship as a Way of Life," *New Directions for Religious Fundraising,* No.17, pp. 21-33.

Transformation: A Newsletter of The Center For Parish Development. 1996. Vol. 3 No. 2.

Zech, Charles E. 2000. *Why Catholics Don't Give…And What Can Be Done About It,* Huntington, IN: Our Sunday Visitor Press.

8

CONCILIATION:
TRANSFORMING CONFLICT THROUGH FAITH

Ed Gaffney

Terri Sortor

Father Henry's leisurely morning coffee was interrupted by Jim's insistent knock on his door. "Father, I'm sorry to bother you so early, but she's done it again!"

Father Henry sighed, realizing that his peaceful start to the morning had been pre-empted by staff conflict—again. "Why can't they just work it out?" he thought.

"Everyone on the staff is familiar with the procedures for approving budget expenditures," said Jim. "Now I've received this bill for educational materials that's almost double Sally's budgeted allotment, and when I just brought it to her attention, she went ballistic!" he said, as he threw the invoice on the table.

"Can't we just find the money someplace?" asked Father Henry. "I'm sure that these materials are important to her program."

"I'll see what I can do," replied Jim angrily. "But shouldn't you talk to her about this? This is the third time in four months that we've been through this with her."

Father Henry sighed deeply and said, "Okay, I'll talk to her," already dreading Sally's usual dramatic response.

He recalled the last time he dealt with Sally's budget excesses—by generally announcing in a staff meeting how tight the budget was and encouraging everyone to stay within their budgetary limits. The other staff members looked puzzled when he said that, but he was more comfortable addressing it to the group than confronting Sally alone. "Didn't she get the point?" he wondered. Now it looked like he'd have to deal with it more directly.

After gulping the last of his now bitter and cold coffee, Father Henry grudgingly headed for his office next door to face the day—and Sally.

Sadly, this scene—or one like it—is all too familiar in church work. Fortunately, God provides us with what we need in these difficult situations.

Our Call to Holiness

Basic to our Catholic faith is our individual and communal call to holiness. Understanding and deeply embracing this call is critical if we are to take God's will for us in conflict seriously. We see this call to holiness articulated in Scripture, the Code of Canon Law, the documents of the Second Vatican Council, and the Catechism of the Catholic Church.

For instance, Scripture tells us, "Before the world was made, he chose us, chose us in Christ, to be holy and spotless" (Ephesians 1:4).

Canon 210 reinforces this, "All the Christian faithful must make an effort…to live a holy life…" (*Code*, 71).

Likewise, the Second Vatican Council and the Church's Catechism remind us of this call: "God has, however, willed to make everyone holy…to make them into a people who might acknowledge Him and serve Him in holiness" (*Lumen Gentium*, The People of God, 9), and "All Christians in any state or walk of life are called to the perfection of charity" (*Catechism*, 2013).

What would a life intentionally striving toward holiness include? Following the Ten Commandments, setting aside regular time for daily prayer, considering how Jesus might respond before taking action, witnessing to Christian stewardship, and persevering in Catholic conscience formation—we do these all in an effort to grow more and more Christlike in our daily lives.

One of our toughest challenges in church work is not to lose this focus of our call to holiness in the midst of interpersonal conflict:

Sally didn't seem surprised when Father Henry asked her to come into his office for a moment.

As soon as she got in the door, Sally unloaded: "I know what you're going to say, Father. I saw Jim going over to the rectory. If I can't get the necessary resources to do my ministry, maybe I'll have to take my talents elsewhere!"

Father Henry looked at her patiently and said, "Sally, remember it's Jim's job to remind us about our budgetary limits and we need to work together on this."

"But I thought you supported the youth program. It just won't be the same without those videos," Sally said as she struggled to keep the anger out of her voice. Father Henry shifted uncomfortably in his chair as Sally continued, her voice rising in frustration, "Do you know how hard it is to compete with what comes through the Internet and cable these days?"

"Well, Sally, I —"

"We might as well just forget the whole program," Sally fumed as she stood up and headed for the door. "Everything I do is for the kids; I'm only thinking of them, and if they're not a priority with anyone else around here, then I just wonder what Jesus would say about this parish," she said as she strode out of Father's office. Father Henry sighed and thought, "Well, that didn't go well," as his secretary announced his first appointment.

Conflicts: Where Do They Come From?

Although there are many complex and varied causes of conflict, a brief exploration of where many conflicts originate may be helpful. Scripture tells us, "Where do the wars and where do the conflicts among you come from? Is it not from your passions that make war within your members? You covet but do not possess. You kill and envy but you cannot obtain; you fight and wage war. You do not possess because you do not ask. You ask but do not receive, because you ask wrongly, to spend it on your passions" (James 4:1–3). While we often think we can identify the causes of our conflicts, the word of God points us to a deeper and more fundamental reality—original sin. Our innate and interior brokenness expresses itself in our interpersonal relationships, frequently in painful and destructive ways. The parable of the prodigal son (Luke 15:11–32) is a study of this dynamic.

This parable is often used as an instruction on the merciful and forgiving love of our Father in heaven. At the same time, it calls us to reflect on how our own attitudes and behaviors are mirrored by the two brothers. While we may easily relate to the squandering of the gifts that God gives us daily, as reflected by the younger son's sins; we are less apt to want to relate to the attitudes and words of the elder son. As we look carefully at his reaction, we see jealousy and resentment toward his brother and toward the mercy of his father. In fact, his very language embodies his disdain, critical judgment, and lack of forgiveness. He rejects his own relationship with his brother with the words, "that son of yours." The father strives to bring him back to love and mercy with the words, "your brother." If we are truly honest with ourselves, we may admit to having more of the older brother's feelings and thoughts than we may initially want to acknowledge. Who of us has not sat in judgment and condemnation of another? Who has not held back forgiveness for the hurts and offenses we've suffered? In these situations, the words from the Gospel of Matthew haunt us as they suggest that relational reconciliation is more pleasing to God than worship: "So then, if you are bringing your offering to the altar and there remember that your brother has something against you, leave your offering there before the altar, go and be reconciled with your brother first, and then come back and present your offering" (Mattew 5:23–24).

In the story of the prodigal son, the elder son's self-righteousness is the sinful passion that keeps him from being able to embrace and forgive his brother and father. Our own sinful passions are often more subtle and frequently take the form of imposing expectations upon and drawing assumptions about others—another source of interpersonal conflict in our lives.

The diagram on the facing page, created by Scott McKenzie of Cargill Associates, illustrates the process we experience when the spoken or unspoken expectations in our relationships and life situations are not met. Generally, before we commit to someone or something, we have explored the possibilities and developed expectations that lead us to make that commitment. What follows is a period of great excitement, creativity, energy, and productivity. Invariably, however, before too long we are disappointed by the reality of broken expectations and changes to our vision. We enter the wilderness, where our behaviors can become fraught with sabotage, withdrawal, and stalemate. Unless we are willing to face reality and let go and grieve our prior expectations, we can remain in this desolation. The path to new opportunity should include prayer and discernment; only then can we achieve the peace that God intends as we consider future action. This future action, rooted in a place of grace and serenity, may include intentional withdrawal or recommitment. It is important to note that the intentional withdrawal here is the result of prayerful reflection and not the reactive withdrawal rooted in emotionalism. Caught up in this cycle of broken expectations, it is easy to see how these situations would lead us into conflict.

Figure 8-1 **Dealing with Broken Expectations & Change**
From: Scott McKenzie, Cargill and Associates

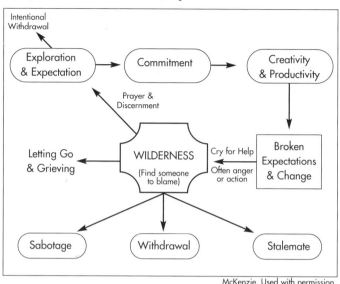

McKenzie. Used with permission.

An all-too-common example of this cycle is reflected in the experiences people have when they come to work for the Church. There is an expectation that Church employees and volunteers will be somehow more Christian in their behaviors than those people working in the secular world. What a shock it is to find human foibles and sin in the Church! So when we face situations in which our expectations have been broken, it is good to remember the cycle through which we move and begin to prepare ourselves for the smoothest, most prayerful passage through it.

Another pitfall is when we draw conclusions and make assumptions about other people's intentions and behaviors. How often do we leap to judgment without consciously thinking through what we are observing and how we are interpreting it? We frequently find ourselves in error when we draw conclusions without validating our assumptions. For example, what does it mean when we pass co-workers in the hall and they ignore our greeting? Do we sometimes jump to the conclusions that either it means that they do not like us, that they are angry with us for some reason, or that they do not believe we are significant enough to acknowledge? The possibility that there may be other reasons for their apparent slight never occurs to us. Having come to our conclusion, we may decide to ignore them in the future or speak ill of them in the present. Now they are left to make their own assumptions about our behavior, thus planting the seeds of interpersonal conflict, which frequently come to full bloom in a very short time (Senge 1994, 243).

These are just some of the causes of our everyday conflicts. Now, let's explore some common responses.

Responses to Conflict

There are three basic ways that people respond to conflict. These responses may be arranged on a curve that resembles a hill. On the left slope of the hill we find the Escape Responses to conflict. On the right side, we find the Attack Responses, and in the center we find the Peacemaking Responses.

Imagine that this hill [below] is covered with ice. If you go too far to the left or the right, you can lose your footing and slide down the slope. Similarly, when you experience conflict, it is easy to become defensive or antagonistic. Both responses make matters worse and can lead to more extreme reactions.

Fortunately, there are two things that you can do to stay on top of this slippery slope: you can learn to resist the natural inclination to escape or attack when faced with conflict, and you can develop the ability to use the peacemaking response that is best suited to resolving a particular conflict (Sande 1991, 17-18).

© Peacemaker Ministries. Used with permission.

Let's first consider the left side of the Slippery Slope where we see the *Escape Responses*.

Denial takes different forms. One example occurs when we deny that there even *is* a conflict. When another person observes our withdrawal and frustration and asks us, "Is there something wrong?" we will deny that there is. Another example of denial is when we deny our own responsibility in the conflict, preferring to cast ourselves in the victim—or even more extreme, the martyr—role. Blaming others is still another example of how denial manifests itself. Related to the avoidance of responsibility, blaming looks to find reasons for the conflict that are outside of ourselves. The denial is implicit in this case.

Another form of escape is *Flight*. There are sometimes legitimate reasons for the flight response in a conflict. If we believe we are in any physical danger, it is wise to remove ourselves from the situation. Another legitimate reason for flight is if we realize that we need to take a "time out" from the situation. We may do this in order to allow emotions to abate or to take time to pray about what is happening and set a time to get back together to work things out. In these cases, the reasons for leaving are justified. On the other hand, there are times when the flight response serves only to help us to escape from the conflict and avoid the situational or relational work that needs to be done. One example of this type of flight is when we try to physically avoid being in the presence of the person with whom we are in conflict. We may avoid meetings where we know the other person may be present, or we might stay away from areas in our office building where we may encounter the person. This physical avoidance never helps to resolve the conflict, of course. It only succeeds in delaying the inevitable—and may serve to make successful resolution that much more difficult. Emotional flight is possible, as well. We may allow ourselves to be in the other person's presence without engaging in truthful and open communication. We may even slip into emotional denial when we're together, all in an attempt to flee from addressing the conflict.

The third and most extreme escape response is *Suicide*, the choice made by those who believe that they have run out of alternatives. Tragically, our country is currently ranked second in the world in teenage suicides; a reality that we must address individually, as a Church, as a community, and as a nation. (We have had the privilege of presenting this process in a Catholic high school, and the openness of the students to gaining faith-based skills to deal with the conflicts in their lives was remarkable!)

On the other side of the Slippery Slope are the *Attack Responses*. Often, those who have been using escape responses will eventually swing over to attack responses when they feel trapped and forced to address the conflict.

The first of these is *Litigation*. We know that we have become a litigious society; taking our adversaries to court has all too often become our first response to conflict. Of course, there is a time when filing a lawsuit is the best response to a conflict; this is when every other attempt to resolve the situation has failed. Some people (other than ourselves, of course) can be so unreasonable that they leave us no other alternative, but we believe that these instances will become very rare if we follow this faith-filled response to conflict.

Another attack response is *Assault*. This would include physical assault, of course, but while common in childhood, the older we get the less likely we should feel drawn to this response. Perhaps the most common type of assault is verbal. We attack one another using painful, hateful, mocking, or sarcastic words; one example of this is name-calling or labeling, which in the Church is most commonly done behind someone's back. By far, however, the most pervasive and destructive types of verbal assault that we have seen in the conflicts we have mediated are gossip and triangulation. At least with in-your-face arguments, those in conflict are honest and upfront with one another. But gossip, triangulation, name-calling, and labeling reflect a deceitfulness and cowardice that we need to eliminate if we are to handle our conflicts as Christians. We engage in these activities when we speak ill of the person with whom we are in conflict, trying to garner allies and get other people to agree and empathize with us. The usual result of this character assassination is a spreading of the conflict that makes it more difficult to reconcile.

The most extreme attack response is *Murder*—physically taking another's life; again, this is not an option for those who are striving to put flesh on the gospel of Jesus Christ. Yet many people feel justified in a more common type of "murder"— killing the reputations of others through malicious speech. We need to begin to recognize that by following the secular world in our responses to conflict, we are losing opportunities for healing and Christ-centered resolution.

So if we are to avoid the Escape Responses, which really embody "peace faking," and the Attack Responses, which are "peace breaking," we should try to remain in the area of the Peacemaking Responses.

Our Christianity calls us to a counter-cultural response to much of what the world values and promotes, including the ways we deal with the inevitable conflicts in life. That is, the world should be able to see our witness in everything we do, of course, but especially in the way we respond to interpersonal conflict. Scripture outlines six particular responses that we can use to resolve differences. The top section of the slope depicts the peacemaking responses to conflict, and are divided into *personal* and *assisted* peacemaking efforts.

The first personal response is to *Overlook*. When a relationship is not substantially broken by the wrong that was done, giving the benefit of the doubt and the gift of forgiveness to the other by overlooking the matter follows the spirit of Proverbs 19:11, "It is good sense in a man to be slow to anger; it is to his glory to overlook the offense." In our humanness, we all make mistakes that have the potential of offending others. Depending upon the severity of the offense, it may be appropriately resolved by simply forgetting the matter and moving on. Note that overlooking the offense is different from denying it, because it is not an effort at ignoring the problem; rather, it first acknowledges that the wrong was committed and then freely makes the choice to forgive.

Sometimes, however, a wrong is great enough to negatively impact the relationship. In these cases, we are guided by the words of Matthew 18:15, "If your brother sins [against you], go and tell him his fault between you and him alone. If he listens to you, you have won over your brother." This direct approach may sound simple, but it is recognizably a difficult thing to do.

The second personal peacemaking response, *Discussion*, calls us to be willing to put aside defensiveness and become vulnerable to the other for the good of the relationship. By explaining how we were hurt by a particular word or behavior, we may make ourselves susceptible to a similar hurt in the future. But being willing to make ourselves vulnerable—for the sake of another and our relationship—recognizes that the relationship is of greater importance to God than the issue that divided us in the first place. And, after all, is it not God's will that we are striving to follow?

Conflict that is substantive in nature, as when allotting limited money, property, time, etc., may be best resolved through *Negotiation*, the third personal peacemaking response. In Philippians 2:4, we read that "each [should] look out not for his own interests, but also everyone for [the interests] of others." Being willing to "give and take" to settle a substantive dispute means that we may end up with slightly less than we had hoped for, but we have once again put the relationship before self-interest. It shows good faith to be willing to come to the table to hear another's interests and consider them when determining an acceptable outcome. Church work abounds with opportunity to resolve the dilemma of limited resources through negotiation.

There are times when the assistance of others is called for to bring about a positive outcome to a dispute. If we have tried to settle the matter through appropriate personal peacemaking strategies but have not been successful, seeking the assistance of another person may be needed. The assisted peacemaking response of *Mediation* is when the counsel of a mutually respected, neutral third party is sought. The eighteenth chapter of the Gospel of Matthew continues in verse 16 with, "If he does not listen, take one or two others along with you, so that every fact may be established on the testimony of two or three witnesses."

Do not confuse this step with the all-too-present habit in conflict, already mentioned, of lobbying others through gossip and triangulation to support one side. The spirit of mediation calls for humility when considering the questions, "Have we considered this issue from all perspectives? Are there places of agreement that we have not acknowledged?" Mediators do not control the outcome of the issue, but rather try to point the disputing parties to see where there are areas of agreement or commonality. This can be done formally, as when hiring a professional mediator, or informally, as when asking a mutually respected friend to help. The resolution is at all times in the control of the disputing parties, which makes it a particularly attractive strategy when other attempts to reconcile have failed.

Another assisted peacemaking effort is *Arbitration*. Appointing one or more arbitrators to listen to both sides of an issue and render a binding decision is another recourse when disputants cannot come to a voluntary agreement. Paul's words in 1 Corinthians 6: 1, 5–6 admonish us to keep our disputes from the publicity of the civil court, which does nothing to recognize or restore relationships. "How can any one of you with a case against another dare to bring it to the unjust for judgment instead of to the holy ones? …Can it be that there is not one among you wise enough to be able to settle a case between brothers? But rather, brother goes to court against brother, and that before unbelievers." Paul's admonishment is twofold: first, Christians are to humbly appoint as a judge a wise person to hear the facts of the matter and render a decision. Second, we are not to discredit Christianity by parading our disputes in the public forum and behaving no differently than people in the secular world.

The final assisted peacemaking strategy is to call upon church leaders to intervene to promote justice, repentance, and forgiveness. *Church Discipline* is practically an alien concept in the Catholic Church because leaders are often not trained to apply church teaching, Scripture, and canon law to settle disputes among its members. It was, however, a strong element in the early Church, as the writings of St. Paul testify. This concept was a source of the Catholic Church's *Code of Canon*

Law, which for many years has been relegated to a secondary role and virtually confined to marriage cases. The teaching of Jesus in Matthew 18:17, however, may prompt us to reconsider the role of the Church in restoring peace among its members: "If he refuses to listen to them, tell the church." Our culture's support for independence of mind and will often reduces the authority previously held by the Church. Certainly, the abuse of this authority through history also has had an impact. But it may very well be an area worthy of reconsideration if Catholic Christians are to take seriously their charge to live *not as the world lives*.

A Four-Step Process

Scripture and Church teaching support a progressive, four-step approach to dealing with life's difficulties. These four steps, also called the Four G's, put our Catholic faith and our personal relationship with God first in all things, but especially when we're challenged by conflict. It is so easy to fall into the trap modeled by the world, which is to approach conflict with an attitude of rights and entitlements. "Hold your ground," "fight for your rights," and "win at all costs" are themes we see repeated constantly on the street, in the news, in the books we read, the music we hear, and the movies we watch. Our society abhors weakness, and it seems to view peaceful means of resolving conflict as weak. For a country that was founded on a deep faith in God, we seem to have abandoned the tendency to follow God's guidance when life's pressures become too great. Remembering our call to holiness when faced with conflict, however, can be the critical step to restoring true peace and reconciling with others.

The First Step: Glorify God. Imagine how different the world could be if we as Catholic Christians stopped to glorify God when disputes arose among us. Asking ourselves the question, "How can I please and honor God in this moment, or in this circumstance?" when we are offended by another is a radical example of truly living our faith. This means that we are to place our trust in God (who sees a much bigger picture than we do) and not in our own selfish desire to be vindicated when wronged. Jesus' life cycle of *withdraw, pray, and act* (WPA) models for us the discipline of stepping aside to consider God's will when discerning the most relationship-building response in conflict. Scripture is full of examples of Jesus taking time to pray as others pressed him for an immediate response. So can we, when conflict seems to demand an immediate reply, take a moment to re-establish our perspective and center ourselves in faith through the WPA process (Sande 1991, 13).

Those who recall the lessons in the Baltimore Catechism will remember that God made us "to know Him, to love Him, and to serve Him in this world, and to be happy with Him forever in heaven." Our very reason for existing is to be in constant relationship with our Creator, though our culture would attempt to convince us to embrace other priorities. "He who dies with the most toys wins" is the anthem of a culture that focuses our attentions on excessive consumption and instant gratification instead of on whatever good God may be calling us to in any given circumstance. When we create idols in our life—things, philosophies, habits, relationships—that interfere with our relationship with God, we lose sight of who we are as God's sons and daughters and the very reason for our being in this world.

In conflict, as anywhere, God's perspective would call us to humility and service, and to true justice, instead. With this mindset, we can begin to view conflict as an opportunity to follow our baptismal call rather than as the dismal situation it would seem at first to be. Prayer affords us an opportunity to know God better, to offer him our praise, glory, and love, and to seek to know how we can best serve as his ambassadors in the world. Prayer at the moment of conflict gets our priorities straight. It is a radical notion, perhaps, but one that honors and reflects our call to holiness—and renders our hearts more open to true reconciliation.

The Second Step: Get the Log Out of Your Own Eye: Another concept radical to our culture is the notion of taking responsibility for our own actions, or our own role in a conflict. Judging others by their behaviors and ourselves by our intentions always shifts the blame in a conflict to the other. Yet Scripture says, "Stop judging, that you may not be judged. For as you judge, so will you be judged, and the measure with which you measure will be measured out to you. Why do you notice the splinter in your brother's eye, but do not perceive the wooden log in your own eye?…You hypocrite, first take the log out of your own eye, and then you will see clearly to remove the splinter from your brother's eye" (Mt 7:1–5) (Sande 1991, 67).

So, while our culture says, "Find someone to blame," our faith tells us, "Look within and acknowledge your own fault in the matter." If we acknowledge the reality of original sin and our own innate woundedness, we will be more inclined to self-reflection than to blaming others.

There are three types of "logs" that we can identify as we reflect on our own role in any given conflict. The first "log" is our *Attitudes*. What types of attitudes might bring us into conflict with others, or at least contribute to a conflict? Have we been overly critical, negative, judgmental, self-righteous, proud, or disdainful? If so, we would do well to reflect upon Philippians 4:8: "Finally, fill your minds with everything that is true, everything that is noble, everything that is good and pure, everything that we love and honor, and everything that can be thought virtuous or worthy of praise." This is what we should focus upon mentally; our attitudes should be ones of hope, trust, love, and humility. Usually, when we are enmeshed in conflict, we lose sight of these dispositions. So as we look for ways that we have contributed to a conflict, we could conduct an "attitude inventory," remembering that Scripture calls us to cultivate an "attitude of gratitude," giving thanks in all things (cf 1 Thessalonians 5:18).

Another "log" we could reflect upon are our *Actual Sinful Words or Actions.* Have we been gossiping about others? Have we reacted with hurtful, angry words toward others? Have we appeared contrite and repentant while we have actually been self-serving? Have we lied or subtly misrepresented the truth? In short, have we again put our own will before God's will? As Scripture tells us, "Guard against foul talk; let your words be for the improvement of others, as occasion offers, and do good to your listeners..." (Ephesians 4:29). If we follow this instruction, God's will, and not our own, will be done.

A third "log" is the *Sin of Omission.* (How many of you just had a nostalgic moment?) These refer to those instances when we know what God is asking of us, but we fail to do it. We may fail to respond in these situations for several reasons: it may be inconvenient, we may not think that we have the time, we may not be sure how our effort would be received, or we may be just plain selfish. Again, Scripture is clear, "Everyone who knows what is the right thing to do and doesn't do it commits a sin" (James 4:17).

Developing the discipline where we pause during the day to identify our "logs"— even when we are not in conflict—will serve us well when conflict rages in our lives. Without this discipline, we tend to revert to our human weakness of pointing a finger at others. Not only is identifying our "logs" good for self-reflection as we journey toward holiness, we can also use the practice to begin resolving conflict by being willing to go to the other and admit our fault.

There are specific elements of an acknowledgment of our own fault in a conflict situation that, if we use them, will help the other person to hear better what we have to say and to be more open to God's grace. These elements, referred to as The Seven A's of Confession (Sande 1991, 109-119), call us to:

Address everyone involved. Those drawn into the conflict through gossip, triangulation, or sinful words and actions need to be addressed in our repentance. This includes God, to whom we go in the sacrament of reconciliation.

Avoid if, but, and maybe. These words excuse our responsibility and discount the other person's pain.

Admit specifically. Focus on all attitudes, words, and actions that have contributed to the conflict.

Apologize. We need to express sincere sorrow for the pain we've caused.

Accept the consequences. We need to realize that we are not finished after we make an apology; relationship re-building takes work, and sometimes other types of restitution are necessary.

Alter your behavior. Most people, when asked how they know others are sincere in their repentance, point to a change in future behavior as the best evidence of sincerity.

Ask for forgiveness. We humbly ask the other for forgiveness, with no demands, expectations, or deadlines.

When we fail to recognize and acknowledge our own sin, we are like a proud and haughty person striding boldly and proudly through life—in a hospital gown with the back undone! Often, we even try to stand before God in that pompous posture.

Our willingness to be vulnerable in front of the other will oftentimes break down more walls that stand between us than any other single action we could take.

If both Father Henry and Sally were aware of the first two steps of this four-step process, now that they have stepped away from one another, their personal thought processes may look very different from their usual responses. Having stepped aside, they may not stay stuck in their initial, angry reaction; they may move to a better place. Although the progression that follows sometimes takes a long time, for the sake of our topic, we have compressed that time in which each of the participants in the conflict comes to this different and better place…

By the time she reached her office, Sally was furious, and grumbled, "Nobody around here cares about our kids as much as I do. Money is their almighty god and I know that's not what Jesus wants. Here I am, a layperson; why do I have to be the one to always have to tell the priest what the church's priorities should be? I can't believe that Father Henry didn't stand up for me or my programs…"

Sally's morning was all but lost as she continued her internal complaining through her tasks and appointments. Late in the morning she slumped back into her chair, and her attention was caught by the crucifix on the wall. "I know I won't be able to get through this one very well by myself; maybe I'll just walk over to the noon Mass," she decided.

The words had barely left the lector's lips before Sally's heart was moved.

"Why are you downcast, O my soul? Why so disturbed within me? Put your hope in God, for I will yet praise him, my Savior and my God" (Psalm 42:5). She began to pray fervently, asking God how she could honor him in this conflict with Father Henry. "What is it you want me to do, Lord?" became her prayer for the remainder of the Mass. As she returned to her office, Sally knew she was in a completely different frame of mind.

"Father Henry always attends so many of my activities. How could I have accused him of not supporting what I do?" she thought. "He's very supportive of my work; a lot of times he even re-schedules meetings to accommodate the kids' functions. But, then, why didn't he defend my position to Jim?" she wondered.

Sally spent a long time thinking about this before she began to realize a bigger picture, "It's not like the youth program is the only one Father Henry has responsibility for; there are more than a dozen program budgets at the parish," she thought, "He's got to take everybody's programs into account, and Jim did say that the Sunday collection has been down from last year."

"I can't believe I blew up again," Sally thought regretfully. "And I stormed out before Father could finish his thought. What did that accomplish? I need to go talk to him."

Father Henry's day had been going no better:

He found it hard to concentrate during his appointments. He even snapped at the parish bookkeeper as she innocently handed him the latest budget reports off the printer. In his dread of conflict, he thought, "Why can't the matter just go away?" and he gulped two more antacids. It was with a heavy heart that he reached for his lectionary and began to review the readings for Mass.

"Do not be anxious about anything, but in everything, by prayer and petition, with thanksgiving, present your requests to God. And the peace of God, which transcends all understanding, will guard your hearts and your minds in Christ Jesus" (Philippians 4:6–7). Father Henry was struck by the timeliness of the words before him. "Boy, this is just what I needed," he sighed. "Lord, I really let conflict get to me; there is nothing peaceful about it as far as I'm concerned," he prayed. "Help me to handle this one differently."

"Maybe it's my avoidance of conflict that keeps me from being a stronger manager; it's probably why we get into these battles in the first place. It's not *fair to the staff or the parishioners when I refuse to deal with unpleasant situations. I should have dealt with this budget issue with Sally the very first time it came up; we could have avoided a lot of grief. I'll sit down with her before the end of the day."*

Father Henry continued his work with a lighter heart—and a more determined attitude.

The Third Step: Go and Show Your Brother His Fault. "If your brother does something wrong, go and have it out with him alone, between your two selves. If he listens to you, you have won back your brother" (Matthew 18:15). It is only after we prayerfully reflect on our own contributions to the conflict that we dare to consider the fault of the other. If our very first reactions are to identify and expose the fault of the other, then we are exhibiting the automatic response that our culture encourages. In fact, blaming others and pointing out their faults is a skill our culture has raised to an art form. Frequently, this third step is our culture's complete, one-step reaction to conflict (Sande, 1991: 129).

But to do it God's way is more difficult. God asks us to lift others up and put their interests first. It requires us to be vulnerable because we are leading with our faults, an admission of our own sin, weakness, and brokenness. It is a risk God asks us to take to deepen and heal our relationships. Moreover, there's no guarantee that it will have the results we desire; we are asked to be true to what God asks of us, not to be wed to our desired outcome. The important thing is to learn how to do it effectively.

To do this third step well, remember to follow these elements:

- Pray for humility and wisdom. Prayer should be a Christian's first response in every situation. It changes our attitudes and our thinking.
- Plan your words carefully. Have a definite idea about what to say and how to say it.
- Anticipate likely reactions. Prepare yourself for the other person's probable responses so that you'll not become flustered as you meet.
- Choose the best time and place. Check with the other to ensure that there is sufficient time to address the situation in a place where you'll likely not be disturbed.
- Assume the best about the person until facts prove otherwise. We generally conjure up everything negative about the person with whom we are in conflict, but if we focus on their positive traits, we will be looking at them the way God does.

• Listen carefully. Ordinarily we spend our "listening time" preparing a rebuttal of some sort, but if we listen for and acknowledge the feelings of the other beneath the words, we will be demonstrating true care and concern.

• Speak only to build others up. Be careful not to attack the other, but use "I" language to relate to the other in a more positive and productive way.

• Ask for feedback. Check for understanding frequently so that your message as well as the one you're receiving is getting through accurately.

• Recognize the other's limits. There may be other obstacles that could prevent final resolution at this time, and our own limits may get in the way as well.

It is good to remember that we are not setting out to change others; only God can do that. As we respond differently to conflict in our lives, however, we give others the freedom to respond differently as well—and it is through that change that God's will can emerge (Sande 1991, 146-165).

As we approach others with whom we are in conflict, we should realize that utilizing our best communication skills would help us to get our message across to the other most effectively. For example, we should remember that we use several channels to communicate any message; these include the *linguistic* channel (the actual words we use), the *para-linguistic* channel (the intonations, emphases, rate, pitch, and tone), and the *nonverbal* channel (gestures, expressions, movement, and posture—where most of the meaning is carried). We should be aware of our personal strengths and weaknesses in communication and work intentionally in each channel to make our message coherent and easily understood. For instance, do we express displeasure with the other's message nonverbally before the other person is even finished speaking? This signals that we have reached conclusions and judgments and have not given the speaker the gift of empathic listening. Do we use sarcasm to drive home our points and in the process diminish others and the perspectives they have shared?

One practice we could strive to follow to improve our communication comes from The Talmud; it is called The Lesson of the Three Gates. In this exercise, we pretend to have a giraffe-like neck containing three gates, each with a question on it. Everything we want to say must pass through these three gates by answering affirmatively to the questions. The question on the first gate is, **"Is it true?"** In other words, we agree not to say anything that is not completely truthful. Assuming that what we want to say is, in fact, true, our message proceeds to the second gate, where the question is, **"Is it necessary?"** This means, "Does it need to be said?" "Does it need to be said by me?" and "Does it need to be said by me now?" Again, let us suppose we can answer "Yes" to the second gate's questions. The question challenging us on the third gate is, **"Is it kind?"** We need to be careful not to mistake "kind" with "comfortable." We sometimes need to share uncomfortable things with others for their and others' good. For example, we need to point out areas where our subordinates need improvement. It would be unkind of us *not* to do this; who wants to be receiving false and empty praise and affirmation all year, only to be fired for poor performance? So we strive to limit our verbal communication to only those messages that are **true, necessary, and kind.** Take up this particular challenge for a period of time—say, one or two days. See if trying to limit yourself to only true, necessary, and kind communication brings you any insights. (Once you have mastered these three gates, the "extra credit" fourth gate's question is, "Is it uplifting?")

We also have to learn how to receive others' communication pointing out our own sin in a conflict. When we pray to God and ask him to reveal our logs, he sometimes reveals those logs through others. We need to be able to hear others' observations and concerns about us without resistance and defensiveness. Instead, we can ask ourselves three important questions:

- What truth might there be in this person's perspective?
- How can I use this input for my good and the good of others?
- What is God saying to me in this experience?

Another principle to keep in mind when we are taking things in that are difficult to hear is that the speakers are also telling us about themselves as they speak. For example, it has been said that 90% of our anger has its roots in hurt or fear. Yet most times, we react to others' angry words and actions rather than hearing and responding to the deeper feelings that are driving them. For example, if someone says, "Listen to me, look at me, don't turn away while I'm talking," we can defend ourselves, be self-righteous, and claim that we were listening, or we can acknowledge that the other may be feeling discounted and ignored and that it feels bad and hurtful and calls us to a better response.

The Fourth Step: Go and Be Reconciled. In our culture merely achieving a truce or coming to some kind of an agreement reflects adequate resolution to a conflict. Our faith does not allow us to stop at this, however. We are expected to work harder to seek healing in the relationship. This usually means seeking forgiveness and being willing to extend it. An obstacle to achieving this level of reconciliation is a false idea about what forgiveness is—and what it is not. There are several misconceptions about forgiveness that prevent us from moving forward in healing and restoring relationships broken by conflict (Sande 1991, 183-188).

One such misconception is that we need to have *feelings* of forgiveness before we extend forgiveness to another. If this were true, we may never—or at least not for a very long time—forgive another. To overcome this misconception, it helps to think of all of the other things we do that we do not necessarily feel like doing. A definition of maturity is "acting in spite of our feelings rather than because of them." It is the same with forgiveness; we are to forgive the other, even if we do not feel like it, simply because God has forgiven us first.

Another misconception is that we do not believe that we will ever *forget* what has happened to us, so we cannot forgive it. Christians are not expected to forget what has happened to them, but when we extend forgiveness to another, God's grace does affect the degree to which the offense impacts us on a daily basis. It has been said that "Christians forgive to forget," and it is God's action that moves us toward forgetfulness.

Still another misconception is the notion that forgiving *excuses* the wrong that was done. Some people think that forgiving is the same as saying, "Don't think anything about it; it was nothing." If it truly were nothing, there would be no need to seek or extend forgiveness. Instead, forgiveness acknowledges the wrong that was done. In some cases, restitution may be necessary and there may still be consequences to face.

A final misconception of forgiveness is that we think we need to have a *guarantee* that the offense is not going to happen again before we forgive. How many of us have ever had to forgive someone for the same offense more than once? More important, how many of *us* have needed forgiveness for the same offense more than once? In our humanity, it is more common for us to fail in our resolutions than to succeed. We are reminded of this in Scripture, "… Peter came up and asked him, 'Lord, when my brother wrongs me, how often must I forgive him? Seven times?' 'No,' Jesus replied, 'not seven times, I say seventy times seven times'" (Matthew 18:21–22).

Now that we have explored some of the misconceptions about forgiveness, it would be good to discuss what forgiveness is. There are many ways to define forgiveness, and we include here examples of what people have shared during our parish mission on Christian Conciliation. One person said that forgiveness is "letting go of anger, resentment, and the desire for revenge." Another said that it is "letting the other person back into your heart." A third said that it is "forever giving up all hope and resentment of ever having a better past." All of these contain essential truths about forgiveness that are important to us as we seek to heal and restore our relationships.

Still, some people do struggle with forgiving others; they nurse grudges long after they can even remember how the conflict originally started. This is not healthy for anyone. One last thought, then, on the lack of forgiveness: "Unforgiveness is the poison we drink hoping the other will die."

What would true forgiveness look like? In order for forgiveness to be effective, we believe it would contain four specific elements or promises that we are extending to the person who has offended us. These four promises are:

1) *I will not think about this incident.* Since we cannot control every thought that comes into our head, what does this mean? Actually, when we say "think," we are referring to dwelling upon or brooding over something, thereby inflaming all of the emotions we first felt during the conflict. This is obviously counterproductive if we are trying to forgive and let go of the hurt.

2) *I will not bring up this incident and use it against you.* It has been said that some people get hysterical in conflict while others get historical, dredging up past offenses as ammunition in the current conflict. Committing to this promise means remaining in the present moment and dealing only with the current issues.

3) *I will not talk to others about this incident.* Once we have forgiven an offense, we are promising not to disclose the incident to anyone else. There is sometimes a great temptation to commiserate with someone who has suffered a similar offense at the hand of the person who had hurt us. But in forgiving, we are vowing not to give in to that temptation. Note, too, that not relating the incident to others after we have extended forgiveness is not the same as seeking another's wisdom in the midst of conflict to learn how to handle it better.

4) *I will not allow this incident to stand between us or hinder our personal relationship.* As we move into the future with the person we have forgiven, we are promising to allow trust to develop again between us. We will decide not to avoid situations that place us in the position of possibly being hurt again, as long as these are not physically or emotionally abusive situations. Instead, we will trust God to help us in the healing we are striving to attain.

It is worth noting here that these four promises apply to *ourselves* as well as to others. We are often our own worst enemies, continually recalling our own shortcomings and condemning ourselves for the mistakes we've made. How wonderful to promise to ourselves that the past will be accepted for what it was, and that today is a new day, full of promise and opportunity—and God's grace.

It is also good to note that, if we are serious about the promises of forgiveness, we should not forgive prematurely. That is, we need to be sure that we are willing to follow through on these promises and not just relegate forgiveness to lip service. Rather than forgiving someone before we are able to commit to these promises, it would be better to explain to the other just what forgiveness means to us, and that we are working toward that goal.

Let's see how following the four steps might work in our "real life" situation:

The afternoon was much more productive for both Father Henry and Sally. Father Henry was pleasantly surprised when his suggestion to meet at 4:00 in Sally's office was met with a positive reaction.

After opening with prayer, Father Henry began the meeting by saying, "Sally, I've been giving a lot of thought to our conversation earlier. No, let me be more honest, to our disagreement earlier. I'm beginning to see that, even in my language, I try to avoid unpleasantness. I owe you an apology; we have a budget problem that has been going on for some time now, and I was never direct enough for you to understand the seriousness of it. The first couple of times that you overspent a line item, I—for all practical purposes—shrugged it off. That wasn't fair to you, to the rest of the staff, or to our parishioners who trust us with their stewardship dollars. We're in a tremendous budget crunch and...."

"Father Henry," Sally interrupted, "I need to let you know that I came to realize that. You and Jim have been reporting our shortfall for some time now. I just wanted the youth program to be the best it's ever been."

"I understand that, Sally, and I'm proud of the program we have. But remember that there are many other ministries in this parish that we need to support. All the ministry leaders want their programs to be excellent. That's why we have such a strong parish."

"I guess I couldn't see past what I thought our kids needed, and I felt I had to be fighting for every penny for my programs," Sally admitted. " I haven't wanted to hear or really face our financial realities. The truth is, I guess I can rent those videos for much less than they cost to buy."

"But another thing I realized," Sally continued, "is that I can get pretty

intense when I'm confronted, and that just makes it more difficult for you to approach me. So, I really want to apologize for blowing up this morning."

"You're right, Sally," replied Father Henry. "I do have a tough time when things get emotional. I know I need to develop better skills to deal with those situations. And I appreciate your acknowledging the impact your anger has, and for agreeing to forgo buying the videos this year. I'm glad to know that you understand the need to follow the budget. In the future, you'll need to follow the policies just like everyone else, and seek approval for special situations."

"You know this isn't easy for me," Father continued. There was a long pause as he hesitated, uncomfortable at having to confront Sally's temper. "But I also need to address something that happened this morning that was really distressing." Father Henry took a deep breath and continued, "It wasn't appropriate for you to storm out of my office when we were speaking this morning. It's not productive at all and it ends up making the matter worse. If you need some time to think or calm down, I'd prefer that you say so rather than just walking away."

Sally replied regretfully, "I know. It's just that I get so angry when everyone's telling me what I can and can't do with my program. And when I get that angry, I have trouble finding the right words, and I feel like I just have to get away. It's gotten me in trouble more than once, and I know it doesn't help. I'll really try to do it better."

"Well, Sally, it seems we've both learned some things that might help us in the future." A smile came to Father Henry's face as he said, "I'm reminded of the Scripture that says 'all things work for good for those who love God.' I guess that means conflict, too."

We recognize that there is a certain fairy-tale quality to this example. People do not usually move through the wide range of emotions beginning with rage and ending with reconciliation as quickly as this story suggests. It often takes us a long time to calm down, to recognize our contribution to a dispute, and to become willing to acknowledge our fault to the other person. But we do know that using the four-step process of Christian Conciliation—a profoundly simple though challenging process—significantly increases the chances of reaching true and lasting reconciliation. We have witnessed dramatic conversions of heart as the Spirit has led people to reach out to others with whom they have been embroiled in bitter and protracted disputes. We know that we do not do this in our own power, but as

Catholics we are called to depend on God's strength.
We are called to be witnesses of Christ's love and to be his ambassadors of reconciliation in the world. Let us remember our individual call to holiness and live it out in every circumstance of life, especially when we find ourselves in interpersonal conflict.

May the words of St. Francis of Assisi be an inspiration:

Make me an instrument of your peace.

Notes

[1] All references to Peacemaker concepts are made by permission of Peacemaker Ministries, www.HisPeace.org (406) 256-1583, 1537 Avenue D, Suite 352, Billings, MT 59102.

References

Code of Canon Law, Latin/English Edition. 1983. Washington, D.C.: Canon Law Society of America.

Confraternity of Christian Doctrine. 1970. *The New American Bible.* New York: Catholic Book Publishing Co.

Flannery, Austin, O.P. 1979. *Vatican Council II, The Conciliar and Post Conciliar Documents,* Northport, New York: Costello Publishing Co. (Fourth Printing).

Jones, Alexander, General Editor. 1966. *The Jerusalem Bible, Reader's Edition,* New York: Doubleday.

McKenzie, Scott. 1999. "Broken Expectations," Cargill Associates, Ft. Worth, TX.

Sande, Ken. 1991. *The Peacemaker.* Grand Rapids, MI: Baker Books.

Senge, Peter et al. 1994. *The Fifth Discipline Fieldbook.* New York: Doubleday.

United States Catholic Conference. 1994. *Catechism of the Catholic Church.* Ligouri, MO: Liguori Publications.

9

PARISH INFORMATION SYSTEMS— RESOURCES FOR MINISTRY

Francis Kelly Scheets, OSC, PhD[1]

On Being Accountable to Mission

Parish ministry depends on money—parishioners' contributions. Does accountability, then, refer only to money—to those annual financial reports? Does accountability refer to ministry? How does a pastor or staff know how "good" their ministry is? What constitutes "good" ministry? What is "better" ministry? Having comparable information relating to the parish mission is more than just useful, it is crucial. This chapter looks at the need for data, which becomes information for improving ministry, which improves on parish accountability both to parishioners and to other parishes, and ends with a strong plea for understanding the administration burden of pastors.

Parishes Need Better Information

Information systems! ... Resources for ministry! ... Over many years I have struggled to show that moneys *are* resources for ministry ... that program-based statistics *are* resources for ministry...that surveys *are* resources for ministry. I have devoted much of my priesthood to developing computer systems to relate finances to ministry resources. Over many years I have devoted tens-of-thousands of hours to showing that parish statistics *are* ministry resources. I have used surveys developed by others as ministry resources. Information tells a story; it promotes accountability; it strengthens stewardship. Data, statistics, information, surveys; and their reliability, use, and dissemination are important for good parish ministry. They need to be understood by all: the pastor, staff, and volunteers.

Before the arrival of the desktop computers in the early 1980s maintaining and gathering parish data was not only boring, it was difficult. Today with contemporary PCs and good computer programs every parish could have more than adequate financial reports and good sacramental and parishioner statistics. Without parish statistics, without financial reports, without surveys, effective ministry among American Catholics is and will continue to be a case of "crippled ministry." Some stories are useful.

Three Case Stories of Decisions Without Data

I want to take you on a journey into the hazy world of parish data—as in numbers. "Numbers?" you say, with a quizzical look, wondering what there is beyond balancing the weekly average budget to the Sunday collection … hoping this chapter does not result in a plea for more data collection forms from diocesan offices. I fear that more data is needed, but first let me tell you a few true stories. These are stories of why and how my priesthood was molded over the past thirty years as I wrestled with parish accountability. "Accountability is not only about money, but also who decides!" as one woman once told her pastor as reported by the *National Catholic Reporter.*[2] I would add that it also is about reporting back to parishioners.

A religious education director for a large suburban parish informed the pastor year after year that the parish had the finest program in the diocese. How did the director know? … She just did. But how could that director be sure? It just "felt" like it was the finest—until the standardized NCEA test showed that program to be "average" for the diocese. The lessons learned were easy: the results of a parish program cannot be compared with others without having a standard and acceptable measure. Without that type of a measure it is not easy to know what aspects of any parish program need to be continued, modified, or dropped.

In another parish the pastor informed me that his parish had one of the most active and outstanding Christian service programs in the area. How did he know? Did he know how many volunteer hours were involved? How many families were helped? He just knew. He showered me with anecdotal stories about how his program compared with other parishes. How could he be sure? The lesson here was easy but the solution was not: the parish needed to devise some sort of numbers to know what is being done and by whom. Accurate comparisons with others require that other parishes should use the same method of counting.

Another time I was engaged as a consultant for a midwest diocese. My task was to revise the annual parish Pastoral Report, which, among other things required pastors to "estimate the percent of parishioners attending Mass on an average weekend." Each year a large number of pastors were pleased to report that that their Mass attendance figures were in the high sixty- and low seventy-percent range. How did they know? They just knew. This lesson was easy: after I revised the annual report, parishes counted all attendees, averaged over several weekends. The result was that many pastors were surprised as well as unsettled when their "average" Mass attendance dropped significantly into the thirty-percent range.

Each of these stories involved dedicated clergy or staff, who needed information that would cast doubt on their present ministry comfort level. Much remains to be noted about parish data, and questions need to surface if data is to be useful: What data is needed? When is it needed? How is it obtained? In what form is it useful?— and perhaps the first question should be: Do all parishes need the same data?

Pastors' Burdens: What is the Pastoral Question?

In the course of this chapter I will set out a lot of questions. I believe the right question is important because it directs the efforts of staff in probing for effective or useful answers. An incomplete understanding of "pastors' burdens" results in an incomplete answer. Simple. In the 1970s, 1980s, and even into the early 2000s many priests and bishops felt the pastoral question was: "Are priests spiritual men?" If the answer is "Yes!" then all would be well. So dioceses embarked on intensive spiritual programs and implemented spiritual support groups.

But, by the early 1980s, all was not well at the parish. Other questions kept intruding. It seems that the spirituality question is not the only one needing to be answered. Spirituality is but one answer to reducing pastors' burdens. Theology schools and universities raised the second question: "Are pastors knowledgeable about theology, Scripture, and liturgy?" If the answer is "Yes!" then all would be well. This answer brought forth many sabbatical programs. Those who have been fortunate to attend such a program uniformly sing its praises.

By the 1990s, however, the answer was *not* a loud "Yes!" Too many pastors still felt burdened. Too many priests were declining assignments in large parishes. So it was that the third question remained unasked because it involved neither spirituality nor theological updating. This third question is, "Do pastors possess the administrative skills to manage parishes?" The failure to appreciate this last question has left pastors of the large parishes on their own to struggle with a hit-miss mentality.

Do All Parishes Need the Same Information?

In 1969 I was elected to the diocesan school board of the Fort Wayne-South Bend diocese and was appointed to chair the finance committee. With my education

background I already knew that adequate data on parish Catholic schools was exis-
tent—if at all—with the school supervisors of various religious communities of
sisters. Parish fiscal data, capable of shedding some insight on the ability of a parish
to support its school, was confined to annual reports on file with the chancery. The
school board had little information beyond anecdotal stories. So I developed a
parish-based information system—with much encouragement and help from laity
who provided me with skilled computer programmers. Over the years I have created parish-based data information for a number of specific projects. I hold that
comparable "parish data" is important for well-functioning parishes. But what,
how, when, and in what form do parishes need data? The answer to this question
requires us to look at the parish as a social system.

Parishes as a Social System

In the 1990s, the Alban Institute of Washington, DC, a well-respected Episcopal
Church consulting firm, developed the concept of a parish as a social system. They
categorized parishes by size (taking into account 1) image in the community, 2)
management style, and 3) administration skills required) into Family, Pastoral,
Program, and Corporate parishes.

Family parishes are small and dominated by the matriarch from one of the "old
families." Liturgies are family gatherings, and minimum administrative skills are
needed.

Pastoral parishes are medium size and the image of the pastor is that of the shep-
herd of the flock. Liturgies are simple, and a moderate degree of administrative skills
are useful.

Program parishes are large and have a professional staff of two or three full-time
persons requiring staff meetings. Their image is in their programs; their leadership
depends on the pastor working well with staff.

Corporate parishes are very large, with a professional staff of five or more directors of ministry. These parishes sponsor many programs—as many as fifteen to thirty or more, and the pastor is the symbol of unity.

This social system concept was intriguing, but was it applicable to Catholic parishes?

During the 1990s, as a planning consultant, I had acquired a database covering 637
parishes from four dioceses encompassing a minimum of five years.[3] This database
contained all the information from the financial and statistical reports for every
parish. After I learned about the "parish as a social system," I applied the concepts to
my database parishes with adjustments made for the size of Catholic parishes.

In determining the size I used the construct developed by the Center for Applied

Research in the Apostolate: small, medium, large, and very large parishes. *Family* parishes number fewer than 450 registered parishioners in fewer than 170 households. These parishes comprised fourteen percent of my database and a mere one percent of registered Catholics. *Pastoral* parishes have between 450 and 1,200 registered parishioners, with 170-450 households and are twenty-two percent of my database with seven percent of Catholics. *Program* parishes number between 1,200-3,000 parishioners comprising 450-1,200 households; this group comprises thirty percent of the database and registers twenty-two percent of the Catholics. *Corporate* parishes number more than 3,000 Catholics in more than 1,200 households; these parishes number thirty-two percent of my database but registered over seventy-one percent of all Catholics.

This seventy-one percent figure surprised me! Thus I began to understand the magnitude in the differences of image, management style, and administration skill among these four social systems. With over seventy percent of registered parishioners the importance of what happens with these *Corporate* parishes should not be underestimated. All parishes need to be cared for and nourished, but the urban and suburban *Corporate* and *Program* parishes present us with special issues.

Communication and Accountability Difficulty Scale

Now, I want to turn our attention to the communication and accountability issues among these very large parishes. Communication with parishioners, historically, has been the responsibility of each parish. It was reasonably simple and straightforward when neighborhoods were stable and parishioners were not so highly educated. Financial accountability was long a concern for diocesan offices, providing standard forms for reporting parish revenues and expenditures, with annual reports signed off by two lay members of a parish. Many dioceses employ auditors to check over these reports and conduct an on-site audit of parish books at the change of pastors.

Family parishes, with one weekend Mass, average about 200 attendees; communication is fairly simple and straightforward with announcements, simple bulletins, and "town hall" meetings after Mass. Accountability for decisions and finances is easy because decisions can be made at those meetings and the average income flow is less than $100,000.

Pastoral parishes, with two weekend liturgies, average from 200–500 attendees; communication is a bit more complex, but is manageable with announcements and bulletins, but "town hall" meetings are not as useful as the parish council, and periodic mailings are frequently helpful. Accountability for decisions rests with the parish council and its communication. Financial accountability rests with the finance council and, with an average of $200,000 income flow, is fairly straightforward.

Program parishes average from 500 to 1,200 parishioners attending two to three weekend Masses. Communication with parishioners is fairly complex and challenging: the usual announcements, bulletins, and parish mailings do not always yield expected results, and so some parishes have turned to web sites or "email your pastor" in their struggle to communicate. Accountability for decisions again rests with the parish council and its communications. Finances require a skilled bookkeeper and are overseen by the finance council. These parishes average over $400,000; if they have a school the number could reach over $1,250,000.

Corporate parishes are large, with 3,000 parishioners, at four to six or more weekend liturgies. Communication with parishioners is extremely complex and often frustrating: the usual means are not entirely satisfactory, for parishioner interest depends on any one of the many ministry programs in which they participate. Accountability for decisions rests with the parish council and implementation with parish staff. Finances, overseen by the finance council, are actually handled by skilled bookkeepers or accountants; average income flow is over $800,000 and can exceed $3,000,000. Let me illustrate.

Figure 9-1 below illustrates the scale of communication and accountability difficulty encountered by parishes as they increase in numbers and income flow.[4] The

Figure 9-1 **Parish Communication-Accountability Difficulty Scale**

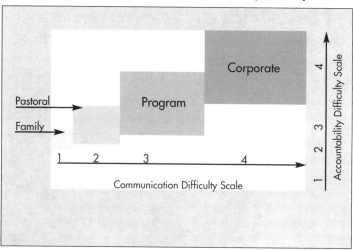

bottom scale represents households increasing by size of parish, while the right scale indicates income flow increases. The Difficulty Scale ranges from "1" for the ease of communication and accountability experienced by *Family* parishes to a "4" for *Corporate* parishes.

A *Corporate* parish with 4,000 Catholics would not encounter a difficulty scale faced by one with 11,000 Catholics with a communication difficulty scale of "4." This suggests that the scale is not a simple "3" or "4," but is more complex. A small *Family* parish with 200 parishioners should have no difficulty with a communication scale of "1" or accountability scale of "1" due to an income flow of $75,000, for a combined scale of "1" (1 x 1 = 1). But a *Program* parish with 2000 parishioners with a communication scale of "3" and an income scale of "4," due to flow of $1,700,000 because of a parish school, would then have a combined difficulty scale of "12." A very large *Corporate* parish with a communication scale of "4" and with an income flow of over $3,000,000 and an accountability scale of "4" would have a combined scale of "16."

Before moving on I want to re-enforce the above concepts by illustrating the distribution of parishes by size and income flow for an actual mid-size diocese for 1996, as shown in Figure 9-2.[5] The distribution of parishes by the number of registered parishioners in this diocese closely parallels that described above and clearly shows that most of the parishes are clustered in the lower left corner—smaller parishes with smaller income flows. The *Corporate* parishes in this diocese, those with over 3,000 parishioners, accounted for thirty-two percent of all parishes but registered seventy percent of parishioners. Twenty parishes had over 7000 registered parishioners! *Program* parishes, with between 1,200-3,000 parishioners, comprised thirty-six percent of parishes, and registered twenty-four percent of parishioners. Between them the *Family* and *Pastoral* parishes constituted the other thirty-two percent of parishes and registered a little over six percent of Catholics. The scatter chart below shows that several *Program* parishes have large income flows, greater even than some *Corporate* parishes. I need to point out that the maximum income flow shown on the left scale as $1,750,000 is usually not the total parish income flow, as diocesan reports generally require net accounting for fund raising (income less expense), diocesan collections (in less out), and diocesan managed stewardship campaigns (excess less assessment).

Figure 9-2 **Parish Communication-Accountability Difficulty Scale**
(Showing the Distribution of all Parishes for a Midwest Diocese, 1996)

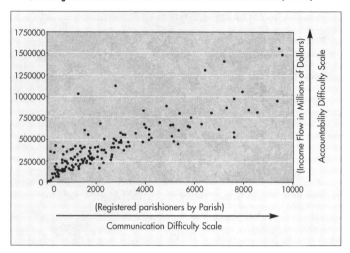

What Questions Should a Parish Ask?

How do parishes know what data is needed? When is it needed? How is it obtained? In what form is it most useful?

Data versus Information

I need to state the obvious: there is a distinction between data and information. Data is not information. Information is data that conveys a relationship, that is useful for evaluating a program, or that is helpful for knowing where the parish is headed by showing current trends. In the course of a year an ordinary parish is capable of generating a lot of numbers: infant and adult baptisms, marriages, funerals, enrollment in religious education programs, Mass attendance, and reams of financial data. A simple example of data becoming information is the popular weekly financial report using just three pieces of data, consisting of weekly "budget collection minus actual collection received" with the difference showing the gain or loss for that week. This is important ongoing information for parishioners—if the budget is to be balanced and parish bills paid. Both the budget and the actual are examples of information designed to convey hundreds of accounting transactions.

Parishes are required by canon law to have "a set of parish books including baptismal, marriage and death registers" (canon 535.1). All dioceses require annual reports on sacramental and parishioner data—the minimum amount is dictated by the needs of *The Official Catholic Directory*. For the collection of data to be reasonably accurate it is necessary that we feel that it will be useful—and, more important, that it will be used. This important point, not usually apparent, is well understood by most pastors I know. Early in my consulting career I had been asked to assist a group of parishes in forming a regional pastoral council. One member of my resources committee, responsible for the accuracy of public school data, decided to check the accuracy of his parish data, such as baptisms and marriages. He was surprised to find the numbers too high by ten to fifteen percent. In conversation with his pastor he was told, "Check with our secretary—she fills in the diocesan forms." And he was told by the secretary, "Father told me to fill in whatever I thought was in the ball park."

And another story on the use of reporting forms: this diocese, with which I worked, was not aware that fifteen percent of the parishes had not bothered to send in their annual statistical report in any given year. And another ten to fifteen percent had not returned their annual financial report. These documents would not have been discovered to be missing unless I wanted them to put them to use. Even where all reports are accounted for each year, in many cases, the reports are months late in arriving. (I must pause to give credit to the one diocese in which I found annual reports were returned on time. Pastors had learned to have their data in on time or they would feel the wrath of the vicar general, who took pride in sending all reports to a bindery on September fifteenth each year—the day he left for his annual vacation. All years were bound and filed on the shelf—but never looked at.)

Three Questions for Efficient Management

To be useful, data must be of assistance in answering questions. Over many years I have found that we frequently do not always know how to ask the right question—and when we do ask that question the data is not readily available. When it is available it is likely to be in a form that is not readily useful. Therefore, my first and most important question is:

1. What data do I need to do my work efficiently?

This question is asking *me* for the data I think *I* need to do *my* work more efficiently. In asking this question some types of data are apparent: the time schedules—for Sunday liturgies or for staff meetings or counseling meetings, appointment calendars—expected numbers for communions, at liturgies or funerals, cash-in-bank for paying bills. This first question brings forth other questions: When do I need it? In what form? How do I obtain it? *When* can mean daily, quarterly, annually. *What form* is most important, as data must be readily useful. For example, a copy of the complete financial activity for the month is not the "right form" for a finance council interested in the over-all budget trend—but it is for the bookkeeper need-ing to make adjustments. Or consider Mass attendance data: raw numbers for sev-eral years is just data, whereas "percent of change" data from year to year is quite useful. An index measuring that percent of change may present a sharper picture. *How obtained* dictates the usefulness of data because it can't be useful if consider-able effort is entailed. There are times when useful data requires considerable effort. Take the example I gave of the weekly collection net gain or loss and then estimate the amount of effort required to obtain that "net" figure to publish in the bulletin. Yet, its importance demands the effort.

2. What do I need to do with data I collect?
> *If I have this information*
> *…what tasks should be done differently?*
> *…what tasks should be abandoned?*
> *…what new tasks should be undertaken?*

Most pastors and staff are concerned with being responsible; they try to be good at what they do, whether it be preaching, counseling, or directing programs. We all gather information to help us evaluate what we are doing; we listen to our friends, overhear conversations, subscribe to favorite journals and magazines. We gather information constantly; most of the time it serves to re-enforce our current opin-ion. We filter out the bad so that we do not have to face this or that question. The "we" in this question is not just the pastor. Every staff individual needs to have that information that helps to answer this question as circumstances change—certainly not daily—but periodically. A recent example about parish liturgical data relating to this question came to my attention. A midwest diocese, in instituting regional plan-ning, conducted a survey in all parishes. Each vicariate received its own results.[6] A major section of the survey for the local vicariate asked this question: *How much do you look for these aspects in a parish?* (Seven "parish aspects" were provided). The highest response rates, with over ninety percent, indicating "very much" or "some-what," were, in order: quality worship, quality preaching, and a welcoming spirit. With this information in hand, a second question clearly suggested that each parish assess these three aspects for themselves: What am I doing that needs to be done dif-ferently … abandoned as unproductive … new ways studied and tested? Certainly no parish can afford not to assess its own results. In one form or another, national, regional, and parish surveys delving into these aspects have been around for a long time, but, with few exceptions, the task of translating their data into action remains. Is this failure because such surveys are not "mine" in the sense that "I" do not feel that surveys involving more than "my" parish really reflect "my" parish?

The third question requires me to consider the sharing of this information:

3. What information do I owe to whom and when?

This question asks parishes to search for people with the need to know—or to whom the information will prove useful. Is it only the diocesan office that sends the annual form to the parish? Is it just those advisory groups that have multiplied over the past twenty years: parish pastoral and finance councils, commissions and committees? For these groups organized information is needed—information that *enables* them to understand. Let us not underestimate our parishioners. With their higher levels of education—over fifty-percent of Catholics under sixty years of age have college degrees or better—their sense of "accountability" means they desire reasons why. These Catholics are not satisfied to be told "all is well." Their education has trained them to seek reasons, data, and statistics. This is why a parish annual report is more than just a report of how money was spent—it needs to be a report of parish programs and ministries, the successes or difficulties. This is why I hold that "money follows programs." As dioceses struggle with aging clergy and the accompanying need to twin, cluster, or merge parishes or resources, this question opens up another: Do parishes owe information to other parishes? If so, what, when, and how? If you think "Yes," then we must be concerned with diocesan data collection at this time—and its use.

Five Questions for Mission Accountability

Important data for any parish is that which is capable of providing information to assist it in answering: "How well are we pursuing our mission?" To provide some assistance in deciding what data might be important, I have devised a set of helpful questions to relate parish mission to the first management question: What data do I need to do my work efficiently?

How will we know when we are accomplishing our mission? Parish mission statements have moved from lofty and lengthy statements of high purpose to a succinct statement of what the parish wishes to accomplish. The mission statement is empty and meaningless without goals to flesh: What do we wish to accomplish over the next six years? Management manuals clearly tell us that goals need to be supported with objectives that are "measurable." But a measurable objective requires data. This question is asking for data that provides insight into its unique mission statement. This first question requires serious discussion regarding the type of data to be collected! Such data, for each parish program, is not often readily available. Assume that the mission requires parish outreach to the poor and needy of the community. What data will be needed over time that will be able to provide information answering this question?

How will we know we have impacted these parishioners? Parishioners are the recipients of many of the programs undertaken as a result of the mission statement —these are people the mission seeks to impact. To be effective, this second question cries out to be supported with data. The question requires data found in surveys, focus groups, and even from anecdotal stories collected from parishioners.

How will we know how effective the parish staff is? Parish staff and volunteers are crucial in addressing the mission for the *Program* and *Corporate* parishes. Data to measure performance also suggests the need for provide for ongoing staff development and training. I surveyed one diocese on computer usage and found that half of the parishes had an average of four computers— yet not half of the secretaries or bookkeepers were judged to have acquired the skills to make use of the available software.

How will we know our programs are effective? Programs are a very important part of parish ministry, and parishioners are encouraged to become involved in various ministries. The importance and quality of parish programs was the object of a study by the Diocese of Rockford (Illinois), as Michael Cieslak reports elsewhere in this volume. Parishioners eagerly responded with 55,000 usable questionnaires. The study found "a strong correlation between parish size and vitality, i.e., the larger the parish the more likely it is that parishioners perceive it as vital.... In order for a parish to score high on this measure, two dynamics must be present: 1) the pastor must be open to share responsibility with others; and 2) there must be various ministries in which people can become involved."[7]

How do we know how many fiscal resources to allocate? Financial resources are "resources for ministry," and parishes with many ministries are faced with deciding on the allocation of those resources. The decision on the allocation of financial resources is important. Parishes need administrative guidelines, which can only be discovered by comparing similar types of parishes. Some years ago the Archdiocese of Detroit suggested limiting parish support to the school to no more than forty percent of school operating costs. In my work with parish information systems I suggest that collections should exceed ninety percent of operating costs. Otherwise fundraising consumes too much of staff time. Collections covering one hundred percent of operating costs would be ideal. With the increase of lay staff, the question of allocation of fiscal resources is assuming a high degree of visibility—and potential conflict between pastor and staff who desire reasonably competitive salaries.

To illustrate the questions for what, when, how, and in what form, I offer the following example.

One Question on Mass Attendance

Why is a Mass count once a year important? I recounted earlier the impact of even asking the terribly wrong question had on pastors in one diocese. Yet I know that someone in that diocese—in times gone by—thought pastors should know something about Mass attendance. I know of dioceses that do not even ask parishes to report on Mass count. I believe that a simple count of Mass attendees over a period of years is an important measure of parish life. Even that count may not be enough. Sister Rosalie Murphy, SND, then director of planning and research for the Archdiocese of Baltimore, taught me that lesson in the early 1990s.[8] She felt that parishes needed to know more than just *how many* attended average parish weekend liturgies—they needed to know *who did and who did not attend*. She thought such information would prove useful—and provoking—to parishes in planning liturgies. She devised a form to make such information available by age and sex for attendees and for registered parishioners. This form was distributed on Mass-count Sunday, tabulated by volunteers, and processed by the planning office. It provided information for over eighty percent of the parishes within three years. Figure 9-3 (next page) illustrates Mass attendance rates for all parishes in the Archdiocese of Baltimore in 1996. Responding parishes across the archdiocese found an impressive average of forty-three percent of registered parishioners attending Mass.

Murphy annually sent each parish this graph using their own data. Among parishes, the difference, when age was factored into the results, was dramatic. Sixty-seven percent of adult Catholics aged 60-69 attended Mass on the count weekend compared to a low of thirty-five percent for the young adults aged 30-39, and twenty-four percent for the twenty-somethings. Children under fourteen averaged forty-one percent—pointing out the importance of parental example and the need for parishes to devise encouraging and welcome programs for young adults with children. The lesson is important: local data has a greater impact on pastors and staff, because it is easier for them to relate to. Obviously, a good census program is required to provide the data on registered parishioners.

What Information Does Parish Mission Require?

For too long a time many Catholic Church leaders have held to the philosophy that "Church is *not* a business." But it is! Income must equal or exceed expenses; parishioners with unmet needs will search for a compatible parish or cease being practicing Catholics. The need for mission information should be apparent but it seems not. So I will take note of four types of mission-information: generation

Figure 9-3 **Mass Attendance by Age Group for All Parishes**

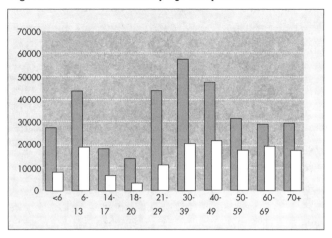

characteristics and attitudes of parishioners, participation in social organizations, comparable inter-parish trends, and reports supporting accountability for mission.

Generation Differences in Characteristics and Attitudes

Over the past five years Catholic sociologists have been probing the concerns of young adult Catholics. Their concern parallels that of marketing specialists. In 1999 the Center for Applied Research in the Apostolate (Bendyna and Perl 2000) undertook to study young adult Catholics in the context of older Catholic generations. The researchers surveyed 2,635 Catholics, who were broken into four seventeen-year generations: Young Adults (ages 22-39), Vatican II (ages 40-57), Silent

Table 9-1 **Selected Characteristics & Attitudes for Four Generations of Catholics**

GENERATION	YOUNG ADULTS	VATICAN II	SILENT	WORLD WAR II
AGE RANGE	22-39	40-57	58-75	75+
Selected Characteristics				
Weekly Mass Attendance	22	35	59	63
Registered with Parish	56	69	77	85
College Graduate or Higher	55	49	32	21
Income Over $60,000	46	47	21	22
Attitudes				
Traditional Forms of Prayer	35	33	59	64
Church Meets Spiritual Needs	34	33	50	69
Opportunities to Help the Needy	48	38	38	40

(ages 58-75), and World War II (age 76 and over). Table 9-1 shows four characteristics and three attitudes for each generation with the percent who responded favorably. These seven aspects of the CARA study are presented to re-enforce parish need for, and understanding of, information as a resource for ministry. National surveys, when done by professionals, have the advantage of indicating important trends. In the case of this study, trends were found among young adults and differences among four generations of adult Catholics that have important consequences for parish ministry now and over the coming decade. Weekly Mass attendance rates start with the twenty-two percent for young adults, increases to thirty-six percent for Vatican II Catholics, then jumps to fifty-nine percent for adults in their sixties, and peaks with Catholics over seventy-five years old. (These latter two groups grew up before Vatican II when attendance rates were in the seventieth percentile). The same general movement, rising from left to right, appears for parish registration, with fifty-six percent for young adults rising to eighty-five percent of Catholics of the World War II generation. However, the trends for college education and income over $60,000 are reversed. From the fifty-five percent of young adult Catholics who have college or graduate degrees, the trend falls to twenty-one percent for the World War II generation. This same trend holds for the youngest generation to the oldest.

The low Mass attendance rate among young adult Catholics should be a concern. There are those who hope that young adults will return to church when their children are born, following the traditional pattern. And there is some truth to this. However, I think the above data suggests "Not so!" I think this for two reasons: 1) young adults are highly educated, and many are the children of educated parents and are more secure in questioning—each generation of college-educated children are more inclined to ask questions and less willing to accept mediocrity; 2) the next generation (age 40-57) also has a low rate of attendance at Mass. Low attendance rates among young adult parents—especially among those who have registered with a parish—translates into low attendance for their children. What attracts these young parents to liturgies will bring the children—at least until they reach their teen years. The impact of secular and Catholic higher education on the minds and attitudes of these young adults has taught them to question—not only traditional church authority, but most sources that insist on authority of the kind that says, "Trust me, I know."

The attitude section in Table 9-1 shows trends regarding forms of prayer, meeting spiritual needs, and help for the needy. The survey data for prayer and spiritual needs show the upward trend rising for each subsequent generation, from the middle thirty percent to the middle sixties. The CARA survey described "traditional forms of prayer" as devotions such as eucharistic adoration or praying the rosary. Slightly over one-third of young adults were "very satisfied" with the way the Church meets their spiritual needs; there is no increase in satisfaction for the Vatican II adults, as theirs drops to thirty-three percent. The older two generations are quite satisfied. There is general agreement for parish programs for helping the poor and needy.

Participation Differences in Social Organizations
Sociologists have long known that members in any voluntary organization are not all equally active—and parishes can identify with this bit of knowledge. Researchers have identified four groups of membership based on their activity: the actives, participants, occasionals, and the infrequents. The actives are the leaders and doers; the participants regularly attend meetings and functions; the occasionals show up periodically; and the infrequents are seen only on special occasions like Christmas or Easter. Figure 9-4, with its suggested percents, is based on my personal experience with parish surveys. It primarily reflects Mass attendance and is only suggestive. In general, between the actives and the participants, parishes experience thirty-five percent attendance rates week after week. The occasionals attend three to four times a month or so. For this reason I believe that a typical parish reaches half of the registered parishioners monthly.

Figure 9-4 **Models for Parishioner Participation by Percent**

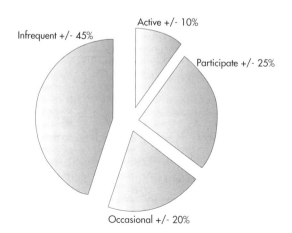

Managing For Mission: Four Suggestions

I found the description of "parish as a social system" to be an important concept because it describes parishes not only by size, but, more important, by its image in a community, and the management systems and administrative skills needed. *Corporate* parishes, with over 3,000 registered parishioners, are similar to each other in image, management, and administration. The difference between them and *Program* parishes is one of scale and complexity. *Pastoral* parishes, with between 450 to 1,200 parishioners, are popular parishes with many priests because their size makes it possible to know the parishioners, and they are generally easier to administer. The introduction of the Communication Difficulty Scale reenforces the need for everyone concerned to understand the magnitude of difficulty encountered. All parishes have three levels of communication: current happenings, special issues, and mission and goals. A word on each.

Current happenings are found in weekly bulletins and special inserts. They are useful for *Pastoral* parishes but a necessity for *Program* and *Corporate* parishes. The vicariate survey I noted earlier, conducted by a midwest diocese, contained the question "How much do these items help you to stay connected with the parish?" Attending Sunday Masses scored highest, but eighty-eight percent of the replies placed the weekly bulletin in second place—to the surprise of many pastors. Fortunately the quality of bulletins, for many parishes, has improved since private firms have taken over the publishing and delivery. With the growing popularity of the Internet, parishes, often working on their own initiative, are setting up their own web sites. Judging from surveys a parish web site has not yet replaced periodic mailings.

Special issues are found among *Corporate* parish "magazines" with monthly or quarterly mailings to all registered households. These magazines can be expensive, but they do reach and communicate with all registered households.

Mission and goals, with their broad statements of hope, need success stories backed up with effective statistics—even with comparisons with past years—if they are to be communicated effectively to parishioners. The annual parish report ought to be the document that blows the trumpet on parish program successes during the past year. It is the document that serves to inform all of how well parish mission, goals, and objectives were accomplished or missed with a description of corrective actions to be taken. In creating a positive attitude among the parishioners, in making them proud to be members, parishioners are encouraged to take an active part in the parish. The extent of this participation ought to be supported with data—how many, how much, how did we compare. If, as I have contended for many years, "money follows programs," the parishes need to tout their successes and communicate them effectively.

My suggestions to parish staff. ***First, every parish program requires trend data.*** No program should be set up that is not accompanied by some number measuring its use or popularity. What is the average attendance rate, or number of individuals involved or helped? Data collected over several years can provide trend information. Is Mass attendance up? What about religious education of children? What is their retention rate?

Second, data must be reasonably accurate. This is no small task, as parishes are not used to making use of data for decisions. My experience with creating databases using parish data is replete with wonderment at the wide fluctuations that exist in such areas as registered parishioners or Mass attendance from year to year (I noted earlier the difficulty I had in obtaining and using baptismal and funeral data available on standard parish reporting forms). To say that the annual financial reports are probably the most accurate parish data available is a sad commentary on our sense of accountability—or the need to have information ready at hand for planning and managing for parish mission and goals. Really, with the sophistication of parish census programs there is little or no excuse for inaccurate parish data.

Third, comparative interparish data is needed to provide comparisons. To be useful, this data requires diocesan assistance. All dioceses collect sacramental data, but management and planning information is urgently needed. It must be collected annually, processed, and returned to parishes as soon as possible. Parish management demands data that allows one parish to compare itself with similar parishes. The complexities that *Corporate* and *Program* parishes encounter in their efforts to communicate call for this diocesan effort. My work with trying to develop parish based information systems has shown that parishes are calling for help—without knowing what to ask for.

Fourth, the data gathered must adhere to these principles:

1) Data gathered by the diocese must be able to provide comparable information about ministry—percentages, trends, per capita, ratios;

2) sacramental and parishioner data should reflect the common need of all parishioners; *Family* and *Pastoral* parishes should be expected to respond to these common data needs;

3) Data should be recorded only once at the parish level;

4) Data must be reported back to the parishes in a form that provides useful information within a reasonable time frame;

5) Numbers should be required; neither percentages nor "yes/no" answers make it possible to provide regional or diocesan summaries for higher and broader level planning.

Accountability for Mission

Accountability for mission implies an ability to know how well parish programs are assisting in accomplishing the particular parish mission. Information, not data, is needed.

First, Corporate parishes require program accounting. This is a crucial need. Is your parish organization structure set up to manage parish programs for mission? Many parish councils are organized around four commissions: worship, stewardship, education, and Christian service. Various committees assist each commission. All data-gathering forms—financial and statistical—must be organized on the same principle: programs undertaken by the parish are necessary or useful for promoting its mission. Program directors cannot ignore—or worse, remain ignorant of—the financial implications when they really need to understand that finances are resources for ministry. Neither can they ignore or remain ignorant of the data trends in their programs. The divorce between the directors of programs, fiscal accounting, and data gathering is really intolerable. Program management becomes anecdotal; directors are left to their own feelings; finance personnel control resource allocation; comparative data is almost non-existent. So, where is accountability hiding?

Second, parish managers need management reports. This may sound trite, but it is not! Reports should be brief but show current trends and be able to provide answers to the questions raised by those who are responsible for the direction of the parish. Thus, a straight-line monthly trend for income or expense is simplistic, but not useful. At the least, monthly or quarterly trends should reflect last year's experience as far as possible. (Reports with decimals need never leave the bookkeeper's office!) Management reports are important for directors of programs to relate their responsibilities to fiscal resources.

Third, pastors and staff of larger parishes need to meet regularly. Thus pastoral associates, directors of religious education, school staff, youth ministers, and Christian service coordinators can share experience and increase their knowledge and understanding of particular issues. It is important for all to understand the signs of our times and how they relate to us. I am afraid that the time when we could think that "one form fits all" has been gone for decades. If Catholicism belongs with and for a well-educated populace living in a democracy, then it behooves parishes to be able to respond to various needs.

Are We Facing the Administrative Pastoral Question?

I recently learned that the Vatican is proceeding to study "the administrative burdens that priests face."[9] I support this effort. Yet I fear that their study will prove fruitless if it ignores the impact of *parishes as a social system*. We, bishops, priests, and laity, cannot continue to look at parishes as simply a "Pastoral" parish gone astray: *Family* parishes as shrunken *Pastoral* parishes; *Program* parishes as overgrown *Pastoral* ones; *Corporate* parishes as gigantic *Pastoral* parishes. In no way are *Program* or *Corporate* parishes just larger *Pastoral* parishes! The pastoral image of parish leadership has only existed for *Pastoral* parishes and in the daydreams of many parish priests as my-Christmas-wish-gift-from-my-bishop! The same liturgical and preaching skills that are useful in communicating with 400 households will not prove satisfactory in addressing the spiritual needs of 1,200 households—let alone prove to be "the answer" to the spiritual hunger of well over 2,000 households week after week. The administrative differences, as identified by "parish as a social system" are different by more than of degree—they differ by magnitudes! Liturgy among *Pastoral* parishes is a weekly connection of parishioners with the pastor. Liturgy among *Corporate* parishes is—and should be—good to excellent, supported by a choir and instrumental music. *Pastoral* parishes do not need written norms and job descriptions for staff and volunteers to function. *Corporate* parish norms have to be found in policy manuals, or the large number of parish programs would not be able to function.

As the bishops study the administrative burdens priests face, I hope they understand the magnitude of the generational differences that exist among American Catholics and the impact this has on *Program* and *Corporate* parishes. The impact of higher education on the Catholic laity is unique in history. Not only are they the best educated generation in Catholic Church history, many of them are second or third generation college or university graduates. Granted, this does not make them even slightly knowledgeable about theology—but it does make them comfortable with questions, and *more* comfortable than their parents. Many of us have friends with college degrees who have remained faithful and practicing Catholics while questioning such teachings as birth control or divorce; yet too many of their children are no longer practicing. They wonder and ask, "What did we—laity and clergy together—do wrong?" Church documents bewail the materialism and individualism of American Catholics, yet studies like the CARA study of young adult Catholics is subtitled, "Living with Diversity, Seeking Service, Waiting to be Welcomed." This study found a high degree of spirituality among young adult Catholics. Their materialism has not prevented these young from wanting to help the poor and needy, and they are looking for useful and meaningful ways. Their individualism has helped them make great sacrifices to obtain their education—an education that forty-three percent of the female college freshman class of 2000 said they wanted so they could make society better.[10]

I am glad that bishops are studying the administrative burdens priests face. I hope they understand the need that pastors and staff have to meet with priests and staff of similar social system parishes on a regular basis to share, not ignorance, but difficulties and successes. When experienced people come together the questions become: What works? What steps made it work? What doesn't work? What can we try? To whom can we go for some insights? This sharing might make it possible for successes that have been developed and tested by the innovative pastors acceptable by the majority sooner than waiting for twenty to twenty-five years for adoption to occur naturally. Such meetings have long been a staple for management programs among successful organizations. The casual meetings for vicariate and deanery clergy and staff are too short and tend to be informational—with the flow from diocesan staff to parish clergy. What are needed are two- to three-day meetings once a year, or every second year, for similar social parishes (e.g., *Corporate*-to-*Corporate*) which provide time for sharing and for learning. What are needed are diocesan structures that bring the parish clergy and staff together to talk and exchange information freely.

Notes

1. © Copyright 2001, Francis Kelly Scheets, OSC.

2. I saved this quote from an article in an early 1990s *National Catholic Reporter* and I have lost the reference. I like this quote as it expands accountability well beyond finances to include who makes decisions, how staff are to be accountable for implementation, and how these actions are communicated to parishioners.

3. At the time I was hired as a consultant to develop a parish database system for producing Parish Planning Reports; I started with the Archdiocese of Baltimore in 1991, the Diocese of Cleveland in 1993, the Diocese of Rochester in 1995, and the Diocese of Grand Rapids in 1997. I think the profile for each type of parish by size, using the CARA data, reasonably reflects the national break out of parishes throughout the United States.

4. I devised the Communication-Accountability Difficulty Scale for this paper. The data for each type of parish in the social system seemed to call for this scale.

5. This scatter chart is for all parishes of the Archdiocese of Baltimore for 1996 as contained in my four-diocese database.

6. Archdiocese of Detroit, The Department of Parish Life / Pastoral Resources, conducted the "Catholic Survey, Summer 2000" by vicariates. This survey drew on a similar one developed by the Center for Applied Research in the Apostolate for St. Daniel Parish of Clarkston, Michigan, and Msgr. Robert S. Humitz, pastor.

7. Cieslak, Michael, PhD, Research Review, *Catholic Research Forum No. 16*, published by the National Conference for Pastoral Planning and Council Development (CPPCD), St. Louis, Mo.

8. Sister Rosalie Murphy, SND, was director for the Division of Planning and Council Services for the Archdiocese of Baltimore during the 1990s. She was an extremely insightful director as she designed the age and sex Mass count card prior to my working with her in developing my Parish Planning Report for parishes. The various age groups were chosen by Murphy and reflect the importance of providing parishes with their own data on young adult Catholics— long before they were to be studied.

9. Cardinal Adam Maida, Minutes of Meeting of the Presbyteral Council, November 15, 2001; Cardinal's comments to the council that he is to give a major paper on the parish priest and his ministry in North America. One of the aspects he will discuss is "the administrative burden that priests face."

10. Chronicle of Higher Education conducts this annual survey.

References

Bendyna, Mary E. and Paul Perl. 2000. "Young Adult Catholics in the Context of Other Catholic Generations: A CARA Working Paper." Washington, D.C.: Center for Applied Research in the Apostolate.

Cieslak, Michael. *Catholic Research Forum Research Review* No. 16. St Louis, Mo: National Conference for Pastoral Planning and Council Development.

Froehle, Bryan T and Mary L. Gautier. 1999. "National Parish Inventory Project Report," Washington, DC: Center for Applied Research in the Apostolate.

Hoge, Dean R, William D. Dinges, Mary Johnson, and Juan L. Gonzales, Jr. 2001. *Young Adult Catholics: Religion in the Culture of Choice.* Notre Dame: University of Notre Dame Press.

Of Related Interest

Vatican II
Forty Personal Stories
William Madges and Michael Daley, editors

Here are the stories of women and men who took part in the council, were there at the time, or saw the course of their lives change dramatically because of it. These storytellers include: Joan Chittister, Martin Marty, Richard Rohr, Thomas Groome, Avery Dulles, Mary Jo Weaver, and Walter Burghardt. .
1-58595-238-9, 240 pp, $19.95

Revised and Updated
Church Emerging from Vatican II
A Popular Approach to Contemporary Catholicism
Dennis M. Doyle

Explains what it means to be a believing, practicing Catholic today in terms of Vatican II ecclesiology and theology.   0-89622-507-0, 368 pp, $19.95

The Parish of the Next Millennium
William J. Bausch

Summarizes the social and cultural forces shaping our lives and church by examining where we are and where we might be going.
0-89622-719-7, 288 pp, $16.95

Four Ways to Build More Effective Parish Councils
A Pastoral Approach
Mark F. Fischer and Mary Margaret Raley, editors

This highly practical collection of essays brings readers up-to-date on the latest developments in pastoral councils and presents four principles that make pastoral councils even more effective. A must-have for pastors and parish councils members.   1-58595-194-3, 224 pp, $19.95

TWENTY-THIRD PUBLICATIONS
185 WILLOW STREET • PO BOX 180 • MYSTIC, CT 06355
TEL: 1-800-321-0411 • FAX: 1-800-572-0788
Bayard E-MAIL: ttpubs@aol.com • www.twentythirdpublications.com